AAT UNITS

20 WORKING WITH INFORMATION TECHNOLOGY

22 MONITOR AND MAINTAIN A HEALTHY, SAFE AND SECURE WORKPLACE

23 ACHIEVING PERSONAL EFFECTIVENESS

COMBINED TEXTBOOK AND WORKBOOK

ISBN 1 85179 928 1

British Library Cataloguing-in-Publication data

A catalogue record for this book is available from the British Library.

We are grateful to the Association of Accounting Technicians for permission to reproduce past assessment material. The solutions have been prepared by The Financial Training Company.

Published by

The Financial Training Company
22J Wincombe Business Park
Shaftesbury
Dorset
SP7 9QJ

Contents

Preface

This text book has been specifically written for:

Unit 22 - Monitor and maintain a healthy, safe and secure workplace

Unit 23 – Achieving personal effectiveness

Unit 20 – Working with information technology

of the AAT's new Foundation syllabus (NVQ Level 2).

It is written in a practical and interactive style:

- ♦ key terms and concepts are clearly defined

- ♦ all topics are illustrated with practical examples with clearly worked solutions

- ♦ frequent practice activities throughout the chapters ensure that what you have learnt is regularly reinforced

- ♦ 'pitfalls' and 'assessment tips' help you avoid commonly made mistakes and help you focus on what is required to perform well in your assessment.

Icons

Throughout the text we use symbols to highlight the elements referred to above.

 Key facts

 Assessment tips and techniques

 Pitfalls

 Practice activities

The text is followed by a workbook which contains two Practice Devolved Assessments and a Mock Devolved Assessment.

SYLLABUS – UNIT 22

Unit 22 Monitor and Maintain a Healthy, Safe and Secure Workplace*

Unit commentary

This unit is about the individual's ability to monitor the workplace to minimise risks to self and others and to maintain a healthy and safe working environment. This includes the identification and rectification, when authorised and competent, of potential hazards and emergencies and adherence to legal and other regulations relating to safe and healthy work practices. Also included is following set procedures for the security of the premises and its contents, identifying security risks and taking appropriate action.

Elements contained within this unit are:

Element 22.1   Monitor and Maintain Health and Safety Within the Workplace

Element 22.2   Monitor and Maintain the Security of the Workplace

Where covered in the textbook

Knowledge and Understanding

Common forms of accident/health emergency (Element 22.1)
Types and uses of fire and emergency equipment (Element 22.1)
Hazards in the use of equipment (Element 22.1)
Methods of minimising hazards in the work area (Element 22.1)
Organisation's procedures for dealing with emergencies (Element 22.1)   **Chapter 1**
Own scope and limitations for dealing with emergencies (Element 22.1)
Methods of reporting emergencies (Element 22.1 & 22.2)
Relevant legal requirements (Element 22.1)

Location of fire and emergency equipment (Element 22.1)
Identification of potential security risks (Element 22.2)
Organisation's security procedures (Element 22.2)   **Chapter 2**
Own scope and limitations for dealing with security risks (Element 22.2)

*This unit is taken from the Council for Administration National Standards for Administration

Unit 22   Monitor and Maintain a Healthy, Safe and Secure Workplace

Element 22.1   Monitor and Maintain Health and Safety within the Workplace

Performance Criteria

i.   Existing or potential hazards are put right if authorised

ii.   Hazards outside own authority to put right are promptly and accurately reported to the appropriate person

iii.   Actions taken in dealing with emergencies conform to organisational requirements

iv.   Emergencies are reported and recorded accurately, completely and legibly in accordance with established procedures   } Chapter 1

v.   Work practices are in accordance with organisational requirements

vi.   Working conditions which do not conform to organisational requirements are promptly and accurately reported to the appropriate person

vii.   Organising of work area minimises risk to self and others

Range Statement

1   Workplace: all equipment, fixtures and fittings within own area of responsibility; all areas within the organisation

2   Emergencies: illness; accidents; fire; evacuation

3   Organisational requirements: instructions provided by the organisation to ensure compliance with legal requirements and codes of practice

Evidence Requirements

◆   All performance criteria must be met

◆   Evidence must be available to prove that all variables within the range have been included in the assessment

◆   Competence must be demonstrated consistently, over a period of time, with evidence of performance obtained from a variety of sources

◆   Evidence for the listed criteria must be made available where it is not apparent from performance

◆   Performance evidence must be available of the candidate identifying potential hazards and emergencies in the workplace and taking appropriate action, in accordance with organisational and legal requirements

Sources of Evidence (these are examples of sources of evidence, but candidates and assessors may be able to identify other, appropriate sources)

- ◆ Observed performance, eg

    - identifying and reporting hazards

    - identifying and reporting emergencies

    - putting right hazards, within limits of own authority

    - taking part in evacuation procedures

    - reporting accidents

    - organising own workstation to reduce hazards - reducing glare, positioning equipment, furniture and materials

    - phasing work activities to minimise risk to self-exposure to VDUs

- ◆ Work products, eg

    - records of potential hazards and/or emergencies and actions taken

    - reports of accidents

- ◆ Authenticated testimonies from relevant witnesses, eg

    - supervisor

- ◆ Personal accounts of competence

- ◆ Responses to questions

- ◆ Other sources of evidence to prove knowledge and understanding where it is not apparent from performance

Unit 22   Monitor and Maintain a Healthy, Safe and Secure Workplace

Element 22.2   Monitor and Maintain the Security of the Workplace

Performance Criteria

i.   Organisational security procedures are carried out correctly

ii.   Security risks are correctly identified

iii.   Identified security risks are put right or reported promptly to the appropriate person

iv.   Identified breaches of security are dealt with in accordance with organisational procedures

> Chapter 2

Range Statement

1   Security systems: personal identification; entry; exit; equipment

Evidence Requirements

♦   All performance criteria must be met

♦   Evidence must be available to prove that all variables within the range have been included in the assessment

♦   Competence must be demonstrated consistently, over a period of time, with evidence of performance obtained from a variety of sources

♦   Evidence for the listed criteria must be made available where it is not apparent from performance

♦   Performance evidence must be available of the candidate following set procedures for the security of the workplace and its contents. Evidence is also required of identifying security risks and taking appropriate action, within limits of own authority

Sources of Evidence (these are examples of sources of evidence, but candidates and assessors may be able to identify other, appropriate sources)

♦   Observed performance, eg

  -   carrying out set security procedures – equipment security, locking cabinets

  -   identifying and reporting potential or actual breaches of security

  -   dealing with security risks, within limits of own authority

♦   Work products, eg

  -   reports of security risks

♦   Authenticated testimonies from relevant witnesses, eg

  -   supervisor

♦   Personal accounts of competence

♦   Responses to questions

♦   Other sources of evidence to prove knowledge and understanding where it is not apparent from performance

SYLLABUS – UNIT 23

Unit 23 Achieving Personal Effectiveness

Unit commentary

This unit relates to the personal and organisational administration aspects of the accounting technician's role. At this level the individual is expected to organise his or her own work, establish good working relationships with colleagues, customers and suppliers, and ensure all the relevant financial information is filed in accordance with organisational and legal requirements.

The first element requires the individual to use planning aids such as diaries, schedules and action plans, and to seek assistance where necessary to meet specific demands and deadlines. The second element relates to the individual developing good working relationships through responding to requests, meeting commitments and using appropriate communication methods. The final element is about the individual maintaining the filing and recording system in line with organisational and legal requirements.

Elements contained within this unit are:

Element 23.1   Plan and Organise Own Work

Element 23.2   Establish and Maintain Working Relationships

Element 23.3   Maintain Accounting Files and Records

Knowledge and Understanding

The Business Environment

- The different types of people : customers; peers; manager; other members of staff (Elements 23.1 & 23.2)
- Relevant legislation : copyright; data protection; equal opportunities (Element 23.2)
- The different types of documentation : incoming correspondence; copies of outgoing correspondence; financial records (Element 23.3)
- Sources of legal requirements : data protection; companies acts (Element 23.3)

} Throughout

Methods

- Prioritising and organising work (Element 23.1)
- Work planning and the use of planning and scheduling techniques and aids (Element 23.1)   } Chapter 3
- Time management (Element 23.1)
- Team working (Element 23.1)   Chapter 3, 4
- Work methods and practices (Element 23.1)   Chapter 3
- Handling confidential information (Elements 23.1 & 23.2)   Chapter 3,4
- Methods of establishing constructive relationships (Element 23.2)
- Seeking and exchanging information, advice and support (Element 23.2)   } Chapter 4
- Handling disagreements and conflict (Element 23.2)
- Using appropriate actions and different styles of approach in different situations (Element 23.2)
- Different communication methods and styles (Element 23.2)   } Chapter 4,5
- Types of communication difficulties and how to resolve them (Element 23.2)
- Employee responsibilities in complying with the relevant legislation (Element 23.2)   Chapter 4
- Methods of classifying information : alphabetical, numerical, alphanumerical (Element 23.3)
- Sorting, handling and storing information (Element 23.3)   } Chapter 6
- The purpose of storing and retaining documents (Element 23.3)

The Organisation

- The organisational and departmental structure (Elements 23.1 & 23.2)
- Own work role and responsibilities (Element 23.1)
- Organisation's administrative procedures (Element 23.1)   } Throughout
- The customer base (Element 23.2)
- Organisational document retention policy (Element 23.3)

Unit 23   **Achieving Personal Effectiveness**

Element 23.1   **Plan and Organise Own Work**

Performance Criteria

i.   Routine and unexpected tasks are identified and prioritised according to organisational procedures

ii.   Appropriate planning aids are used to plan and monitor work

iii.   Where priorities change, work plans are changed accordingly   Chapter 3

iv.   Anticipated difficulties in meeting deadlines are promptly reported to the appropriate person

v.   Assistance is asked for, where necessary, to meet specific demands and deadlines

Range Statement

1   Planning aids: diaries; schedules; action plans

Evidence Requirements

♦   Competence must be demonstrated consistently, over a period of time, with evidence of performance being provided of planning own work and changing plans in line with organisational priorities

Sources of Evidence (these are examples of sources of evidence, but candidates and assessors may be able to identify other, appropriate sources)

♦   Observed performance, eg

-    assessing work load and prioritising tasks

-    preparing action plans

-    coordinating own work with that of colleagues

-    checking achievement against plans and adapting plans to meet changing circumstances

-    requesting assistance when unable to meet specified work loads or deadlines

♦   Work produced by candidate, eg

-    action plans

-    diaries

-    records of communications with colleagues

♦   Authenticated testimonies from relevant witnesses

♦   Personal accounts of competence, eg

-    reports of performance

- ◆ Other sources of evidence to prove competence or knowledge and understanding where it is not apparent from performance, eg

  - answers to questions

Unit 23   Achieving Personal Effectiveness

Element 23.2   Establish and Maintain Working Relationships

Performance Criteria

i.   Information is provided to internal and external customers in line with routine requirements and one - off requests

ii.   The appropriate people are asked for any information, advice and resources that are required

iii.   Commitments to others are met within agreed timescales

iv.   Communication methods are appropriate to the individual situation   } Chapters 4 and 5

v.   Any communication difficulties are acknowledged and action is taken to resolve them

vi.   Opportunities are taken to promote the image of the department and organisation to internal and external customers

vii.   Confidentiality and data protection requirements are strictly followed

Range Statement

1   Internal customers: peers; manager; other members of staff

2   External customers: suppliers; customers; external agencies

3   Communication methods: written; verbal; electronic

Evidence Requirements

♦   Competence must be demonstrated consistently with evidence of performance being provided of relationships with at least two types of both internal and external customers being established

Sources of Evidence (these are examples of sources of evidence, but candidates and assessors may be able to identify other, appropriate sources)

♦   Observed performance, eg

    -   communicating with customers

    -   obtaining information and advice

    -   obtaining resources

    -   resolving communication difficulties

    -   undertaking measures to ensure confidentiality

- co-operating with other staff on work activities

♦ Work produced by candidate, eg

- copies of external correspondence

- internal memos

- details of information that has been provided to customers

♦ Authenticated testimonies from relevant witnesses

♦ Personal accounts of competence, eg

- reports of performance

♦ Other sources of evidence to prove competence or knowledge and understanding where it is not apparent from performance, eg

- answers to questions

- performance in simulations

Unit 23   Achieving Personal Effectiveness

Element 23.3   Maintain Accounting Files and Records

Performance Criteria

i.   New documentation and records are put into the filing system in line with organisational procedures

ii.   Item movements are monitored and recorded where necessary

iii.   Documentation and records are kept according to organisational and legal requirements

iv.   Out of date information is dealt with in accordance with organisational procedures

v.   Opportunities for improving filing systems are identified and brought to the attention of the appropriate person

} Chapter 6

Range Statement

1   Documentation: incoming correspondence; copies of outgoing correspondence; financial records

2   System: manual; computerised

3   Legal requirements: document retention; confidentiality

Evidence Requirements

◆   Competence must be demonstrated consistently with evidence of performance being provided of documentation and records being kept in line with organisational and legal requirements

Sources of Evidence (these are examples of sources of evidence, but candidates and assessors may be able to identify other, appropriate sources)

◆   Observed performance, eg

    -   filing documentation

    -   recording item movements

    -   dealing with out of date information

    -   discussing improvements to the filing system

◆   Work produced by candidate, eg

    -   records of documentation put into the system

    -   records of item movements

    -   reports relating to improvements in the system

- ♦ Authenticated testimonies from relevant witnesses

- ♦ Personal accounts of competence, eg

  - reports of performance

- ♦ Other sources of evidence to prove competence or knowledge and understanding where it is not apparent from performance, eg

  - reports

  - answers to questions

SYLLABUS – UNIT 20

Unit 20 　　　**Working with Information Technology,**

Unit commentary

This unit is about using information technology as part of the accounting technician's role.

The first element involves inputting data into the computer system using accountancy packages, in line with the organisational requirements. The element also requires the individual to generate unique codes as necessary, identify and correct errors in inputting and make use of search facilities. The individual is also expected to output data as both a hard copy and on disk, and to send it electronically via fax and e-mail.

The second element relates to the security aspects of information technology, in particular in terms of unauthorised people accessing information, work being lost from the system, and both hardware and software being removed from the organisation or department. To minimise these risks the individual is expected to take responsibility for saving and making back-ups of their own work, using passwords to limit access to sensitive information, and securing hardware and software. The individual is also required to identify and report other potential risks, such as viruses or risks to confidentiality.

Elements contained within this unit are:

Element 20.1 　　Input, store and output data

Element 20.2 　　Minimise risks to data held on a computer system

Knowledge and Understanding

General Information Technology

◆ The relationship between different software packages: accountancy packages; spreadsheets; databases, word processors (Element 20.1)	Chapter 8
◆ The purpose and application of different software packages: accountancy packages; spreadsheets; databases, word processors (Element 20.1)	Chapters 8, 14, 15, 16, 17
◆ Types of data held on a computer system (Elements 20.1 and 20.2)	Chapters 9, 10, 15
◆ How to save, transfer and print documents (Element 20.1)	Chapters 12, 14, 15
◆ Relevant security and legal regulations: data protection legislation; copyright; VDU legislation; health and safety; retention of documents (Elements 20.1 and 20.2)	Chapters 8, 11
◆ The purpose of passwords (Element 20.2)	Chapters 8, 9
◆ Different types of risks: viruses; confidentiality; hardware; software (Element 20.2)	Chapter 13
◆ Causes of difficulties: necessary files which have been damaged or deleted; printer problems; hardware problems (Element 20.2)	Chapters 12, 13

The Organisation

◆ House style for the presentation of documents (Element 20.1)	Chapters 12, 14, 15
◆ Location of information sources (Element 20.1)	Chapters 9, 15
◆ Organisational security policies (Elements 20.1 and 20.2)	Chapters 8, 10, 13
◆ The organisation's computer software, systems and networking (Elements 20.1 and 20.2)	Chapter 8
◆ Organisation procedures for changing passwords and making back-ups (Element 20.2)	Chapter 11
◆ Location of hardware, software and back-up copies (Element 20.2)	Chapters 11, 13

Unit 20   Working with Information Technology

Element 20.1   Input, store and output data

Performance criteria

i.	Data to be input into the computer system is clarified with, and authorised by, the appropriate person	Chapters 8, 11, 13, 17
ii.	Data is input and stored in the appropriate location	Chapters 9, 10, 15, 16, 17
iii.	New unique codes are generated as necessary	Chapters 9, 10
iv.	All vital fields are completed	Chapter 9
v.	Errors in inputting and coding are identified and corrected	Chapter 10
vi.	Data required from the computer system is clarified with the appropriate person	Chapters 12, 14
vii.	Effective use is made of available search facilities	Chapters 12, 14
viii.	Confidentiality of data is maintained at all times	Chapters 11, 12, 14, 17
ix.	Data is output as required in line with agreed deadlines	Chapters 12, 14

Range Statement

1.   **Input**: manual source documents; computerised source documents

2.   **Output**: print; e-mail; fax; disk; to other systems

Evidence requirements

♦   Competence must be demonstrated consistently with evidence of performance being provided of data being input and stored, and then output as a hard copy and on disk, and sent electronically

Sources of Evidence (these are examples of sources of evidence, but candidates and assessors may be able to identify other, appropriate sources)

♦   Observed performance, eg

  -    Inputting information into a computer system

  -    Generating new unique codes

  -    Correcting errors in inputting and coding

  -    Using search facilities

♦   Work produced by candidate, eg

  -    Bar chart

  -    Pie chart

  -    Histogram

- Invoice

- Remittance advice

- Pay run

- Statement of accounts

- Infringement report

- Flexitime report

- E-mails or faxes which have been sent

♦ Authenticated testimonies from relevant witnesses

♦ Personal accounts of competence, eg

- Report of performance

♦ Other sources of evidence to prove competence or knowledge and understanding where it is not apparent from performance, eg

- Reports

- Performance in simulation

- Answers to questions

Unit 20   Working with Information Technology

Element 20.2   Minimise risks to data held on a computer system

Performance criteria

i.	Work carried out on a computer is saved on a regular basis	Chapters 9, 11, 13
ii.	Back-ups of work are made in accordance with organisational procedures	Chapter 11
iii.	Passwords are used where limitations on access to data are required	Chapters 9, 11
iv.	Passwords are kept secret and are discreetly changed at appropriate times	Chapter 9
v.	The computer is closed down in a way so as not to cause loss of information or damage to the computer system or storage media	Chapters 11, 13
vi.	Immediate assistance is sought in the case of difficulties	Throughout
vii.	Hardware and software are securely located	Chapter 13
viii.	Potential risks to data from different sources are identified and the appropriate person is promptly notified	Chapter 13

Range statement

1. **Appropriate times:** on a regular basis; if disclosure is suspected

2. **Difficulties:** failure of equipment

3. **Potential risks:** viruses; confidentiality; hardware; software

4. **Sources of data:** internal; external

Evidence requirements

♦   Competence must be demonstrated consistently with evidence of performance being provided of potential risks to data from both internal and external sources being identified and minimised

Sources of Evidence (these are examples of sources of evidence, but candidates and assessors may be able to identify other, appropriate sources)

♦   Observed performance, eg

-   Saving data

-   Backing-up work

-   Closing down the computer

-   Seeking assistance

-   Relocating hardware or software

- Work produced by candidate, eg

  - Report on potential risks

  - Back-ups of data

- Authenticated testimonies from relevant witnesses

- Personal accounts of competence, eg

  - Report of performance

- Other sources of evidence to prove competence or knowledge and understanding where it is not apparent from performance, eg

  - Reports

  - Answers to questions

AAT UNITS 22 & 23

MONITOR AND MAINTAIN A HEALTHY, SAFE AND SECURE WORKPLACE

ACHIEVING PERSONAL EFFECTIVENESS

TEXTBOOK

CHAPTER 1

Health and safety in the workplace

ASSESSMENT FOCUS

This chapter covers the following Knowledge and Understanding and Performance Criteria of the AAT Syllabus.

Existing or potential hazards are put right if authorised (*Performance Criteria element 22.1*)

Hazards outside own authority to put right are promptly and accurately reported to the appropriate person (*Performance Criteria element 22.1*)

Actions taken in dealing with emergencies conform to organisational requirements (*Performance Criteria element 22.1*)

Emergencies are reported and recorded accurately, completely and legibly in accordance with established procedures (*Performance Criteria element 22.1*)

Work practices are in accordance with organisational requirements (*Performance Criteria element 22.1*)

Working conditions which do not conform to organisational requirements are promptly and accurately reported to the appropriate person (*Performance Criteria element 22.1*)

Organising of work area minimises risk to self and others (*Performance Criteria element 22.1*)

Common forms of accident/health emergency (*Knowledge and Understanding*)

Types and uses of fire and emergency equipment (*Knowledge and Understanding*)

Hazards in the use of equipment (*Knowledge and Understanding*)

Methods of minimising hazards in the work area (*Knowledge and Understanding*)

Organisation's procedures for dealing with emergencies (*Knowledge and Understanding*)

Own scope and limitations for dealing with emergencies (*Knowledge and Understanding*)

Methods of reporting emergencies (*Knowledge and Understanding*)

Relevant legal requirements (*Knowledge and Understanding*)

Location of fire and emergency equipment (*Knowledge and Understanding*)

In order to cover these, the following topics are considered:

health and safety legislation;

hazards in the office;

fire;

risks from new technology;

reporting accidents and hazards.

1   *Health and Safety legislation*

1.1   Introduction

Health and safety at work is important to all employees, whether they work in a factory, a shop, an office or on a building site. The main piece of legislation covering health and safety is the Health and Safety at Work Act. This has been the law since 1974 and has been amended fairly frequently.

The law puts the responsibility for health and safety on *both* the employer *and* the employee.

1.2   Employer's duty

The employer has a duty to provide the following:

(a)   safe ways in and out of the place of work;

(b)   a safe working environment;

(c)   safe equipment and procedures;

(d)   arrangements for the safe use, handling, storage and transport of articles and substances;

(e)   adequate information, instruction, training and supervision;

(f)   adequate investigation of accidents.

1.3   Employee's duty

The employee has a duty to:

(a)   be responsible for his or her own health and safety;

(b)   consider the health and safety of other people who may be affected by the employee's actions;

(c)   co-operate with anyone carrying out duties under the Act (including the employer).

As you can see, your employer has a duty to provide a safe working environment, but you, the employee, have a duty to look after yourself and other people within that environment. Any breaches in the law come under criminal law, which means an offence has been committed and this could lead to a prosecution by the Crown.

1.4   Health and safety manual

In addition to a safe working environment, your employer must provide a health and safety manual which describes the company's rules and procedures (see 1.7). Your employer must also display a health and safety notice in a prominent place. This summarises the responsibilities of employers and employees.

Activity 1 *(The answer to this activity can be found in Chapter 7)*

Mitchell & Co is a partnership of solicitors. They have five offices situated in various parts of the country.

(a)   What information would you expect to find in their health and safety manual, a copy of which is provided for all new employees?

(b)   What conditions and facilities do you think Mitchell & Co should provide for their employees?

1.5   Civil law

Under civil law, employees may be able to sue their employer for negligence if they are involved in an accident at work. This is in addition to any criminal proceedings which might arise from the *Health and Safety Act*. This also applies to members of the public who have an accident on the employer's premises.

1.6   Employer's liability insurance

Your employer must also take out Employer's Liability Insurance and display the insurance certificate on the premises. This insurance will cover the employer for any accidents you might have at work.

1.7   Health and safety policy

Every employer should have a document setting out health and safety procedures. This document outlining the company's rules, regulations and procedures will include the following:

(a)   details about how to report accidents;

(b)   where the accident book is kept;

(c)   the position of the first aid box;

(d)   details of qualified first-aid personnel;

(e)   the names and duties of the official safety representatives and the manager in charge of safety policy;

(f)   information on working practices throughout the organisation.

It is important that each employee has a thorough knowledge of the employer's health and safety procedures.

2   Hazards in the office

2.1   Introduction

Every year in the UK there are thousands of accidents in the office which result in injury. The latest estimates amount to around 50,000 office accidents each year.

2.2   Types of hazard

Typical hazards might include:

(a)   desks/chairs too near to doors;

(b)   unsafe electric plugs;

(c)   trailing wires, cables and leads;

(d)   torn carpets and other floor coverings;

(e)   unlit or poorly lit corridors and stairs;

(f)   top-heavy filing cabinets;

(g)   untrained operators using machines such as guillotines;

(h)   unmarked plate glass doors;

(i)   projecting door and drawer handles;

(j)   wet floors.

There are, of course, potentially many others; this list is not intended to be fully comprehensive.

Activity 2 *(The answer to this activity can be found in Chapter 7)*

What do you think are the causes of most accidents in the workplace?

2.3   Being aware of hazards

Obviously an office does not have the same hazards as a building site or factory but, to be able to operate safely within the workplace, you need to be aware of what is potentially hazardous.

Become aware of any hazards around your own workstation. Is the area around you free from hazards, eg objects lying on the floor, overloaded electrical sockets, trailing leads, top-heavy bookcases, overloaded filing cabinets? This is known as good housekeeping and is vital if you are to protect yourself and others.

Remember that you have a duty to look after yourself and others in your environment.

2.4   Personal safety checklist

The following questions should be considered:

(a)   do you know how to operate equipment properly;

(b)   do you always ask for assistance when using dangerous machinery for the first time;

(c)   do you always look at the manual before carrying out any unusual procedures (eg clearing paper jams from the inside of a photocopier);

(d)   do you always report hazards and leave any electrical work (eg repairing equipment) to qualified electricians;

(e)   do you know how to move objects and equipment safely within the work environment;

(f)   do you keep your back straight and bend your knees when you pick up objects;

(g)   do you ask for help when you need it, eg when carrying heavy objects, or negotiating doors or stairs.

Much of this is common sense but you do need to be aware of it when in the working environment.

3   Fire

3.1   Introduction

Fire is probably the greatest danger we face, both at work and in the home. One spark, a forgotten burning cigarette or an electrical fault are all that is needed to start a disastrous fire.

To guard as much as possible against fire there must be provided the means of:

(a)   warning;

(b)   fighting the fire;

(c)   escape.

3.2   Warning

The means of warning may be manual or automatic. Manual methods include breaking the glass on fire alarms, bells, rattles and sirens. Automatic methods include smoke and heat detectors. Some large organisations install personal computer based control systems, which monitor unusual occurrences such as fires, in addition to preventing unauthorised access.

All organisations must have someone who, in the event of a fire, has a duty to check that the building is completely empty. There must also be a check that all persons are assembled at arranged positions.

3.3   Fighting the fire

Extinguishers, sand buckets, hosepipes and sprinklers must be examined regularly to check that they are in working order. In the event of a fire that cannot be put out quickly, the fire brigade must be called without delay.

3.4   Escape

The effectiveness of the means of escape depends on how and where they are situated. Escape routes must be labelled and signposted and ideally should have emergency lighting. Fire exit doors must not be obstructed or locked from the outside.

You should ensure that you know where the fire exits are in your working environment.

3.5   Fire procedure

Most organisations will have a laid-down procedure for all matters relating to fires. The main points to remember are as follows:

(a)   all employees must know their fire drill: the escape routes, the location of the nearest fire exit and where they have to assemble when evacuating the building (for whatever reason);

(b)   fire doors must be kept closed;

(c)   gangways and passages must be kept clear;

(d)   rubbish should not be allowed to accumulate;

(e)   'No Smoking' area regulations must be observed;

(f)   inflammable items must be stored away from anything that will cause them to ignite;

(g)   waste paper baskets must not be used as ashtrays;

(h)   damaged gas and electrical appliances must be reported immediately.

Each individual in an organisation must know the procedure to follow in the event of a fire.

Activity 3 *(The answer to this activity can be found in Chapter 7)*

Describe your actions in the following situations:

(a)   if you discover a fire;

(b)   if you hear the fire alarm.

---

4   Risks from new technology

4.1   Introduction

Sitting at a VDU presents a particular risk to the health of employees. Employees who spend a large part of their working day working at a VDU risk various problems including eye strain, back problems and repetitive strain injury (RSI). RSI appears to arise from making the same movements over and over again and affects hands and arms.

If you ever suffer any pain or discomfort while working at a VDU, then you must take a break. It would also help if you could move on to a task not involving the VDU.

4.2   Reducing the risk

If you work at a VDU, there are certain things you can do to reduce the risk of problems:

(a)   use a five-leg swivel chair (preferably with an adjustable back rest) set at the correct height;

(b)   sit with the keyboard and monitor directly in front of you (do not sit in a position which means you have to turn your head to see the screen);

(c)   adjust the monitor so that it is on the same level as your eyes;

(d)   avoid a position which means there is light reflected directly from windows;

(e)   sit with your feet slightly raised on a support or book;

(f)   use the keyboard in its tilted position. Your forearms should be level with the work surface and your wrists should rest on the work surface;

(g)   make sure you have enough space on your workstation for books and papers you are working on; tidy away any other items which you are not actually using;

(h)   take regular breaks and avoid looking at the screen continuously for long periods of time.

These are simple things that each employee can do to minimise the potential problem of working at a VDU.

4.3   VDUs and the law

With effect from 1 January 1993, employers have a responsibility for the health and safety of their employees in relation to VDUs. This includes both new installations and existing equipment. The use of equipment must not be a source of risk for workers. The requirements for each type of equipment will now be considered.

4.4   Display screen

The requirements are that:

(a)   the characters on the screen must be well-defined and clearly formed, of adequate size and with adequate spacing between characters and lines;

(b)   the image on the screen must be stable, with no flickering or other forms of instability;

(c)   the brightness and/or the contrast between the characters and the background must be easily adjustable by the operator;

(d)   the screen must swivel and tilt easily and freely to suit the needs of the operator;

(e)   it must be possible to use a separate base for the screen or an adjustable table;

(f)   the screen must be free of reflective glare and reflections likely to cause discomfort to the user.

4.5   Keyboard

The keyboard must be tilted and separate from the screen so as to allow the worker to find a comfortable working position. The space in front of the keyboard must be sufficient to provide support for the hands and arms of the operator, the keyboard must have a matt surface to avoid reflective glare and must be easy to use with clear characters.

4.6   Work desk or work surface

The work desk or work surface must have a sufficiently large, low-reflective surface and allow a flexible arrangement of the screen, keyboard, documents and other equipment. The document holder must be stable and adjustable and must be positioned so as to minimise the need for uncomfortable head and eye movements, and there must be adequate space for workers to find a comfortable position.

4.7   Work chair

The work chair must be stable and allow the operator easy freedom of movement and a comfortable position, the seat must be adjustable in height and the seat back must be adjustable in both height and tilt. In addition, a footrest must be made available to anyone who wishes to use one.

4.8   Workstation

The workstation must provide sufficient space for the user to change position and vary movements. In addition:

(a)   room lighting and/or spot lighting (work lamps) must ensure satisfactory lighting conditions and an appropriate contrast between the screen and background environment, taking into account the type of work and the user's vision requirements;

(b)   possible disturbing glare and reflections on the screen or other equipment must be prevented;

(c)   noise emitted by the equipment belonging to the workstation shall be taken into account when a workstation is equipped, in particular so as not to distract attention or disturb speech;

(d)   equipment belonging to a workstation shall not produce excess heat which will cause discomfort to workers;

(e)   all radiation must be reduced to negligible levels from the point of view of the protection of workers' safety and health;

(f)   an adequate level of humidity must be established and maintained;

(g)   workers must take breaks or change activity at regular intervals.

4.9   Operator/computer interface

In designing, selecting, commissioning and modifying software, and in designing tasks using display screen equipment, the employer must take into account the following principles:

(a)   software must be suitable for the task;

(b)   software must be easy to use and, where appropriate, adaptable to the operator's level of knowledge or experience;

(c)   systems must provide feedback to workers on their performance;

(d)   systems must display information in a format and at a pace which are adapted to operators;

(e)   the principles of software ergonomics must be applied, in particular, to human data processing.

In addition, employers must offer a free eyesight test (at regular intervals) and provide any special glasses which employees need for VDU work. Training in the proper use of computer equipment must also be provided.

Employers now have considerable responsibilities when their employees are using computer equipment.

5   Reporting accidents and hazards

5.1   Introduction

If you come across an accident, then your first action must be to get help (unless you are a qualified first-aider). Trying to move someone who is injured may make their injuries worse.

5.2   Medical facilities

The medical facilities available will depend upon the size of the organisation. Some large companies (particularly those in manufacturing companies) employ a nurse. Other organisations have appointed first-aiders and a first aid box.

First aid boxes can only contain a limited number of things (by law). For instance, drugs (eg paracetomol or aspirin) should not be kept in a first aid box or given to anyone who feels unwell. If that person has an allergic reaction to the drugs, then he or she could sue.

5.3   Recording accidents

Employers must keep some form of accident book or log. If you have an accident you will probably be asked to complete an accident form. The details of the accident will then be recorded in the accident book.

Activity 4 *(The answer to this activity can be found in Chapter 7)*

Which details do you think should be recorded in an accident book?

5.4　*Reporting hazards*

If you become aware of any potential hazards either to yourself or other employees, then you should report them immediately. You should report them to the person identified in company procedures.

5.5　*Safety representative*

In a large organisation, there will generally be a safety representative in each department. Any employee who notices anything hazardous should report it to the representative so that it can be dealt with appropriately.

As an exercise, you could walk around your department or building and make a list of anything which is potentially dangerous. Things to look out for include:

(a)　piles of rubbish left near an entrance way;

(b)　drawers to filing cabinets left open;

(c)　sand levels in the fire buckets dangerously low;

(d)　fire doors jammed open;

(e)　electric plugs overloaded.

CHAPTER 2

Security of the workplace

ASSESSMENT FOCUS

This chapter covers the following Knowledge and Understanding and Performance Criteria of the AAT Syllabus.

Organisational security procedures are carried out correctly (*Performance Criteria element 22.2*)

Security risks are correctly identified (*Performance Criteria element 22.2*)

Identified security risks are put right or reported promptly to the appropriate person (*Performance Criteria element 22.2*)

Identified breaches of security are dealt with in accordance with organisational procedures (*Performance Criteria element 22.2*)

Identification of potential security risks (*Knowledge and Understanding*)

Organisation's security procedures (*Knowledge and Understanding*)

Own scope and limitations for dealing with security risks (*Knowledge and Understanding*)

In order to cover these, the following topics are considered:

the importance of security;

security of premises;

security of property;

security of computer systems.

1 The importance of security

1.1 Security awareness

You may ask why security is important; after all, most people are relatively honest. Unfortunately, there are always people who steal and cheat; large scale theft is possibly more prevalent than ever before. The amount of violence used in pursuit of theft is also on the increase.

In the workplace, millions of pounds are lost every year through thefts of money, stock, equipment, vehicles and information, as well as by shoplifting, fraud and forgery, and bad housekeeping (eg failure to keep proper records of stock movements). If not checked, thefts and frauds lead to lower profits, possibly higher prices, higher costs for insurance and certainly less overall prosperity in the organisation.

1.2 Security policy

One of the performance criteria for this unit is to carry out organisational security procedures correctly. An understanding of the meaning of procedures may help you satisfy the requirements of this part of the course.

An organisational policy is generally a principle laid down for the guidance of executives in handling their jobs.

1.3 Security procedures and rules

Policies find expression in procedures and rules. Procedures are the formal arrangements by which the policies are put into effect. They provide a sequence of activities that employees are required to follow. Rules or regulations are the laws with penalties attached by which procedures are enforced.

It may be easier to compare rules, procedures and policies to the ground, middle and top floors, respectively, of a three-storey building.

It is important to remember that:

(a)   policies are broad in content and are the concern and responsibility of top management;

(b)   procedures are less general and are suitably detailed, they prescribe action in respect of situations and govern both management and workers, and it is the responsibility of middle and lower management to carry them out;

(c)   rules are detailed, regulating the conduct of all employees in the various situations in workroom and office.

1.4 Example of a security policy

A suitable safety and security policy for an organisation might be worded as follows: 'The company recognises the need for all people at work to understand the importance of health, safety and security at work and to be committed to maintaining high standards. In addition to the provision of necessary facilities, information and adequate supervision, safe and secure working depends on staff attitudes and job training at all levels. It is the policy of the company to provide and encourage adequate safety and security training in all activities and at all locations'. Because this is quite a general policy, the procedures detailing the actions may vary from one department to another.

Procedures may not always be written down and easily accessible, but employees will be expected to know what to do in certain circumstances. If you are unsure of the procedure to follow where security is involved, it will only show how competent you are if you ask for some clarification from your supervisor or manager.

1.5 Personnel

Some of the best methods of safeguarding the organisation's possessions revolve around the staff. Efficient managers will do their utmost to make all employees mindful of the importance of security. Involving staff in decisions which affect them and are related to their jobs, treating people as more than numbers and setting a good example all help towards the creation of a loyal workforce.

Careful recruitment, staff training and the operation of incentive schemes relating to security in supervision and constant alertness all lead towards better security. From an individual's point of view, it is often easier for an employee to know when colleagues are a potential security risk: for example, if they are unhappy and wanting to leave the company, especially when their feelings are strongly negative and they feel they have an axe to grind.

1.6   Inefficiency

Not all the losses in companies are caused by criminal activities, nor covered in general procedures. In many instances, losses can be attributed to bad practices, carelessness and general inefficiency. Examples include the following:

(a)   clerical errors, such as failing to check goods properly when they are delivered, can lead to payment for goods not received;

(b)   careless treatment of stock and equipment could lead to items being written off before they should have been;

(c)   treating customers badly can lead to incalculable losses in future, and possibly present, business: consumers who are badly treated tell others.

Security of the assets of an organisation can be encouraged through security policy and procedures and also by careful training and treatment of staff, and efficient working procedures.

2   Security of premises

2.1   Unauthorised access to buildings

Many thefts and burglaries, often accompanied by damage to property and equipment, are not well planned crimes. Simple security precautions could prevent them. For example, windows and doors left open or unlocked, and ladders left lying about, all help the illegal entry of intruders. By being alert to these risks, you could prevent a breach of security in your company.

Depending on the size of the organisation, there are a number of access controls that could be used. Sophisticated control systems provide for control by card access at a single door, or a network of doors, parking places, lifts and turnstiles. Less sophisticated systems include burglar alarms, some of which may be connected to the local police station.

2.2   Visitors

Many large companies have a gatehouse where security staff check visitors as they enter the premises and issue a special visitors' badge or card. These identity cards may be colour coded, or have a built in control, to only allow access to distinct areas of the building. The visitor will be asked to sign in, using a visitors' book, stating their name, company and other relevant details of their visit. Often the car registration number of the visitor is included if the car is parked in a company car park. Highly security-conscious companies may insist that any large bags are left in the gatehouse and collected on departure. They may also insist on escorting visitors from one department to another.

It is important that, as an employee, you are aware of the security procedures for dealing with visitors to your company. Any breaches of this security which you can identify should be reported to the appropriate person immediately, even if it is only a case of someone being over-polite and keeping a door open so that a visitor can pass through without using a pass.

2.3   Bomb threat

The Metropolitan Police have issued a guide for small businesses which includes an action checklist for anyone receiving a bomb threat over the telephone. If you can't find any written procedures for this type of situation, you should ask your local Crime Prevention Officer to obtain a copy for your company.

Points to note are as follows:

(a)   try to keep the caller on the line, but try not to cut off the conversation or ask the caller to hold;

(b)   do not ring off or become flustered or excited because you will need to report the details;

(c)   ask if there is a code to verify that this is not a hoax call;

(d)   take the message about where the bomb has been planted and the time it is to go off;

(e)   ask what the device looks like;

(f)   ask why the caller is doing this;

(g)   ask the caller's name;

(h)   make a note of all the caller's characteristics: for example, male or female, alone or with others, approximate age, accent, whether intoxicated, laughing or serious, inconsistent or rational, and whether it sounds like the message is being read or is spontaneous;

(i)   pay attention to background noises (eg interruptions from someone else, music, children, machinery, road noises).

After the call, you must collect the notes you made during the conversation and inform your immediate superior and, of course, the police. Even bogus calls must be taken seriously.

3   Security of property

3.1   Stock

An organisation can suffer stock losses because of:

(a)   the dishonesty of its staff and customers (eg at the checkout points);

(b)   shoplifting;

(c)   burglary and fraud;

(d)   poor management (eg failure to keep proper records of goods and raw materials received).

Many of these losses, referred to as leakages, are caused by poor practices being used when goods and raw materials are received. Saying 'Thank you' and asking the driver to put the package out of the way is not good enough when a delivery is made to the organisation. It can lead to the company paying for goods which have never been received.

3.2   Goods in procedures

To check the stock losses, the organisation should have a set of goods in procedures to follow. The types of check that might be included are as follows:

(a)   all goods must be delivered to the company's delivery area between certain times (eg 10 am–1 pm, 2 pm–5 pm);

(b)   a note of damaged or opened parcels must be made on the delivery sheet;

(c)   goods must be checked against the advice note when they are delivered;

(d)   where stock is valuable, it should be locked in secured rooms;

(e)   goods should never be left outside store rooms;

(f)   waste should be cleared regularly.

3.3   Receiving parcels

Companies differ in their policy about whether parcels and packages should be delivered unopened or opened by the mail room staff. If you receive a parcel, you will be expected to sign for it. Unopened parcels should be signed for with an additional note to say 'contents not checked'. Parcels which are already opened should be checked carefully and a note made of any discrepancies. If possible, a damaged parcel should be refused on delivery and returned to the sender. The alternative is to sign for it as 'damaged on delivery'.

3.4   Suspicious packages

Certain organisations face the problem of receiving suspicious packages in the mail (eg suspected letter bombs). If you work for an organisation which considers itself vulnerable, there is probably a screening device which scans all mail before it is opened. The machine will discriminate between potentially harmful contents and routine items such as paper clips and staples. The Post Office routinely scans mail.

Even companies which are not involved in sensitive areas of work should be aware of the threat of a letter bomb or package arriving through the mail. You should check whether the company that you work for has information, leaflets or posters to remind staff of the problem and the correct procedure to follow. Because a letter bomb or package is designed to kill or maim when opened, everyone should be alert to the possibility that a letter or package is an explosive device. There are a number of indications that should rouse your suspicions:

(a)   a smell of almonds or marzipan;

(b)   grease marks on the wrapping;

(c)   visible wiring or tin foil seen through the outer wrapper;

(d)   excessive wrapping;

(e)   heavy for its size;

(f)   too many stamps for the weight of the package;

(g)   delivery by hand from an unknown source;

(h)   posted or delivered from an unexpected source;

(i)   poor handwriting, typing or spelling.

If you are suspicious, you should inform your supervisor immediately. If this is not possible because you are on your own, you should treat the package with caution, isolate it in a locked room, preferably on a table and away from the windows. Leave the room or building and telephone the police.

3.5   Equipment

Good equipment is both costly and vital to the efficient working of the organisation. Within the office environment, great care must be taken with the maintenance, operation and custody of equipment.

At the end of the day's work, small valuable pieces of equipment, such as calculators, should be securely stored away. Filing cabinets and desk drawers must be locked when work is finished. The keys must be removed and held by a responsible employee; keys must not be hidden in the office. Where it is possible, offices should also be locked when they are empty.

3.6   Suspicious behaviour

Access to offices is far too easy. Thefts are carried out by people posing as cleaners, decorators, delivery or repair personnel, window cleaners, and gas, electricity and telephone officials. If you see anyone who appears to be acting suspiciously, or whose presence in the office you cannot account for, politely ask the nature of their business and whether or not you can help. If you are still not satisfied, you should report the matter at once to one of your superiors.

3.7 Cheques

Your organisation will hold a supply of cheques which it issues to suppliers and to its staff. The cheques will probably be kept in a fireproof safe, with a lock or unique security number, which can only be opened by the cashier or assistant cashier. Whilst the arrangements will differ from organisation to organisation, there will always be safeguards for protecting the cheques.

3.8 Petty cash

Petty cash is the term given to the money, often kept in a tin, to cover small day-to-day items of expenditure in an office, which would not be paid for by cheque (eg. tea, coffee or magazines for the reception area). The amount kept is generally sufficient to cover expenditure for a week or a month, depending on the company policy. To make sure that only correct amounts for authorised payments are paid out, petty cash vouchers are used to record the money spent. These vouchers are numbered and issued in numerical order.

3.9 Security over petty cash

Strict control must be kept over the petty cash tin itself and the money paid out to prevent loss of money through mistakes, pilferage or deliberate fraud. If it is part of your duties to look after petty cash, there are a number of rules which should be adhered to:

(a)   the petty cash tin should be locked when not in use and kept in a secure place; although its whereabouts are often common knowledge within an office, you should not discuss where it is kept with anyone else;

(b)   unused vouchers should be kept safely, preferably within the tin;

(c)   completed vouchers should be filed and kept in a secure position;

(d)   any lost or missing vouchers should be reported immediately;

(e)   payments must not be made without an accompanying voucher and requests for 'advances' from petty cash by any colleague should be denied and reported to your superior.

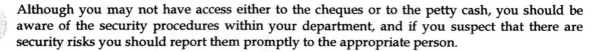

Although you may not have access either to the cheques or to the petty cash, you should be aware of the security procedures within your department, and if you suspect that there are security risks you should report them promptly to the appropriate person.

4   Security of computer systems

4.1 Introduction

Safeguards must be applied to a computer system to protect the hardware and the data which is held on the computer files. The loss of the system could be catastrophic for the organisation and consequently security of all aspects must be maintained.

4.2 Physical security

Normally a computer system, or at least the central processing unit of a large system, is housed in a separate room where it can be protected. It is necessary to take precautions against natural hazards, such as fire or water. Consequently, a computer room should be a 'no-smoking' area and have heat and smoke detectors, fire extinguishers and rules to ensure that tapes and disks be returned to the fireproof safe after use. Only those authorised to work in the computer room should have access, and strict physical security often includes a security device on the door to control entrance and exit. The damage to hardware usually occurs by accident and deliberate physical damage can be minimised by general security measures.

16

The biggest problems associated with computer systems are the corruption and destruction of software and information.

4.3   Information

The importance of the organisation's commercial and trade information cannot be over-estimated. The leaking of a company's trade secrets, such as its production processes, to its competitors might seriously affect its performance and its profits.

The safeguarding of information kept in files and filing cabinets will be dealt with later in the text. However, computers are used by most organisations to store information of all kinds, ranging from details about employees to financial accounts. If such information is lost or destroyed, the consequences might be disastrous.

4.4   Computer-stored information

Information stored in a computer is often confidential, for example:

(a)   bank account details;

(b)   staff wages and salaries data;

(c)   personnel details, such as police criminal records;

(d)   customer accounts.

4.5   Security procedures

Where computers are used, certain procedures may be taken to safeguard the information they hold. These include the following:

(a)   only staff responsible for the information are permitted to operate or change the computer programs;

(b)   back-up copies of vital information are kept separately;

(c)   a system of passwords is available to authorised users - this helps to stop unauthorised persons gaining access to the information;

(d)   visitors are denied access to any rooms where computers are used.

4.6   Passwords

Access to certain types of information held on computer is controlled by the use of passwords or other types of secret code. Because different people within a department have separate responsibilities, there may be several passwords within one program.

4.7   Example: wages and salaries department

In a wages and salaries department using a payroll package, you may find the following:

(a)   one password is required to get into the program giving access to hourly paid employee records;

(b)   a second password is needed for access to information on salaried staff;

(c)   a third password is required for information on managers' and directors' salaries.

4.8   Passwords and security

To ensure confidentiality, there are certain procedures about the implementation and use of passwords, or any other personal identity number, for example:

(a)   passwords should not be known by other people;

(b)   passwords should not be written down;

(c)   passwords should be changed frequently;

(d)   passwords should not be too obvious (eg the name of the password-holder) - many organisations have had security breaches because they have chosen passwords connected to the month or time of the year (eg Easter), or they have continued to use passwords issued by the software company which wrote the program (eg letmein).

Security in an organisation does not just relate to physical items. Security of information is just as important.

CHAPTER 3

Planning and organising work

ASSESSMENT FOCUS

This chapter covers the following Knowledge and Understanding and Performance Criteria of the AAT Syllabus.

Routine and unexpected tasks are identified and prioritised according to organisational procedures (*Performance Criteria element 23.1*)

Appropriate planning aids are used to plan and monitor work (*Performance Criteria element 23.1*)

Where priorities change, work plans are changed accordingly (*Performance Criteria element 23.1*)

Anticipated difficulties in meeting deadlines are promptly reported to the appropriate person (*Performance Criteria element 23.1*)

Assistance is asked for, where necessary, to meet specific demands and deadlines (*Performance Criteria element 23.1*)

Prioritising and organising work (*Knowledge and Understanding*)

Work planning and the use of planning and scheduling techniques and aids (*Knowledge and Understanding*)

Time management (*Knowledge and Understanding*)

Team working (*Knowledge and Understanding*)

Work methods and practices (*Knowledge and Understanding*)

In order to cover these, the following topics are considered:

time management;

work planning;

agreeing timescales;

planning methods;

routine and unexpected tasks.

1 Time management

1.1 Introduction

Commitments to others should be met within agreed timescales. Work planning is necessary to ensure that work is carried out in accordance with the organisation's requirements and needs, whether those requirements are clearly defined or are merely implied. It ensures that commitments to others are met within agreed timescales and necessitates planning and organising on the part of the organisation and the employee.

1.2   Timetabling tasks

Your time needs to be properly managed if you are to work efficiently and effectively. The first way to start to organise your time is to plan your use of time.

1.3   Example

Here is Joe's diary for the coming week:

Mon	Tues	Wed	Thurs	Fri
9am	3pm	2:30pm	Mum's	
Meeting	Group	Visit	birthday	
Mr Green	meeting	other site		

This shows his meetings with other people but not how he will use the rest of his time.

1.4   Solution

Here is a more useful version of his diary for the same week:

	Monday	Tuesday	Wednesday	Thursday	Friday
9am / 10am	Meeting Mr Green	Record cash	Record cash	Record cash	Record cash
11am / 12 noon	Record cash	Update cash book	Bank reconciliation	Finish bank reconciliation	Prepare cash flash figure
1pm	Lunch	Lunch	Lunch	Buy card	Lunch
2pm	Record cash continued	Prepare for meeting	Site visit	Prepare info for report	Prepare journals
3pm / 4pm	Speak to Pat about new systems?	Group meeting			Count petty cash
5pm	Home early				Request cash

Notice how all the major tasks have been timetabled. Joe has estimated the amount of time to complete each task and blocked out that time. This ensures that Joe has sufficient time to complete tasks before the necessary *deadline*.

1.5   Timing of tasks

Whatever function you perform at work, you will always have tasks which fall into *four* categories:

Category	Examples
Daily	Recording cash received
	Recording sales invoices in sales day book
	Recording purchase invoices in purchase day book
Weekly	Preparing journal entries to post totals from books of prime entry to nominal ledger
Monthly	Sales ledger reconciliation
	Purchase ledger reconciliation
	Bank reconciliation
One-off	Information for reports

Joe also keeps a list of quick tasks to do at appropriate times. As he does them, he crosses them off his list.

1.6   Review of work plans

Each evening before he goes home, Joe reviews his work schedule and updates it for:

(a)   things to carry over;

(b)   any other changes (eg meeting times changed).

Even if you do not have the opportunity to schedule your work, try scheduling your studies and your free time! You should find you get more out of your time.

1.7   Dealing with deadline problems

Sometimes you will find that your schedule shows that you do not have enough time to complete all your work. In this case, you *must* tell your supervisor as soon as a crisis appears. You must not wait until the crisis happens.

Remember to be polite, even if you are under pressure.

It is much better to inform the person for whom you are working that there is a problem meeting a deadline sooner rather than later, however tempting it is to put off such an admission.

Activity 1 *(The answer to this activity can be found in Chapter 7)*

Today is Friday.

Thomas has three tasks to complete, each of which will take two hours. His supervisor is expecting him to have completed them all by 10am on Monday.

Thomas was unable to perform any of the tasks on Friday morning because the computer was not working. It is now 2pm on Friday. Thomas normally goes home at 5pm.

What should Thomas do in these circumstances?

A   Complete one of the tasks and start one of the others. He should be able to complete all of them by noon on Monday.

B   Complete the most urgent task and take home the other two tasks. He is bound to be able to find time to finish them over the weekend.

C   Contact his supervisor immediately and explain the problem. He should suggest that he finishes what he considers to be the most urgent task first before starting one of the others.

D   Start all of the tasks and do parts of each of them. This way he has at least done something towards each of them before he goes home.

2   Work planning

2.1   Objectives of planning work

Planning work has the following objectives:

(a)   the determination of priorities;

(b)   the effective treatment of priorities as priorities;

(c)   the achievement of work deadlines;

(d)   the attainment of goals;

(e)   the co-ordination of individual tasks within the duties of single employees or within the activities of groups of individuals;

(f)   the mechanism and means to re-schedule ordinary work to facilitate and accommodate new, additional or emergency work.

2.2   Planning approach

The majority of organisations approach work planning methodically. Employees, however, often do not realise that if they do not plan their own individual and personal approach to work then the results desired by the organisation will not be achieved despite the efforts of the organisation.

As a well organised employee you should, as a general guideline, be:

(a)   neat and tidy;

(b)   orderly;

(c)   able and willing to follow an established routine.

You should try to ensure that your desk, shelves, cabinets, etc are tidy. This not only has the advantage of a pleasing appearance but, provided items are tidied in order, assists retrieval and efficiency.

2.3   Order of work

There are distinct advantages to be gained from tackling your tasks in some semblance of order, be it chronological or priority. Once a task has been commenced, it should be completed as far as is practically possible. Efficiency is impaired by moving from one task to another. Efficiency is improved if work is grouped into batches of the same type and carried out at the same time.

It is important that routine should be established in all aspects of your work. The following items typify the approach to be adopted:

(a)   important and difficult tasks should always be attempted when you are fresh, normally during the morning;

(b)   tasks, requests and instructions should be written down - memory often proves defective;

(c)   the adage 'never put off until tomorrow what can be done today' should be put into action;

(d)   often there are tasks which need to be done daily - these tasks should indeed be carried out each day, preferably at the same time;

(e)   the regular routine, once established, should be written down to enable you to use it as both a reminder and a checklist.   Additionally, if you are absent or leave the organisation, the written routine will enable a substitute or replacement to function more effectively.

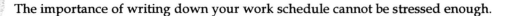

The importance of writing down your work schedule cannot be stressed enough.

3   Agreeing timescales

3.1   Introduction

The planning of work involves the allocation of time to the requirements of work to be done. This must be applied to the organisation as a whole, to individual departments and sections, and to single employees. Planning must be geared to periods of time, and the degree of flexibility built into planning will vary according to the length of time being planned for. The principles of planning will revolve around:

(a)   determining the length of time covered by the plans;

(b)   planning by departments and groups of individuals;

(c)   planning by individuals.

3.2   Time ranges

There are three time ranges which are normally involved in planning work:

(a)   long-term;

(b)   medium-term;

(c)   short-term.

These three terms are really only expressions of convenience. Time is relative. For example, a length of five years might be considered long-term within an organisation producing footwear but short-term in, say, the aviation industry. It must be remembered that all time ranges are relative. It may well be that three years is short-term to an organisation but to a department within that organisation it may be medium-term whilst to an individual employee it may be long-term. It is important that, whatever the relevant time span may be to a group or individual, work is allocated accordingly.

3.3   Planning by departments and groups of individuals

Within organisations, departmental plans are devised to meet specific objectives, the origins of those objectives stemming directly from the goals, aims and objectives of the organisation as a whole. There are two aspects which should be considered here:

(a)   the internal departmental/group planning via the determination of schedules, etc;

(b)   the co-ordination of the work of all the departments/groups within the organisation to ensure that the overall objectives of the organisation are attained.

3.4   Planning by the individual

It is all very well to state, perhaps blandly, that the objectives of departments/groups must be determined, co-ordinated and ultimately attained, but this may only be achieved by those individuals comprising departments and groups attaining their own goals, a task which will necessarily require planning at that individual level.

It is essential to note well this fact that the objectives of the organisation will only be met in any time span if individual organisation members (employees) plan and implement appropriate actions effectively.   The individual should plan for the long term by ascertaining the requirements over, say, the coming year. The equivalent of medium-term planning would be perhaps on a quarterly basis and this would be broken down into monthly, weekly and daily plans (ie the equivalent of short-term planning). Priorities must be identified.

Individuals can only successfully plan their own work in the context of the plans of the department or group within which they work.

4   Planning methods

4.1   Introduction

Different organisations, groups and individuals have individual characteristics, tastes, styles, preferences and objectives. These particular objectives may well be attained via different methods and systems of scheduling work.

As a method of planning group work, it is vital that these efforts are co-ordinated – not only with each other but with all actions taken. The method used can be a means of communication and support within the group, assuring all members of the group progress towards their goal.

The following planning methods and systems are probably the most common:

(a)   checklists;

(b)   bar charts;

(c)   bring-forward, bring-up and follow-up systems;

(d)   activity scheduling and time scheduling;

(e)   action sheets;

(f)   other systems, including planning charts and boards, and diaries.

Each of these methods and systems will be discussed individually below. However, any combination may be in use at any one time within an organisation or by an individual employee. It is vital therefore that these efforts are co-ordinated, not only with each other but with all actions taken.

4.2   Checklists

Checklists are often used on an individual basis and are perhaps the simplest system, being essentially a list of items or activities. The preparation of a typical checklist would involve the following:

(a)   the formulation of a list of activities and tasks to be performed within a given period;

(b)   the identification of urgent or priority tasks;

(c)   the maintenance of a continuous checklist with the addition of extra activities and tasks as and when required.

This system is obviously limited in its application because of its simplicity. It is suited to fairly mundane or routine tasks, but it is these tasks which are often the very essence of the attainment of objectives.

Typical uses of checklists would include the following:

(a)   purchasing requirements;

(b)   points to cover at an interview;

(c)   points to cover at a meeting (eg an agenda);

(d)   organising a conference or meeting.

Activity 2 *(The answer to this activity can be found in Chapter 7)*

Prepare a checklist of information you would store relating to a meeting at some other organisation's premises.

4.3   Bar charts

A bar chart has two main purposes:

(a)   to show the time necessary for an activity;

(b)   to display the time relationship between one activity and another.

Bar charts are particularly useful for checking the time schedules for a number of activities which are interdependent. A bar chart for the building of a house extension might be shown over a period of six months and an example is given below.

Task	March	April	May	June	July	August
Dig foundations	▬					
Walls/floors		▬				
Windows			▬			
Door frames				▬		
Roof				▬		
Electric wiring				▬		
Plumbing			▬			
Glazing					▬	
Plastering						▬

This illustrates the importance of bar charts in showing:

(a)   overall progress to date, thus assisting in monitoring;

(b)   the progress attained at an individual stage of a multi-stage process.

4.4   Bring-forward, bring-up and follow-up systems

These systems are more sophisticated than checklists and bar charts. They are particularly useful for coping with documentation and are utilised in many offices. The systems involve the filing of details of work to be done and the dates on which this work is to be done. A routine is established with a view to allocating necessary tasks to the precise day.

The systems all operate around the following principles:

(a)   a note is made of anything to be done in the future, showing details of the appropriate action or format (eg make a telephone call or write a letter);

(b)   the note is filed away in a concertina folder with separate files for each day;

(c)   each appropriate file is checked at the start of each day and the action required that day noted;

(d)   the action is carried out.

4.5   Activity scheduling

Activity scheduling is concerned with the determination of priority and the establishment of the order in which tasks are to be tackled. The establishment of an order of priority is not as easy in practice as it may appear in theory. Some tasks must be completed before others may be commenced, some may need to be carried out at the same time as others and some may need to be completed at the same time as others but factors such as finance or manpower may prevent this. A typical problem which is particularly suited to activity scheduling is the arrangement of an interview where, say, three panel members are required and six candidates have been short-listed for interview. Obviously, mutually convenient dates must be found when all nine parties are available and the room which is to be used for the interview must be free for use on these days.

Activity scheduling involves the identification of key factors and their assembly on a checklist. In the example given above, the two key factors are room availability and people availability. It may be used for any task which involves a number of actions which must necessarily be undertaken in some sequence.

4.6   Time scheduling

Time scheduling is an extension of activity scheduling by indicating the required time for each task. It follows the preparation of an activity schedule and involves the determination of time required for each activity. Given that within an activity schedule some tasks will be performed simultaneously, it should be noted that the time period in which the series of activities will be completed may not equate to the total of the individual activity times.

Effectively a time schedule determines the order in which activities are scheduled on a checklist, the time required for each activity also being shown alongside each item. Tasks that can be done in parallel are noted. The total of the individual activity times, with allowances for simultaneous activities, will produce the time allowed for one complete group of activities.

Time scheduling is thus particularly useful in the process of planning, especially as it enables the initial deadlines to be set.

4.7   Action sheets

This system is a natural progression from activity and time scheduling. Action sheets summarise the time that the stages of the individual task should take, and contain estimates of the start and finish dates of each stage.

The example below depicts an action sheet for a wedding.

Activity number	Detail	Number of weeks in advance	Certification of completion (initials or signature)
1	Book church	26	
2	Book reception hall	26	
3	Send out invitations	12	
4	Receive replies	4	
5	Order food/refreshments	3	
6	Check arrangements	2	
7	The wedding day	–	

Action sheets are widely used and are often utilised in conjunction with bar charts.

4.8   Planning charts and boards

These usually show information in summary form and any required item of information may be seen at a glance. They are often used to show details of future events which affect departments (eg to plan staff holidays).

4.9   Diaries

The diary is an obvious and consequently often overlooked aid to planning. Diaries can be small pocket-size type, large diaries with a page for each day or computer diaries such as Microsoft Outlook.

Diaries are especially suited to individual employees but only if the employee ensures that all relevant details of any appointments are entered as a matter of course. This matter of full details is important because the failure to note down full and appropriate information regarding a particular appointment could have serious repercussions for the organisation, particularly if an appointment has to be rescheduled or handled by someone else. It is sensible to have a routine for making appointments and indeed to create a 'checklist for appointments'.

5   Routine and unexpected tasks

5.1   Introduction

Much office work is of a routine nature, although there are exceptions. Most routine work is cyclical. Priorities must be established with regard to:

(a)   the cyclical components of routine work;

(b)   unexpected demands.

5.2   Routine work

The cyclical aspects often mean that certain tasks have to be completed by a certain time. In such cases, other work may have to be left in order to ensure that the task with the approaching deadline date is given priority. Such tasks might include:

(a)   the preparation of payroll sheets for a weekly computer run;

(b)   the despatch of monthly statements to account customers;

(c)   the checking of stock levels at predetermined intervals and subsequent appropriate action, such as reordering.

5.3   Unexpected tasks

Unexpected demands are often made at departmental, sectional or individual level. If management requires urgent or additional work to be carried out, then obviously some other tasks will have to be postponed.

Where tasks or events of an emergency type arise, the main problem facing an individual will be that of deciding which of the routine tasks should be postponed. Additionally, it must be remembered that the postponement of one routine task will automatically delay successive tasks.

5.4   Identifying priorities

In determining priorities, the following should be noted:

(a)   wherever it is possible for a priority to be anticipated, associated difficulties will usually be overcome by sensible, logical planning;

(b)   plans should be formulated and implemented to ensure that the routine work which has had to be postponed is carried out as soon as possible, resulting in minimum disruption to the normal routine;

(c)   often situations may arise in which one priority comes into conflict with another - the task deemed more important by a responsible individual should take preference;

(d)   individuals within one department or section often become blind to the needs of other departments or sections. A task that is classed as low priority within one department or section may be of the utmost priority to another. Thus, in arriving at any decision, the individual making that decision must ensure that the effect on each department is included in the decision-making process.

When an unexpected task is given to you then you must have the flexibility to be able to reschedule your routine work in order to complete this task.

CHAPTER 4

Working relationships – internal customers

ASSESSMENT FOCUS

This chapter covers the following Knowledge and Understanding and Performance Criteria of the AAT Syllabus.

Information is provided to internal and external customers in line with routine requirements and one-off requests (*Performance Criteria element 23.2*)

The appropriate people are asked for any information, advice and resources that are required (*Performance Criteria element 23.2*)

Commitments to others are met within agreed timescales (*Performance Criteria element 23.2*)

Communication methods are appropriate to the individual situation (*Performance Criteria element 23.2*)

Any communication difficulties are acknowledged and action is taken to resolve them (*Performance Criteria element 23.2*)

Opportunities are taken to promote the image of the department and organisation to internal and external customers (*Performance Criteria element 23.2*)

Confidentiality and data protection requirements are strictly followed (*Performance Criteria element 23.2*)

Methods of establishing constructive relationships (*Knowledge and Understanding*)

Seeking and exchanging information, advice and support (*Knowledge and Understanding*)

Handling disagreements and conflict (*Knowledge and Understanding*)

Using appropriate actions and different styles of approach in different situations (*Knowledge and Understanding*)

Different communication methods and styles (*Knowledge and Understanding*)

Types of communication difficulties and how to resolve them (*Knowledge and Understanding*)

Employee responsibilities in complying with relevant legislation (*Knowledge and Understanding*)

In order to cover these, the following topics are considered:

dealing with people;

teamwork;

communication;

rules for good communication;

written communication with internal customers;

distributing information internally.

1 Dealing with people

1.1 Introduction

Business relationships refer to the professional working relationships you will be expected to create and maintain with all the people including colleagues, customers and other people who may visit your workplace.

We will start by concentrating on the relationships with line managers, immediate colleagues and other members of staff with related work activities. These are your internal customers.

When dealing with other people in your organisation you should be as courteous and polite as when dealing with external customers.

1.2 Organisation charts

An organisation must be set up in a formal manner to give it some authority or some standing. This means that those within the organisation must be organised so that they know what to do and whom to ask for advice. Generally you find in most organisations there are two types of organisational structure, which are often referred to as:

(a) functional organisation;

(b) line organisation.

1.3 Functional organisation

The functional organisational structure relates to the specialists or specialisms in a particular part of an organisation. For instance, a finance division or group can be described as a functional organisational structure.

We can usually identify a number of different areas which can be referred to as specialist functions. A large company may have the functional organisation below.

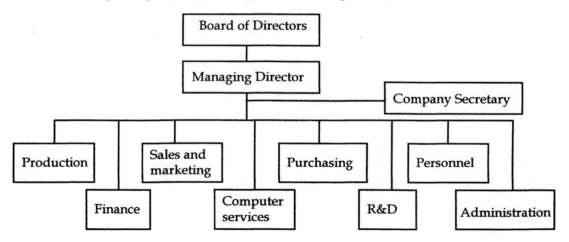

1.4   Line organisation

A line manager is a member of the organisation with direct responsibility for the success or failure of a section of the organisation in performing part of the principal work of the organisation. For instance, the line manager for a finance section is the manager responsible for this particular area. Line managers have staff above and below them.

The easiest way to visualise a line organisation is to think of a line from the accounting clerk to the managing director. All the intermediate staff have to have discussions with those above and below them, but the senior gives the direction to the business and the discipline within the particular area or group.

This type of line organisation can be found within the whole organisational structure and the actions of the staff stem from the line management decisions. The senior line managers' decisions should be complied with as their authority carries more weight.

1.5   Example

You should be aware of the line and staff relations in your organisational structure. Draw an organisation chart of your company, putting names and a brief job description beside the line managers, immediate colleagues and other members of staff with related work activities.

Knowing who does what and where, enables you to:

(a)   communicate more freely and efficiently;

(b)   transfer telephone calls to the right person;

(c)   deliver mail accurately;

(d)   handle any enquiries effectively.

1.6   Working relations

You will see that social skills are important to the organisation, as well as to the individuals employed and this is what we mean by working relations. There will be jobs where co-operation with colleagues is highly essential. It would, of course, be no good to have a large number of employees who all argue and disagree with each other. Apart from the disruption caused to each other, the organisation would also suffer since the amount of work carried out would probably be very small and perhaps even counter-productive.

1.7   Social skills in the line management structure

What is meant by social skills? It means the ways in which we discuss work-related matters with others, or obtain information from them. You will be aware of the situation when you want to take some annual leave and need to ask your supervisor whether you can have the time off when you require it. The supervisor may tell you right away, ask you to put it in writing or need to ask the boss later. What is important is the way you 'get on' with your supervisor and perhaps the way in which they recognise you. If the approach is right, then you might be told right away there are no problems, even though there may be some particular way in which you should go about it. Your social skills or the way you put the question over is important, not only to you – especially if you want time off – but to the organisation because it is in this way that a certain amount of confidence builds up between you and the supervisor.

It is not unknown to find a clash of personality between individuals in a line organisation, and it is up to the senior officer in the organisation to take the appropriate action. Whilst there can be no hard and fast rules on what should be done, the interests of the organisation must take priority, although there may be certain circumstances where the individual's interests should be taken into consideration.

1.8   *Carrying out instructions*

An employee who will not carry out instructions will not be welcomed by most firms. The instructions are given so that the work to be performed can be understood and will fit into the total workload of the department. Failure to carry out instructions may:

(a)   delay a piece of work needed urgently by a customer;

(b)   completely wreck the rest of the work performed by everyone else;

(c)   endanger lives or health of other employees or customers (eg by operating a machine without following instructions or smoking in 'non-smoking' areas).

Employees should expect their employers to give proper instructions at the right time, in the right manner and in the right place. Failure to do so can mean that the employees might lose pay bonuses because they are unable to complete the work within a prescribed time. It can also lead to poor morale due to workers arguing about what should be done, rather than being fully aware of their commitments.

In addition, instructions to protect employees' physical well-being which are not given properly, or not given at all, can result in disability or even death.

1.9   *Asking for clarification when necessary*

It is possible for instructions genuinely to be misunderstood or for completely wrong instructions to be given. If this happens to you at any time, you should ask for clarification of the instructions. Simply to carry on with the job when the instructions are genuinely not clear, or where they are obviously wrong, can cause all sorts of problems. Your employer or supervisor would therefore expect you to question the instructions in such cases.

Of course it is possible to be obstinate and obstructive by deliberately trying to misinterpret instructions. You must be careful to ensure that your manager or supervisor understands your proper concern at the lack of clear instructions and does not mistakenly assume that you are being unnecessarily awkward.

If you are ever unclear about instructions that you have been given you should always check them with the appropriate person.

2   Teamwork

2.1   Introduction

There are very few jobs in which it is not necessary to work as part of a team.

Being part of a team means dealing with people at all levels within your organisation and building professional relationships with them. It takes time to build this association with people but there are a few guidelines which might get you off to a good start:

(a)   be tactful and courteous;

(b)   treat with respect people who are your senior in either age or position;

(c)   have a pleasant and helpful manner;

(d)   make allowances for others having personal problems which may affect their work, but do not joke about it or expect them to tell you why they might be having a 'bad day';

(e)   communicate with people using the correct words and tone.

2.2   *Personality differences*

Having a professional relationship with someone is different from a social relationship. In a social relationship you can choose how well you get to know someone, even whether or not you get to know them in the first place.

At work you will inevitably have to deal with people whom you would not necessarily choose as friends. This does not mean that you have to treat them as friends, but as colleagues. This means being polite to other people and speaking to them in an appropriate tone of voice. It also means offering to help them if you can see they need help.

It can be difficult if you do have a personality clash with someone at any level, but you must keep it in proportion. One of the worst things you can do is to dwell on the problem. You will quickly become unpopular with your other colleagues if you talk continually about your problems with another member of staff. It may also mean that the other person hears about your complaints which makes the matter worse.

2.3   *Complaints*

Staff morale is very important wherever you work and you can contribute to it. In the short term, everyone likes to complain about things, but in the long term this can cause tensions within the office.

In some cases, however, you may have a genuine cause for complaint. You should discreetly arrange to see your manager or personnel manager to discuss the problem. Remember that they will not necessarily have all the answers but will expect you to suggest solutions. Think carefully first about what you want to say and be positive.

2.4   *Responding to requests*

To be able to communicate effectively you must have the ability to:

(a)   pass on information accurately and without delay so that all concerned are aware of the situation and the correct action can be taken;

(b)   talk to a wide range of people with whom you have had little or no previous contact;

(c)   converse with your colleagues in a way which will promote and maintain a harmonious working atmosphere;

(d)   interpret non-verbal communication gestures and their meanings;

(e)   put people at their ease.

Even if you can schedule a lot of your own work, you will inevitably be asked to do things by your supervisor or other managers. In any job, you will have to do things you do not like. The important thing is to accept that everyone is in the same position and so you should try to carry out unwelcome tasks without complaining.

The way you act is very important. Do you appear disinterested when other people ask you to do something or do you appear attentive? Do you interrupt or do you let the other person finish first?

When dealing with colleagues, it is important to think about not only what you say but also the way you say it.

2.5   *Asking for help*

Sometimes you will need help from other people, but think carefully before asking. You may waste other people's time if you ask them for simple factual information which you could find elsewhere.

If you do need help, do not be embarrassed to admit that you do not know the answer.

Activity 1 *(The answer to this activity can be found in Chapter 7)*

Darren is the supervisor of a travel shop. When his staff take a customer booking, they have to add on a charge for airport taxes. The charges are different for each airport but are found in the company's fares manual.

One afternoon Fiona, who has worked in the shop for six weeks, asks Darren for the charge for Oslo airport. Darren gets angry. What could explain his outburst?

2.6 Listening

When asking for help it is important that you listen to the help or advice given.

Most of us have poor listening skills. We listen to the first part of what we are being told and then spend the next few seconds waiting for the other person to stop speaking so that we can say the next thought that has come into our heads. During this latter part of the other person's speech, we have totally switched off from what is being said.

Without effective listening, there can be no effective communication. It has been discovered that people forget most of what they have heard within a couple of days. This can be improved by better messages, repeated messages and also by helping the receiver to learn to be a more efficient listener.

Among the many ideas for better listening are the following:

(a)   concentrate on what is being said, not on the person saying it;

(b)   ask for something to be repeated if you do not understand;

(c)   try to concentrate on the meaning of the message;

(d)   do not become emotionally involved;

(e)   remember that thoughts are quicker than words and you can evaluate what is being said without missing anything;

(f)   do not take many notes, just the key points.

Listening is not the same as hearing. It involves a more conscious assimilation of information and requires attentiveness on the part of the interviewer. Failure to listen properly to what someone is saying will mean that probing questions (in an interview) may become a worthless exercise. In preparing to listen you should ask 'What new things can I learn from this person?'.

2.7 Problems with listening

Barriers to listening include the following:

(a)   scoring points – relating everything you hear to your own experience;

(b)   mind-reading;

(c)   rehearsing – practising your next lines in your head;

(d)   cherry-picking – listening for a key piece of information then switching off;

(e)   daydreaming – you can think faster than people can talk and there is a temptation to use the 'spare' time to daydream;

(f)   labelling – putting somebody into a category before hearing what they have to say;

(g)   counselling – being unable to resist interrupting and giving advice;

(h)   duelling – countering the other's advances with thrusts of your own, eg 'Well at least this department is never over budget';

(i)   side-stepping sentiment – countering expressions of emotion with jokes or hollow clichés, such as 'Well it's not the end of the world'.

There are also health factors that may cause difficulties in concentrating on what is being said. People who are suffering from stress, who are in pain or are anxious about something will not be at their best when it comes to effective communications.

If you are to do your job properly then it is important that you listen carefully to all instructions, help and advice.

Activity 2 *(The answer to this activity can be found in Chapter 7)*

Diana's supervisor is explaining a new accounting procedure to her. Suggest some things which Diana might do which would suggest that she is not listening properly.

How might her supervisor react to these?

2.8   Passing on information

We have already mentioned the importance of passing on information because inefficiency may affect the organisation's business. It can also affect your relationships with your colleagues. You may make someone waste a considerable amount of time if you do not pass on information correctly and on time.

Passing on information may be by note or memo. Your organisation may use special pre-printed pads for telephone messages.

```
┌─────────────────────────────────────────────────────────────┐
│                   TELEPHONE MESSAGE                           │
│                                                               │
│   Message for . . . . . . . . . . . . . . . . . . . . . . .   │
│                                                               │
│   From . . . . . . . . . . . . . . . . . . . . . . . . . . .  │
│                                                               │
│   Company  . . . . . . . . . . . . . . . . . . . . . . . . .  │
│                                                               │
│   Date . . . . . . . . . .   Time  . . . . . . . . . . . . .  │
│                                                               │
│   Urgent              ┌──────────────┐                        │
│   Please call back    ├──────────────┤                        │
│   Will call back      └──────────────┘                        │
│                                                               │
│   Message    . . . . . . . . . . . . . . . . . . . . . . . .  │
│                                                               │
│   . . . . . . . . . . . . . . . . . . . . . . . . . . . . . . │
│                                                               │
│   . . . . . . . . . . . . . . . . . . . . . . . . . . . . . . │
│                                                               │
│   Taken by   . . . . . . . . . . . . . . . . . . . . . . . .  │
└─────────────────────────────────────────────────────────────┘
```

2.9 Using the internal telephone system

Most organisations have their own internal telephone systems. All extension numbers will be listed in an internal telephone directory.

The internal telephone system should only be used for professional matters.

Many systems have different features. Here are a few of the features you might find:

Call back   Used when the caller wants to speak to someone whose line is engaged. The caller dials a special code. When the other person puts the phone down, that phone calls back (ie both phones ring).

Conference call   Three or more people can talk to each other at the same time.

Call forwarding   Used when someone is working at a different workstation. Calls are automatically diverted to a chosen extension.

2.10 Confidentiality

There will be times at work when you are told something and asked to 'keep it to yourself', either by a colleague, your supervisor or a visitor.

Sometimes this will be in the context of a message you may have to pass on, but at other times it may be in the form of a confidence which is entrusted to you. It is vital that you keep your word and do not pass it on to others at the earliest opportunity.

Working as part of a team will inevitably mean that you must pass information on to other members of the team. This must always be done accurately and promptly.

2.11 Maintaining good relationships

Once you have created a good relationship with other staff, this must be maintained because it is important for the following reasons:

(a)   staff who are happy and co-operate with each other work harder and are more productive;

(b)   morale and motivation are improved.

Be the ideal member of staff that everyone appreciates by:

(a)   communicating with people in a mature and professional manner;

(b)   thinking through the consequence of your words and actions before you say or do anything that you might later regret;

(c)   carrying out requests promptly and willingly, explaining fully and politely when you are not able to help;

(d)   asking others for help and assistance politely and only when necessary;

(e)   informing others about anything you have said or done on their behalf;

(f)   bearing no grudges, not being moody or difficult to work with;

(g)   knowing the difference between telling tales and reporting unethical behaviour or problems to your superior.

3 Communication

3.1 Introduction

One of the most important elements in establishing and maintaining good working relationships is the ability to be able to communicate. Therefore in this section we will consider the main methods of communication and their suitability for different purposes, and also some of the barriers to good communication.

3.2 Oral communication

Oral methods form a major channel in business communications. Some examples of oral methods are purely voice to voice:

(a)   telephone conversations;

(b)   public address announcements.

Most methods are face to face:

(a)   interviews;

(b)   lectures and presentations;

(c)   sales visits;

(d)   formal group meetings;

(e)   informal contact and discussions;

(f)   briefing sessions;

(g)   the grapevine.

3.3 Advantages of oral communication

Important advantages of oral communication are as follows:

(a)   there is the personal touch of seeing the face and/or hearing the voice;

(b)   there is instant feedback with the opportunity to respond quickly to questions of misunderstanding and disagreement;

(c)   because of the strong personal aspect, it is a good persuasive medium encouraging people to take a certain course of action;

(d)   the message can be unique to you as an individual - no-one else is likely to select your mix of words or emphasise the same key phrases.

3.4   Disadvantages of oral communication

Obvious disadvantages of oral communication are as follows:

(a)   there is no permanent record, so disagreement can easily arise as to what was said;

(b)   vocabulary shrinkage occurs, in that we use only 66% of our full vocabulary when communicating orally - the full vocabulary is available to us only when writing;

(c)   we do not have the facility, as with writing, to go back, cancel out and replace an earlier sentence because we wish to amend its meaning.

3.5   Written communication

Written forms of communication in business are familiar to all of us. Examples are:

(a)   reports;

(b)   letters, general external post;

(c)   memoranda, general internal post;

(d)   e-mail (internal and external);

(e)   procedures manuals;

(f)   notice board, house magazine, wage packet inserts;

(g)   forms;

(h)   books.

3.6   Advantages of written communication

Major advantages of written communication are:

(a)   it provides a permanent record;

(b)   it enables a difficult piece of communication to be reworded and rewritten over a period of time, so that the exact shade of meaning can be conveyed;

(c)   the same message is conveyed to everyone;

(d)   it is the cheapest form of contacting a range of individuals.

3.7   Disadvantages of written communication

Disadvantages of written communication are:

(a)   there is no means of knowing whether the message has been received and understood by the person notified;

(b)   a written message tends to invoke a written response so timescales are extended.

3.8   *Visual communication*

Visual forms of communication include:

(a)   posters, charts, graphs;

(b)   video, TV, slide projection;

(c)   product demonstration.

3.9   *Advantages of visual communication*

Main advantages of visual communication are:

(a)   impact – you will notice and remember the picture long after you have forgotten the words and figures;

(b)   it has the highest retention rate (ie recall after the event);

(c)   the availability of colour and moving images enables the communicator to add drama and grab attention.

3.10   *Disadvantages of visual communication*

Disadvantages of visual communication are :

(a)   it is a limited method in that the amount of content that can be included on one slide, poster, etc is restricted;

(b)   as in advertising, where you may remember the advert clearly but forget the product, so with visual communication: the receiver may be so interested in the illustration that the facts become secondary.

Owing to the advantages and disadvantages that relate to each method, companies commonly use several methods in combination. A good example is the sales launch of a new product as illustrated below:

(a)   initially, visual methods are used (slide projector, films) to grab attention and provide impact to the main message;

(b)   then verbal methods of briefing, lectures, question and answer sessions are used to persuade and motivate the salesforce, to answer any questions and to show senior management's personal backing;

(c)   finally, each salesperson is sent home with a fact pack, containing a written record of all the details, test results, etc for later reference.

4   *Rules for good communication*

4.1   *Communication should be to the right person*

Most companies can produce examples of instructions, data sheets or control reports which are distributed in accordance with predetermined lists of recipients, often on the basis of seniority or status. Very often some of the recipients have no use for the information and may indeed be led to investigate matters which have no relevance to the job they have to do. If one considers specific requests or complaints coming upwards in the chain of management, the possibility of a helpful response depends on the approach being made to the person with the relevant functional responsibility.

Certainly some types of information – for example, on economic factors of general interest – can be given a wide circulation because they assist the lateral discussion of common problems, but this is only a particular instance of the general rule that information should be related to the use the recipient is expected to make of it.

4.2 Communication should be accurate and complete

Any information contained in a communication should be factually correct, otherwise wrong conclusions may be drawn or wrong decisions taken. As a corollary of this, all the facts should be stated, ie the communication should be complete. What is 'correct' will depend on the nature of the information and the use to be made of it. A report that overtime work increased by 20% between April and May may be inaccurate to the extent that the actual percentage was somewhere between 17.5% and 22%. If the purpose is to stimulate an investigation, then the precise amount of overtime can be left to emerge when the investigation takes place.

4.3 Communication should be timely

When the communication is intended to result in action, then the speed of communication will be related to the urgency of that action. A report that a machine is out of action is of little value if it is delayed while several hours or days of production are lost.

Similarly, communications may be intended to prevent ill-informed actions. Reports downwards on the progress of wage negotiations should be made available **before** workers decide to stop work in protest at apparent delays. On the other hand, there is no advantage in issuing daily reports on material spoilage if what is required is a weekly summary for a management meeting.

4.4 Communication should be understandable

Communication always needs care in its presentation. Not everyone has the capability of logical analysis and this is why well-designed, formal presentations are often more effective than oral communication without a recognisable sequence of thought. In upwards and lateral communication, however, a disordered emotional outburst will sometimes give a clearer general impression, to be clarified in further discussion, than a simple recital of facts.

4.5 Communication should be brief

This is true to the extent that a brief message will generally be more acceptable than a verbose one. The length or brevity of communication must be related to the recipient's interest in the subject, ability to make a logical analysis, knowledge of the subject matter and the personal preference for a single summary or a fully argued or documented case.

4.6 Communication should not involve excessive cost

It is to be considered whether the benefits expected to result from the communication are greater or less than the cost of obtaining the relevant information and putting it into an acceptable form. This comparison can seldom be made with precision and will often be a matter of subjective judgement.

4.7 Barriers to communication

Poor communication can be the result of barriers to and breakdowns in communication which should always be analysed to prevent continuing occurrence. Typical barriers and breakdowns are:

(a)   lack of preparation and planning before communication;

(b)   unstated or incorrect assumptions;

(c)   wrong method of communication;

(d)   poorly phrased messages;

(e)   loss in transmission or poor retention by receiver;

(f)   biased interpretation;

(g)   poor listening skills (see earlier in this chapter);

(h)   mistrust and fear (can be clearly seen in many widely publicised trade union and company confrontations);

(i)   natural reserve and status barriers which can result in reluctance to pass information upwards for fear of incurring criticism;

(j)   information overload resulting in individuals receiving too much information to be able to assess what is and what is not important.

4.8   Noise

'Noise' is full or partial loss of communication. It can arise at the collecting and measuring point, or there can be errors or omissions in transmission and/or misinterpretation or misunderstanding, or blatant disregard of communication. The two principal types of noise are verbal and technical.

4.9   Verbal noise

Verbal noise is the misunderstanding of words. Examples are:

(a)   the misspelling or omission of an important word in a communication, so as to obscure or alter its meaning;

(b)   technical persons (such as accountants, who are some of the worst offenders) using jargon that is incomprehensible to non-technical persons;

(c)   the incorrect use of English, written in a style that is difficult to follow.

4.10   Technical noise

Technical noise is created by the information itself during communication. Examples are:

(a)   in response to a request for a simple piece of information, a voluminous report may be prepared obscuring the vital information (accountants' monthly reports frequently have this failing);

(b)   a message is left that is not sufficiently clear to convey its meaning when its intended recipient returns;

(c)   damage to an organisation's communications centre, such as its telephone exchange, prevents information from being transmitted clearly.

Failure to transmit information can have serious consequences on a company's operations. Some noise can be reduced, if not overcome, by using more than one channel of communication, so that if a message fails to get through by one channel, it may succeed by another. For example, a managing director may need the latest stock figures. To confirm the information from the accountant, the figures from sales and production may be analysed personally to find the relevant stock figures.

4.11   Overcoming barriers to communication

The barriers to effective communication can be removed if all members of an organisation understand the channels and methods available.

This can be achieved by setting up and publicising adequate information channels, which might include briefing groups, joint departmental committees and specific project groups with members from the various sectors of the organisation.

Management can also reduce communication barriers by being aware of their existence and always actively encouraging their subordinates to communicate.

In addition, all employees should be trained in how to use communication techniques.

5 Written communication with internal customers

5.1 Introduction

As with any form of communication you need to consider:

(a)   who will be receiving it;

(b)   what facts do you want to convey;

(c)   what sort of response do you expect?

The most common form of internal communication is a memorandum. However on occasion you may also need to make notes to support verbal communication.

5.2 Notes

You may need to write notes for a talk or a presentation. Other occasions when note taking is required might be in the preparation of a report or in connection with a meeting or a telephone call. Whatever the context, notes should suit their purpose and be neither too detailed that they resemble an essay nor too compressed that their meaning is lost.

Notes are not written in complete sentences. They must, however, be:

(a)   legible;

(b)   organised logically;

(c)   easily understandable.

To achieve this, it is recommended that you use:

(a)   headings and subheadings;

(b)   underlining of key words;

(c)   numbered or bullet points;

(d)   common abbreviations.

Notes that are going to be used very soon after they have been written down can afford to be more condensed than notes which will have to wait before they are written in a more acceptable form. Telephone messages tend to suffer from brevity and, with each hour that passes, recollection of the conversation will fade.

5.3 Telephone messages

When taking a telephone message, remember to check the notes with the caller before the call is concluded. This is to make sure that you have all the correct information, especially if there are dates, references, unfamiliar names and figures. Failure to clarify these details may necessitate a call back or lead to an incorrect message being passed on.

5.4 Summarising

Summarising is a form of note taking in which you reduce the amount of original information so that you are left with only the key facts - all the irrelevant details are omitted.

When summarising you should:

(a)   make sure you read and fully understand the original information before you start to summarise;

(b)   make a note of the key points;

(c)   check any unfamiliar words or abbreviations;

(d)   leave out examples and illustrations unless they are necessary;

(e)   write a draft version and check that it contains the key facts and reads well.

5.5   *Memoranda*

Memos are the most common form of inter-office communication, whether in written or e-mail form. (Memo is short for memorandum; the plural is memoranda or memos.) They are used to:

(a)   pass messages from one person to another;

(b)   report on action taken;

(c)   confirm arrangements;

(d)   ask for ideas and/or comments;

(e)   make suggestions;

(f)   keep people updated with what is happening.

Some organisations have pre-printed memo pads with headings as below. These remind the writer to include certain basic information. They also speed up the writing process.

MEMORANDUM
TO: FROM: DATE: SUBJECT:

5.6   *What to include in a memo*

The main points to note with memos are as follows:

(a)   the subject heading, which should be brief and precise, is important as it acts as a focus to the message and makes it easier to file;

(b)   there is no need for an address or salutation;

(c)   the wording should be written in simple language, even in note form;

(d)   no complimentary close is required and the sender's signature or initials are optional;

(e)   if there is an enclosure, this should be indicated with the abbreviation Enc after the initials of the sender;

(f)   if the memo is confidential, the word Confidential should be placed at the top so that it is seen quickly, and the memo must be placed in a sealed envelope (also marked *Personal* or *Confidential*).

Memos can be of any size, from one line to several pages long. For the longer varieties, consideration should be given to the way the information is organised and displayed. The outline below may be a useful guide:

MEMORANDUM

TO: Jo Parker

FROM: Chris Triggs

DATE: 14 July 20X8

SUBJECT: Layout of long memo

BEGINNING

Open with an introduction to the subject and the reason for it. Make references to any earlier discussions, phone calls, meetings, etc that are relevant.

MIDDLE

The middle section or sections are for the information:

(a)   use headings and sub-headings;
(b)   use numbers or bullet points to list points;
(c)   underline the important text for emphasis.

END

The last section should round off the memo, drawing attention to deadlines or further action which may be required.

Whatever form communication takes it should be accurate, understandable and timely.

6   *Distributing information internally*

6.1   *Introduction*

The method of presenting the information to be distributed and the method of passing it on will depend upon what you have been asked to do and the way your office works.

You may present information in many forms, including:

(a)   notes;

(b)   a memorandum;

(c)   a letter (usually for external communication).

Now we will look at ways in which documents are distributed within an organisation.

6.2   Noticeboards

If an announcement, memorandum or letter is addressed to all employees, it may be posted on a noticeboard unless it is of a sensitive nature, in which case each employee should receive his or her own copy or should be told face-to-face by the department head.

6.3   Internal mail

Any document to be sent to individuals will have to be distributed in the office in some way. This may mean a proper internal mail system, particularly if the business is on more than one site.

Employees leave the items to be distributed in their out trays or at a central collecting point in the department or building. These are collected at set times and distributed to other sites and departments.

Individuals might get their internal (and external) mail put in their in tray or they might have to collect it from a central point. Their mail might be stored in pigeonholes while it is waiting to be collected.

Some organisations save money by distributing internal mail in re-usable envelopes. These have spaces to write on as many as a hundred names. Each time the envelope is used the previous name is crossed out and the new name added, as shown below.

INTERNAL MAIL ENVELOPE			
~~RB~~			
~~CR~~			
KL			

6.4   Fax machines

Fax machines can be an alternative to posting documents, although there may be security problems.

6.5   E-mail

This is a method of sending information from one computer to another. The computers must be linked through a network (most usually an internet service provider, or ISP), but they do not have to be within the same organisation.

E-mail can be used to send messages or to gain access to large commercial databases, such as Prestel, and the Internet.

6.6 Good internal distribution

If you have been asked to pass on information, particularly a message to someone else, it is vital that you do this quickly and efficiently.

It is very inefficient to keep a message or other document on your desk for an unnecessarily long time before passing it on. This can lead to time and money being wasted within the business, but it can also lead to a loss of goodwill with customers or clients.

6.7 Deadline problems

The difficulties that may arise are when:

the exact information you need does not seem to be available;

the deadline you have been given looks difficult to meet;

you are unable to find the information anywhere.

The best procedure when difficulties are encountered is to keep the person who made the request informed of progress or problems. You can then make other suggestions, offer additional help or reschedule your plans to cope with any delay.

Dealing with an urgent deadline will put you under pressure. These situations require you to keep calm, plan before you start and avoid getting distracted.

6.8 Confidential information

You may handle information which is clearly confidential, such as payroll details.

Some information may not appear to be confidential at first sight but could cause embarrassment or problems internally or externally if revealed, so it is best always to err on the side of discretion. Such information might include:

(a)   reports on purchases of new machinery whose introduction might lead to fewer jobs;

(b)   details of price rises not yet sent to customers;

(c)   news of changes in key personnel not yet communicated to customers and suppliers.

When dealing with customers and suppliers, you must also respect their own right to confidentiality. For instance, do not reveal details of a customer's account or type or level of purchases to another customer.

Remember that, if someone appears to be asking for confidential information or for information which does not concern them, it is always best to refer them to your supervisor.

CHAPTER 5

Working relationships - external customers

ASSESSMENT FOCUS

This chapter covers the following Knowledge and Understanding and Performance Criteria of the AAT Syllabus.

Information is provided to internal and external customers in line with routine requirements and one-off requests (*Performance Criteria element 23.2*)

The appropriate people are asked for any information, advice and resources that are required (*Performance Criteria element 23.2*)

Commitments to others are met within agreed timescales (*Performance Criteria element 23.2*)

Communication methods are appropriate to the individual situation (*Performance Criteria element 23.2*)

Any communication difficulties are acknowledged and action is taken to resolve them (*Performance Criteria element 23.2*)

Opportunities are taken to promote the image of the department and organisation to internal and external customers (*Performance Criteria element 23.2*)

Confidentiality and data protection requirements are strictly followed (*Performance Criteria element 23.2*)

Methods of establishing constructive relationships (*Knowledge and Understanding*)

Seeking and exchanging information, advice and support (*Knowledge and Understanding*)

Handling disagreements and conflict (*Knowledge and Understanding*)

Using appropriate actions and different styles of approach in different situations (*Knowledge and Understanding*)

Different communication methods and styles (*Knowledge and Understanding*)

Types of communication difficulties and how to resolve them (*Knowledge and Understanding*)

Employee responsibilities in complying with relevant legislation (*Knowledge and Understanding*)

In order to cover these, the following topics are considered:

presenting information externally;

business letters.

---

1 Presenting information externally

1.1 Introduction

Organisations supply information to their customers or clients for a range of reasons. The customer may want to:

(a) enquire about the products or services;

(b) order goods or services;

(c) chase their order;

(d) sort out problems with their account;

(e) complain.

1.2 Customer service

Good customer service is vital in any organisation. Regardless of how good the products or services of the business are, customers will still want good service.

Customers will not make allowances for problems within the organisation. They do not want excuses for why you or someone else has been unable to do something. They will judge the whole organisation by your actions.

The information that you give the customer may be presented verbally or in writing.

1.3 Importance of external customers

The main point to remember when dealing with external customers is that the business will cease without them and most organisations have competitors who could provide the goods or services just as well, if not better!

When you are assisting a customer, you need to convince them that their problem or query has received your full attention and will be dealt with promptly.

1.4 Knowledge of your organisation

If you are to deal with customer requests effectively, then you will need to know certain things about the organisation. You should be familiar with the following:

(a) organisation charts – the structure of the company shows the levels of authority and responsibility, along with the name of the post holder who deals with queries at that level;

(b) brochures and catalogues - should give details of the products or services which your organisation offers (if you are in a position which relies on your knowledge of certain aspects of the product or service, eg price, availability of stock, then you must be up-to-date on the facts);

(c)   procedures manuals - should enable you to grasp the system, for example some companies forego the postage charges when orders are over a certain value;

(d)   internal telephone directory - this can give you pointers to people who can help you or the customer;

(e)   legal constraints – you need to know what information you can and cannot divulge to the customer.

You obviously cannot know the answer to every customer's query, but you should at least know where to find the answer or someone who can deal with the query.

Be aware of what your limits are. Do not give a client information about an area beyond your responsibility or which is not covered by procedures of the business.

1.5   *Providing accurate information*

Any information you provide to customers and clients must be accurate. This means that you must not give information on areas outside your responsibility or commit the organisation to any unusual terms or conditions.

Always refer any queries about which you are unsure to your supervisor.

If you provide any complex calculations, ask someone else to check them first.

1.6   *Keeping records*

Whenever you pass on any information to clients or answer queries, you should make a written record. The format of this will tend to be decided by the organisation. It might be a report or notes.

1.7   *Dealing with customers on the phone*

Dealing with people over the phone is a skill which you can learn, even though it may be very difficult or frightening at first.

Here are some points to think about:

(a)   be friendly and enthusiastic;

(b)   answer the phone properly giving your name, or the name of the department, or using the words required by your organisation;

(c)   do not interrupt the caller;

(d)   ask questions if you are not sure of exactly what the caller wants;

(e)   note down the main points of what the caller is saying so that you can brief the person to whom you transfer the call (if necessary);

(f)   if you cannot deal with the query, do not let the caller go on for too long as they will only have to repeat most of the query to someone else which will waste the caller's time;

(g)   when transferring calls, ask the caller to hold the line but take their name and number first in case they get cut off. If the other line is busy, tell the caller what is happening and ask if they prefer to hold or would like the relevant person to call them back later;

(h)   if you tell the caller that someone will call them back, make sure that you pass on the message and follow up that it has happened;

(i)   if you have a conversation with a customer which you think someone else should be aware of (eg your supervisor), send that person a note or memo as soon as possible;

(j)   never be rude to a caller, even if they are rude to you.

By the end of the phone call you must feel that you have identified the caller's needs and can deal with them. If you cannot deal with the caller's query, you should have identified the person who can deal with it.

1.8   Dealing with letters from clients

Some clients may make queries by letter. If you receive a query by letter, you must decide how best to deal with it. Points to consider include:

(a)   should the letter be dealt with by your department or another department;

(b)   if the reply comes from your department, should it be drafted by you or your supervisor (the letter will probably be signed by your supervisor);

(c)   do you have the information required to hand (eg customer's file) or do you need to refer to another department;

(d)   do you need to obtain copies of any of the business's publications.

Remember that the reply must be prompt. If you cannot deal with a query, holding on to the letter will not make the problem go away.

Any correspondence received should be filed as soon as possible.

Writing business letters in reply to customer queries will be considered later in this chapter.

1.9   Face-to-face contact

Dealing with customers and clients face to face can be difficult at first, but you should become more relaxed with practice. Try to remember the following:

(a)   be friendly and polite, and try to put the customer at ease as this will help them to feel more relaxed with you;

(b)   try to interpret the customer's body language and think about your own - if the customer appears nervous try to put them at their ease, and always project a positive image;

(c)   some matters are best not discussed in public areas - these include financial, personal and health matters (it is only fair that these interviews take place in a private office or interview room);

(d)   information received from clients is confidential. If you tell other people information about that client, you are betraying their trust in you. Even if the information is not of a personal nature, but is connected with their business, that information is still confidential.

1.10   Checking eligibility

Confidential information may include information on eligibility for certain items.

To check the eligibility of a customer or client (eg for a loan or for credit terms), you may have to take certain details. Your organisation may feel that the best way to obtain and summarise that information is to use a form.

There are two ways in which a form can be completed. The customer may be allowed to take the form away to complete at home. You would then have to check the completed form, or you might help the customer to complete the form on the premises. Either way, you must be aware of the contents of the form and the *exact* meaning of each question. Alternatively, if you are asking the customer for information which you then write directly onto the form, make sure you use good interviewing techniques.

Whatever type of contact you have with external customers it is important to be polite and yet appear efficient and confident.

2   *Business letters*

2.1   *Introduction*

Most written communication with external customers will be in the form of a business letter.

Good business letters are clear, concise and courteous. They should help to promote the right image of the organisation.

2.2   *Layout of letters*

The layout of business letters depends upon the house style of a particular organisation.

House style will affect:

(a)   layout;

(b)   spelling (eg dispatch *or* despatch);

(c)   punctuation (decision making *or* decision-making; Eg *or* eg).

Although some people prefer one style compared to another, no style can be described as wrong as long as it is consistent. The components of the letter are always the same and are always typed on headed paper.

2.3 **Main elements of a letter**

Name and address of organisation	THE TRAINING FIRM 123 Lecturer Row London NW2 4LR Tel: 020 732 3232 Fax: 020 723 2323
Our ref. *Their ref.*	REF NM/WPP Your Ref MK/LM
Date	25 January 20X8
Recipient's name, position and address	Mr S Brown Office Manager First Line 22 Plain Street Swindon S42 7KJ
Salutation	Dear Mr Brown
Subject heading	Business letter layout
Opening paragraph	Acknowledge any previous letter and introduce the subject
Main body of letter	In a logical manner, give or ask for the required information
Closing paragraph	Conclude the letter in a suitable manner
Complimentary close *Name of organisation*	Yours sincerely THE TRAINING FIRM
Name of writer *Designation (position)*	John Jones Sales Co-ordinator
Enclosure mark	Enc
More details may be printed here	Reg office: Brick House, Mill Lane, Bromley, Kent

(logo)

2.4 **Yours sincerely or yours faithfully?**

Although lots of things depend upon *house style*, it is important to note the following points:

(a)   if you are writing to someone whose name you know put it at the top of the address of the business you are writing to, eg *George Brown Esq* or *Mrs T Weymouth* (in this case, use Esq instead of Mr) and when you address the person, use *Dear Mr Brown* or *Dear Mrs Weymouth;*

(b)   if you do not know the name of the person, put the name of the position of the person to whom you are writing and start the letter *Dear Sir* or *Dear Madam* if you know you are writing to a woman (never use *Dear Sir or Madam* - this is unnecessary);

(c)   when closing the letter, match phrases as shown below.

Dear Sir Dear Madam	Yours faithfully
Dear Mr Brown Dear Mrs Weymouth Dear George Dear Tina	Yours sincerely

2.5   Style

You must match the style of the letter to the person you are addressing and the situation concerned. A letter to a prospective customer is very different from a letter to a slow-paying one.

Since there are many different types of business letter, we will continue by looking at examples of the main ones.

2.6   Letter of enquiry/reply

When writing a letter of enquiry, you should include all the relevant points so that you get the information that you want. The following example should not need further explanation.

                                                  Own address

                                                     Date

Tour operator
Travel Company
Address

Dear Sir

Para 1   Introduce subject by referring to their
           recent advertisement in the Sunday paper
           about classical holidays

Para 2   Focus on reason for writing: forthcoming
           wedding anniversary, price range affordable
           and spouse's fear of injections

Para 3   Request further information and seek advice

Para 4   Conclude suitably

Yours faithfully

Naomi McLeod

2.7   *Letters conveying information*

The reply to the enquiry above should be answered promptly and courteously. The reply should answer all of the questions and points raised by the sender.

Sometimes you may make a short remark to personalise the letter, such as 'If you need any further information, please do not hesitate to let me know'.

Travel Company
Address

Ref
Date

Mrs McLeod
Address

Dear Mrs N McLeod

Heading

Para 1   Acknowledge: Thank you for ...

Para 2   Name the holidays most suitable, bearing in mind
             the date of the anniversary, their budget and her
             husband's fear of injections

Para 3   Link the recommendation to the brochure that you
             are enclosing, along with the Health Advice to
             Travellers leaflet

Para 4   Refer to enclosures and conclude suitably

Yours sincerely

Maggie Cooper
Classical Tours Manager

When a customer requests information about your organisation's products or services, in your reply you must aim to match the request. In the above example, if Maggie Cooper had sent details of holidays in India or Africa, then the customer's request would not have been matched with the correct information. Even if you don't work in a travel agency, you would have enough knowledge to realise that a dislike of injections and exotic holidays do not always go together. If you wanted to be really helpful in this situation, you would find out what sort of immunisation was needed for certain places and then also find out what method of immunisation was available. Some methods are by tablet (malaria) and some are fluid taken orally (polio).

Wherever you work, you should make it your business to find out as much as possible about the product or service so that you can answer queries from customers.

2.8   *Letters of confirmation*

This type of letter is usually sent after arrangements have been made verbally. To prevent any misunderstanding and confusion, it is better to re-state all the main points which were agreed verbally. These points will include:

(a)   the day and date;

(b)   the time;

(c)   reference to the person who agreed the details.

An example of a letter of confirmation is given below.

Busy Bee Agency
10 St Peter's Avenue
Harpenden AS2 3GG
01703 789022

HB/PV
14 March 20X8

The Holton Hotel
High Road
Reading

Dear Sir

Following my telephone conversation earlier today with Mark, I wish to confirm the reservation of two single rooms for two nights: Monday and Tuesday 22 and 23 March 20X8.

The rooms should be booked in the names of Miss Adams and Mr Stevens.

Their time of arrival on 22 March will be about 3.30 pm.

Yours faithfully

Diane Soames
Office Manager

Activity 1 *(The answer to this activity can be found in Chapter 7)*

Here is a letter which contains all the necessary information but which has not been very well planned. You are required to re-write the letter in a more concise and straightforward style.

Dear Mr Wigmore

The cakes are not exactly what you wanted, but they'll be there on Saturday anyway. I know you said you were concerned about it on the phone last Friday. I can replace the Eccles cakes with apple turnovers (2 dozen). The van will deliver them to the three shops (Leigh, Wigan and Warrington). Let me know if this is OK.

2.9   *Letters in draft*

You may sometimes be asked to submit your letters in draft to your supervisor for review. This will normally involve preparing letters in draft and passing them on to someone else to produce the final typed copy. The draft copy which you prepare for review and typing must be:

(a)   complete (names, addresses, etc);

(b)   legible;

(c)   properly laid out according to house style.

2.10   *Standard letters*

Many of the letters you are asked to prepare may be standard letters. This means that they are to be sent to a number of people over a period of time with *no* or *few* amendments.

Some letters may have boxes to tick. These make the letter relevant to each individual.

Whatever the type of letter sent out to external customers its style must always suit its purpose, and it must be factually correct and timely.

Activity 2 *(The answer to this activity can be found in Chapter 7)*

You work in the accounts department of a large mail order clothes company. You have been asked by your supervisor (Kim Walsh – Accounts supervisor) to design a standard letter to be sent to customers who have sent incorrectly completed cheques. The letter is to be sent in her name.

CHAPTER 6

Maintaining accounting files and records

ASSESSMENT FOCUS

This chapter covers the following Knowledge and Understanding and Performance Criteria of the AAT Syllabus.

New documentation and records are put into the filing system in line with organisational procedures (*Performance Criteria element 23.3*)

Item movements are monitored and recorded where necessary (*Performance Criteria element 23.3*)

Documentation and records are kept according to organisational and legal requirements (*Performance Criteria element 23.3*)

Out of date information is dealt with in accordance with organisational procedures (*Performance Criteria element 23.3*)

Opportunities for improving filing systems are identified and brought to the attention of the appropriate person (*Performance Criteria element 23.3*)

Methods of classifying information: alphabetical, numerical, alphanumerical (*Knowledge and Understanding*)

Sorting, handling and storing information (*Knowledge and Understanding*)

The purpose of storing and retaining documents (*Knowledge and Understanding*)

In order to cover these, the following topics are considered:

filing;

filing system;

computer files;

index systems;

methods of filing;

maintaining a filing system;

data protection.

1   Filing

1.1   Introduction

It is impossible for any one individual to remember all the relevant details of business transactions. It is therefore necessary to install some system of record-keeping which is logical, easy to operate and maintain, safe and cost-effective.

1.2   Definition

Filing is the storing of business records, including letters and documents. The purpose of an efficient filing system is to keep papers safe and clean, and to ensure that the information held on file can be produced without delay when required. If the material is not likely to be required again then it should be destroyed, and not filed unless there is a legal requirement to keep it.

1.3   What is a file?

A file is a collection of related data records with similar characteristics. Examples of files include:

(a)   correspondence on a particular topic;

(b)   personnel records;

(c)   sales ledgers;

(d)   price lists;

(e)   stock records.

1.4   Recording method

Whatever the information to be recorded there are several alternative recording systems existing and commonly used. They include:

(a)   paper;

(b)   card;

(c)   the filing of originals;

(d)   magnetic tape;

(e)   magnetic disk (including floppy disk, hard disk and CD ROM);

(f)   optical disk;

(g)   microfilm.

1.5   Types of record

A whole variety of different details and information may be recorded. Records commonly maintained in organisations might include the following:

(a)   financial transactions and documentation – the book-keeping and accountancy system, which may be computerised;

(b)   legal documentation – employee contracts, property titles and deeds, insurance policies and other agreements;

(c)   company documentation – the shareholder register, the company Memorandum and the Articles of Association;

(d)   staff details and personnel records;

(e)   statistical information – past performance and budgets;

(f)   minutes of formal meetings;

(g)   details of informal meetings;

(h)   correspondence – all internal and external communications including memoranda;

(i)   stock records;

(j)   management information as desired.

2   Filing systems

2.1   Introduction

Many organisations have one department responsible for sorting and filing most of the papers and documents. The only files kept by other departments are personal and current files. This is a centralised filing system.

2.2   Centralised filing system

The advantages of a centralised system include:

(a)   fuller use of equipment;

(b)   staff trained in the filing methods of the organisation.

2.3   Departmental filing

In a departmental system, each department keeps its own files. This enables members of each department to use the filing methods most suitable to their needs. In addition, the files are immediately available for personal reference. This can be particularly useful in departments such as sales, where price lists, quotations and customer details may be required quickly (eg during a telephone enquiry).

2.4   Methods of filing

The most common methods of filing are probably:

(a)   vertical;

(b)   lateral;

(c)   horizontal;

(d)   rotary.

2.5   Vertical

This is the method used in *filing cabinets*. Files are stored one behind another in a number of drawers. Documents and files are normally kept in suspended pockets.

2.6   Lateral

Files are stored like books on shelves, or in suspended pockets. The spine of the file (and therefore the label) is usually visible.

2.7 Horizontal

Files or documents are stored in shallow drawers. These vary in size from A4 upwards.

2.8 Rotary

Files are stored on a revolving stand or carousel.

If you are not used to working with any of the methods described above, obtain a stationery catalogue or visit an office furniture supplier to get an idea of what they look like.

Activity 1 *(The answer to this activity can be found in Chapter 7)*

Which method of filing is likely to be the most suitable for the following files and documents:

(a)   document wallets containing photographs used in the company brochure;

(b)   box files containing supplier brochures;

(c)   manila folders containing personnel details.

2.9 Concertina file

This type of file is divided into sections which are labelled alphabetically. They are normally used as temporary files to pre-sort documents before processing or to hold documents awaiting matching with other documents (eg goods received notes and suppliers' delivery notes).

2.10 Box file

This is a large box used to store loose documents which cannot or must not have holes punched through them (eg brochures, clippings from magazines). The file often contains a large clip to hold the contents in place.

2.11 Lever arch file

This is a large version of a ring binder, but with an additional clip to keep papers secure inside the file. It also has a lever to make opening the rings easier. This type of file can be sub-divided by using file dividers (cards with tabs for labelling).

2.12 Document wallet

This is a large cardboard *envelope* (with or without a flap). It is normally used for temporary storage only.

2.13 Manila folder file

This file is used in suspended pockets. Documents are punched, then secured onto the prongs inside using a clip. The latest document is placed on top.

All of these types of files are used for the filing of actual documents in a manual system.

Activity 2 *(The answer to this activity can be found in Chapter 7)*

Which type of file is most suitable for:

(a)   pre-sorted correspondence from clients awaiting filing;

(b)   copies of sales invoices;

(c)   an individual employee's personnel file;

(d)   booklets received from HM Customs and Excise on accounting for VAT.

3   Computer files

3.1   Introduction

A computer file can be almost anything that is stored for use at a later date. There are program files, data files, spreadsheet files, and text files used in word processing.

3.2   Classification of files

Files can be classified into transaction, master and reference files.

3.3   Transaction file

This file contains records that relate to individual transactions that occur from day-to-day. Examples include:

(a)   stock transactions file – details relating to stock movements;

(b)   wages transactions file – details of wages;

(c)   orders file – items required by customers.

Such details are input for processing, including computing the value of stock movements, gross wages and the value of goods sold to customers. These values are then used as part of the information printed out on documents as well as being recorded on the relevant records in the master file to which they relate.

3.4   Master file

This file is a group of related records, such as stock file, employee file and supplier file. This type of file is periodically updated with current transaction data to show the current status of each record in the file.

In a purchase ledger system the master file is the purchase ledger itself, consisting of:

(a)   standing reference data for each supplier (ie name and address, reference number, account status);

(b)   transaction data for each supplier, recording purchases, purchase returns and payments made.

3.5   Reference file

As its name suggests, this file contains reference data, which is seldom altered (updated). It contains no transaction data. Examples of reference files include:

(a)   price list;

(b)   names and addresses of customers and suppliers;

(c)   wage rates;

(d)   a manual of company procedures and regulations.

Reference files are often classified as a type of master file because they both contain standing data.

3.6   Data storage media on computer

The central processing unit (CPU) of a computer has a certain amount of internal storage, but generally the business computer files are larger than the internal storage can handle, so there has to be a method of holding data on file when it is not required inside the CPU. These files must be able to hold the data in a machine-sensible form until it is needed for further processing.

Before looking at the media used for the storage of data on computer, it is useful to consider the requirements of any large-scale storage system.

3.7   Storage requirements and characteristics

The main requirements and characteristics are:

(a)   low access time - the average time needed to gain access to the stored records must be low enough to enable the processing of the data to be accomplished within an acceptable time;

(b)   storage capacity - this must be sufficient to hold all the data needed during any processing run;

(c)   security - the storage media must hold the data without fear of loss, damage or deterioration over long periods whether it is in use or not;

(d)   transfer rate - the data has to be transferred to and from the storage media at a high enough rate to meet the time restrictions on the work;

(e)   cost - the cost per unit of stored data must be low enough to make the system economical.

The above requirements have resulted in a variety of storage media being developed. As with most decisions, when deciding which method is most suitable it is a matter of balancing one characteristic against another whilst keeping within the acceptable cost.

The principles of storage and access noted above can also be applied to manual filing systems.

3.8   Magnetic tape

Imagine a domestic tape recorder on a much larger scale and you can picture a magnetic tape unit as a computer peripheral.

Tape is a very versatile recording medium used for input and output as well as storage. Unfortunately, it is a form of storage that only offers serial access, ie it is read from one end to another like a domestic tape cassette and therefore lacks the flexibility of magnetic disk.

Computer magnetic tape is very similar to ordinary tape-recorder tape, being made of the same material but of a far higher quality so that much more information can be packed into a small length of tape. A typical packing density is 1,600 characters per inch but may be up to 6,250 characters per inch.

3.9   Magnetic disks

A much more common method of file storage is to hold magnetically encoded information on the surface of a disk which has been coated with a material that can be magnetised (magnetic as opposed to optical disk). Disks hold information on both surfaces, and the information is recorded in a series of concentric circles or tracks. Disks were developed more recently than magnetic tape and at present two types of disk unit exist:

(a)   hard disks;

(b)   floppy disks (sometimes known as diskettes).

3.10   Hard disks

This type of disk device is found in PCs. A number of disk platters are permanently sealed into an airtight enclosure. This keeps the disk surfaces dust-free, and the close positioning of the read/write heads enables a high density of data to be stored. Even the small units will typically hold more than 500 million characters (Megabytes or MB).

3.11   Floppy disks

Floppies are widely used as back-up storage on PCs. Although the PC will usually have a hard disk drive, it will have one or two floppy disk drives as well. The floppy disk provides a cost-effective means of storage for computer business systems. These disks are available in two sizes, 5¼" and 3½", to fit the different types of disk drive, although 5¼" disks are now nearly obsolete.

Typically a 3½" disk stores 1.44 MB.

Floppies can be 'write protected' (ie overwriting can be suppressed). The 3½" disk has a small plastic clip which can be moved to prevent overwriting the disk by accident (see below).

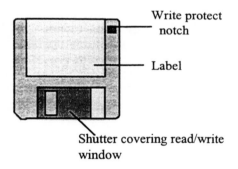

Write protect
notch

Label

Shutter covering read/write
window

3.12   Optical disks

There are four types of optical technology:

(a)   video disk;

(b)   CD ROM;

(c)   WORM;

(d)   re-writable optical disks.

3.13   Video disk

These disks are about 12" in diameter and data is recorded as minute patterns along each track. Reading is carried out by shining a laser onto the disk and capturing reflections of the patterns which are then translated by logic circuitry into a binary code. Unlike the traditional magnetic disk which records data in consecutive tracks, the recording groove on an optical disk is one continuous spiral, which on some systems is around 45,000 tracks. Each track is sub-divided into sectors. An important feature to note here is that, unlike the conventional magnetic disk, data once recorded cannot be erased - these are read-only devices.

To access the disk, the laser unit is moved across the surface of the disk, counting the number of tracks scanned. The relevant sector is then found by reading the pre-recorded numbers of the tracks and sectors to find the precise address required.

These disks possess the properties of being cheap, durable, of high capacity and robust. They are covered with a plastic coating which enables them to be handled without the attendant risks associated with the conventional magnetic disk.

3.14   CD ROM

This is like the video disk but smaller in size. The principle is similar to the compact disk used for audio recording. It is a read-only disk, the data being recorded at manufacture. The storage capacity is about 650 MB characters (equivalent to 100 bibles). These disks are used mainly as a medium for publishing large amounts of reference data, eg *Microsoft Small Business Consultant* contains tax, accountancy and legal information.

3.15   WORM (Write Once Read Many times)

Unlike with the CD ROM, users can write to these disks. However, the material cannot be erased. If the device is used to contain data of a variable nature, one or more versions of the file may be kept on disk as the storage capacity is very large. This technology is used to archive data, especially where permanent records are required for legal or taxation reasons.

3.16   Re-writable optical disks

These disks are re-usable, in that the data can also be erased. A small variant of this is the 3½" floptical disk, which is similar to a floppy disk (though more expensive) but with a storage capacity of 21 MB.

3.17   Microfilm

Here documentation is photographed and reduced and the information thus retained on miniature photographs. Reference may be made to the records by viewing the miniature films through an enlarger. Many modern viewing machines have print-out facilities to provide a more permanent form of information.

There are several types of microfilm available.

(a)   film roll – this is the most obvious and is akin to the roll of film used in a normal camera. It is a cheap and easy form but retrieval of information may be slow;

(b)   cassette – in the same way that many camera systems have changed from roll to cassette format, so too with microfilming. Although slightly more expensive than film roll, it is easier to handle and also offers more protection;

(c)   jacket – here microphotos of, perhaps, a series of documents are placed in strips in transparent folders;

(d)   microfiche – this system is often used to display inter-connected plans, diagrams and maps. It is often used within, for example, the spare parts sections of garages. One sheet is maintained for one section;

(e)   aperture card – this system involves a link-up with a punched card system and aids swift retrieval and reference.

4   Index systems

4.1   Introduction

All files should be labelled to distinguish them from other files. In the case of manual files, the title is often printed on the front of the file.

4.2   Computer systems

In order that data from the right computer file can be read for a particular process, most systems will require the file to be given a file name. This, together with other information, is held at the start of a file in an area known as the file label or header label. Typically, this consists of:

(a)   some code to identify the label as the label;

(b)   file name and number;

(c)   date last updated;

(d)   purge date, ie the date from which the information is no longer required;

(e)   password;

(f)   generation number (in tape systems).

If, for example, a payroll file is loaded when it is intended to run the debtors file, the header label will be read and, if this does not correspond with the file required, the system will signal an error to the operator.

4.3   Finding files

Locating files quickly within any filing system is very important. An index is therefore used to keep track of which files exist. It can also be used to cross-reference files.

For example, orders received from customers and any related correspondence may be kept in manila files within a vertical filing system. Each file is marked with the order number. Filing is in numerical order.

A separate index is kept of customers in alphabetical order. Each time a new file is opened the order number is recorded in the index against the customer's name.

Any indexing system needs to be flexible to allow extra entries to be included. There are four main types of manual indexing system as follows:

(a)   rotary index - cards are stored on a revolving carousel. Each card can be removed and replaced as needed, and extra cards can be added when necessary;

(b)   strip index - strips are held within a frame and can be removed or new ones added as required;

(c)   card file - cards are stored vertically in a box, tray or drawer. They can be added or removed easily and the cards can be separated into sections using *divider cards*;

(d)   visible edge - cards are held in a tray. They can be updated in the tray.

The key to an index system is that it is set up in such a way that the correct file can be located quickly and easily.

4.4 Using an index

The index may be used to store other information as well as information about the filing system (eg customer addresses, telephone numbers, etc).

Sometimes cross-referencing cards may be used where there may be uncertainty as to where a particular piece of information may be found. For example, a business might have changed its name in the recent past. The following cards might be found in an index:

```
BROWN OFFICE SUPPLIES LTD

Correspondence file opened
23/6/W2
File closed 6/9/W8

See under Office Supply
Company Ltd
```

```
OFFICE SUPPLY COMPANY LTD

Correspondence file opened
6/9/W8

See also Brown Office Supplies
Ltd for previous file
```

For more examples of cross-referencing by subject matter and by name, look in telephone directories, in particular in *Yellow Pages*.

4.5 Borrowing files

When files are borrowed, it is important that their location is known. A record of all files borrowed must be kept. There must also be some way of monitoring the return of files. It is usually best to set a limit for when the files must be returned.

Let us look at different systems which may be used.

4.6 Card index

A pre-prepared card is filed in a box or drawer under the return date. As files are returned, the cards are removed leaving only the cards relating to files which have not yet been returned. Overdue files are chased up regularly, eg by sending a reminder slip or a postcard.

4.7 Diary or returns book

This lists files removed either under the return date or in chronological order as they are borrowed. Each entry is crossed out as the files are returned.

4.8 Absent cards

Some filing systems allow cards to be inserted where files have been removed. This depends upon the type of equipment used. It is probably best used in a lateral filing system where the cards stick out as a reminder. Colour-coding can be used to indicate the return date.

4.9   Computerised database

Most organisations now have a computerised database to keep track of files. Files may be labelled with bar codes which are read with a light-pen.

For example this system is used by public libraries to record the borrowing of books. On removing a book, the borrower and the latest date of return are recorded. Once the return date is passed, the book is identified by the system as overdue. When required, reminder cards are generated to be sent to borrowers whose books are overdue.

In the filing system it is important that a file can always be located even if it is has been borrowed.

5   Methods of filing

5.1   Introduction

There are five methods of filing documents and files:

(a)   alphabetical;

(b)   chronological;

(c)   numerical;

(d)   by subject;

(e)   geographical.

5.2   Alphabetical

The problem with alphabetical filing is knowing how to deal with certain *exceptions*. Have a go at putting these customer names into alphabetical order!

> C Browne
>
> J Brown
>
> Mary Brown
>
> M Brown

The answer is:

> J Brown
>
> M Brown
>
> Mary Brown
>
> C Browne

Please note the following rules.

For names of businesses and other organisations:

(a)   numbers are treated like words, eg 7 Stars is filed as if it were Seven Stars, or (in the telephone directory) they come before the As;

(b)   the word The is ignored;

(c)   where two businesses have the same name, the address is used;

(d)   public bodies (eg local authorities) are filed under the name or the town or district, eg Oldham (Metropolitan Borough Council), Social Security (Department of);

(e)   letters come first, eg M1 Cash and Carry comes *before* all the other Ms;

(f)   the names Saint and St are all filed as Saint;

For names of people :

(a)   file by surname;

(b)   shorter names come first (eg Brown before Browne);

(c)   for the same surname, use first names or initials (eg J Brown before M Brown);

(d)   initials come before full first names (eg M Brown before Mary Brown);

(e)   all Macs and Mcs are treated as Mac and come before all the Ms (but *after* the letters);

(f)   apostrophes are ignored (eg O'Leary would come between Oldman and Oliver);

(g)   de, D' and similar are also ignored (eg De'Ath would be found in the As). Note that in telephone directories, they might come under D;

(h)   note that if the name of an organisation contains a person's name but only includes their initial (eg H Goodman Supplies) it is normally filed under the surname (ie G). If an organisation's name contains the full first name (eg Henry Goodman Supplies) it may be filed under either initial (ie H or G).

5.3   Chronological

Chronological filing is used where the order of events is important, eg filing of birth certificates at a Register Office or correspondence. Correspondence is normally filed chronologically by client/customer. The customer/client file is then filed as part of an alphabetical or numerical system.

In an accounts department, chronological order may be used for petty cash vouchers.

5.4   Numerical

This method is very widely used in accounts departments, eg filing of purchase invoices received, sales invoices sent out.

The only drawback of a numerical system is that it requires forward planning if it is to be easily expanded.

One of the most famous numerical systems is the Dewey Decimal System used in libraries.

5.5   By subject

This system is not really practical for large filing systems, but it can be used in parts of a system. For instance all correspondence, documents and invoices relating to the letting maintenance of a particular building may be kept in one file.

This is the system which you are most likely to use in your own notes.

5.6   Geographical

This method is used by organisations which divide their operations up into areas.

5.7   Alphanumerical

This is a system of coding using letters or numbers.

Activity 3 *(The answer to this activity can be found in Chapter 7)*

Avon and Walker Ltd trades under the name of Cut Price Stores. They have a number of retail outlets selling clothes, toys and fancy goods.

The purchasing department processes all purchase invoices received from suppliers. These are given a consecutive number on receipt. On the 7 July 20X5 the last number used was 33566. Invoices are filed in numerical order.

The warehouse deals with the recording of all stock items received. Each new line is given a new number. The last number used was 66388.

What are the disadvantages of using this numbering system for stock?

Suggest a better method of numbering stock items.

6   Maintaining a filing system

6.1   Preparing new files

New files should be opened only when required. This may be because an existing file is full and needs to be closed or because a new subject has occurred.

The correct type of hardware should be selected. The file should be labelled immediately. It should be recorded in the index (including any cross-reference cards).

6.2   The daily routine

Filing should be carried out daily. This avoids a backlog and keeps files up to date.

The most efficient way to file is to pre-sort documents into the same order as the files.

It is important to punch documents carefully so that they do not stick out from the files.

There should be some way of identifying when documents received from other businesses can be filed. This should be a tick, signature, stamp or other mark to show that staff have finished with the document.

6.3   Care of files

A new file should be started when the old file is full. This will help to keep papers in good condition. Mark the closed date on the front of old files.

It is best to remove paper clips from documents as these may tear other documents. Use staples instead.

Any damaged documents should be repaired immediately.

Care should be taken to make sure documents are filed in the correct place. If in doubt ask a supervisor.

Filing cabinets, drawers and shelves should not be allowed to become overloaded with files.

Files are extremely important to an organisation and should always be kept in good condition.

6.4   Confidential files

Security over confidential files is very important. Most confidential files will be kept in locked filing cabinets. Some will be kept in a safe. Highly confidential files should only be available to selected people.

Confidential files kept on computer will have restricted access controlled by the use of passwords.

Several passwords may be required when processing certain transactions, such as payroll. The company procedures may necessitate one password being used to access the weekly paid staff records. Another may be used for salaried staff and a further password may have to be entered for access to directors' salaries.

6.5   Legal constraints

Instances have occurred of individuals suffering from inconvenience and embarrassment because data concerning them, held on computer, has been inaccurate. For example, wrong (and detrimental) information about a person's creditworthiness might be stored on computer. As a result, that person may be refused credit. Data kept on file in a computer is covered by the Data Protection Acts 1984 and 1998 (see later in this chapter).

6.6   Retention policy

It is not necessary to keep all records forever. Some may be disposed of after a relatively short period of time, some may have to be kept for a statutory period of time, whilst others should be kept permanently. The necessity to distinguish between the varying lengths of retention dictates the need for an established retention policy.

Some documents, such as legal contracts, should be retained for a period of not less than six years as they may affect future litigation. As many financial documents also form the basis of a contract, they too should be kept for six years.

Some documents will be concerned with the original establishment of the organisation and should be kept permanently. Annual financial statements and reports should also be kept permanently.

A laid-down retention policy would involve the maintenance of a list detailing the various types of document and the length of time for which they should be retained.

6.7   Long-term storage and disposal of files

Most files have a limited life. How long files are kept within the office area will depend upon the type of file and the amount of storage space available.

Files which are no longer current or for which there is no longer enough space in the office are transferred to long-term storage or stored in another way. Long-term storage might be in the basement or in another building.

Documents can be stored on microfiche or on a computer.

6.8   Disposal of files

Files which are no longer needed should be destroyed as few organisations can keep every document for ever.

Confidential paper-based files should be put through a shredder.

Some companies try to ensure that as much paper as possible is recycled. There are various paper-recycling companies which collect office waste paper. This may mean separating out any files containing plastic or metal parts, but these files may then be reusable by the organisation.

Some paper-recycling businesses can even deal with confidential files which removes the need for shredding.

How long files are kept will depend upon both the organisation's own rules and legal requirements. It is important that files are never disposed of without authorisation.

7   The Data Protection Act 1998

7.1   Introduction

The Data Protection Act 1998 exists to protect individuals from the misuse of personal data held (mainly) on computer files. The 1998 Act came into force on 1 March 2000 when it replaced the original Data Protection Act 1984.

7.2   Personal data

The Data Protection Act only covers **personal data**, ie data which relates to an identifiable living individual (called the **data subject**), and which is:

♦   being processed by computer or other automatic equipment, or

♦   recorded with the intention that it should be so processed, or

♦   part of a relevant filing system (including some manual systems).

7.3   The data protection principles

All personal data is required to be processed in accordance with eight principles. These require that data must be:

♦   processed fairly and lawfully

♦   processed for limited purposes

♦   adequate, relevant and not excessive

♦   accurate

♦   not kept longer than necessary

♦   processed in accordance with the data subject's rights

♦   secure

♦   not transferred to countries without adequate protection.

7.4   Sensitive personal data

The 1998 Act introduces a new category of **sensitive** personal data, meaning any personal data which includes information on:

♦   racial or ethnic origin

♦   political or religious beliefs

♦   physical or mental health.

Sensitive personal data should normally only be processed if the data subject has given his or her explicit consent to the processing.

7.5 Data controller

Every organisation holding personal data must appoint a data controller (ie a person) who is responsible for overseeing the processing of the data, and who must register the organisation with the Data Protection Commissioner (who has taken over from the Data Protection Registrar established by the 1984 Act).

7.6 Rights of data subjects

Data subjects are entitled to be informed, on request, of all personal data being held about them, the purposes for which it is being held, and to whom it might be disclosed.

Any person who knowingly or recklessly obtains or discloses personal data without authority is guilty of an offence.

7.7 Conclusion

The Data Protection Act 1998 has strengthened the protections afforded by the previous 1984 Act. Data subjects are given the right:

♦   to be informed whether a data user holds information on them

♦   to be given a copy of that information

♦   to obtain compensation if they suffer damage due to a failure to comply with the Act

♦   to have inaccurate personal data rectified or erased.

CHAPTER 7

Answers to activities

Chapter 1

ANSWER 1

(a)   It would include information on:

   (i)   the people in charge of health and safety within the firm and their specific responsibilities;

   (ii)   safe operating practices (eg the operation of electrical equipment);

   (iii)   the system for recording accidents in the accident book;

   (iv)   details of first aid available, including the names of qualified first aiders and the position of the first aid box.

(b)   Adequate premises which are structurally sound, have adequate fire exits and safety equipment.

Suitable accommodation: suitable temperature, enough space for number of people, proper ventilation, blinds for windows, adequate lighting and safe floor surfaces in good condition.

Appropriate furniture: safety stools to reach items stored on shelves, adjustable chairs for VDU operators and filing cabinets in which only one drawer can be opened at a time.

Adequate toilet and welfare facilities.

Separate accommodation for noisy or dangerous equipment (eg photocopiers which give out fumes) or substances (eg cleaning materials).

Safe equipment which is serviced regularly by trained technicians.

ANSWER 2

Most likely causes are:

(a)   people tripping up, slipping or falling off equipment or furniture;

(b)   people being hit by falling objects or colliding with equipment, furniture or other people;

(c)   people using electrical equipment incorrectly;

(d)   people using equipment or materials incorrectly.

ANSWER 3

(a)   Discovering a fire:

   (i)   decide whether or not it can be dealt with using a fire extinguisher or fire blanket - these methods are only successful for small fires;

   (ii)   ensure that no one else is in immediate danger;

   (iii)   if the fire is in one room only, close the door;

   (iv)   raise the alarm and follow company procedure on who must ring the fire brigade;

   (v)   leave the building as quickly as possible - do *not* stop to collect any personal belongings.

(b)   Hearing a fire alarm:

   (i)   close all windows and doors and leave the building as quickly as possible - do *not* stop to collect any personal belongings;

   (ii)   remain calm and go to the assembly point;

   (iii)   follow the instructions of your managers or the fire brigade officers - do not re-enter the building until you are authorised to do so.

ANSWER 4

Details of the injured person (name, address, age, etc).

Injuries sustained.

Details of the accident (date, time, place, narrative, diagram if necessary).

First aid or medical treatment provided on site.

Names of witnesses (if any).

Chapter 3

ANSWER 1

C

ANSWER 2

Ensure that the following information is included:

(a)   the full name and title of the person you intend or are required to see;

(b)   the full and precise name and address of the relevant organisation;

(c)   the telephone number of the organisation together with the area code (STD code) and the extension of the person you must see;

(d)   the time, date and anticipated length of the meeting;

(e)   the exact location of the meeting (eg which room on which floor in which block);

(f)   outline details of the matter to be discussed;

(g)   travel directions and details of entrance points and security procedures.

It is, of course, equally important for those details to be sent to people who may be intending to visit you.

Chapter 4

ANSWER 1

Darren might be used to giving his staff this information (particularly as Fiona is a new employee) but on this day one of the following may apply:

(a)   he is very busy himself;

(b)   he has personal problems.

He might expect all staff to look up information for themselves and several other people might already have asked him.

ANSWER 2

Diana might:

(a)   look away or out of the window;

(b)   play with a pencil or other item;

(c)   continue writing;

(d)   interrupt unnecessarily.

Her supervisor might assume that she is either not capable of doing the job or not interested. Her supervisor might decide not to give her some more interesting work as a type of punishment.

Chapter 5

ANSWER 1

Dear Mr Wigmore

Delivery of cake order

Further to our telephone call last Friday, I can now confirm the following details.

We will make the delivery using our own vans on Saturday. We will deliver to the three shops at Leigh, Wigan and Warrington.

Your original order included two dozen Eccles cakes. I cannot supply these but I can supply the same number of apple turnovers. Please let me know if this is not acceptable.

If you have any queries, please do not hesitate to contact me.

Note how letters should always:

(a)   refer to previous letters or phone calls (although it is best to give dates);

(b)   encourage the recipient to contact you if he or she has any queries.

ANSWER 2

ON COMPANY LETTERHEAD

Order ref

Date

Customer name
Customer address

Dear *

Order received

Thank you for your order. Unfortunately we have been unable to despatch the goods as we were unable to accept your cheque.

The following problem(s) were noted on your cheque:

Date inappropriate (post-dated)	
Payee incorrect	
Amount incorrect	
Words and figures do not agree	
Signature missing	

I enclose your cheque. Once we have received your new cheque, we will despatch the goods to you as soon as possible.

Yours sincerely

Kim Walsh
Accounts supervisor

Chapter 6

ANSWER 1

(a) horizontal – photographs or plans are less likely to be damaged if kept flat in individual drawers;

(b) rotary or lateral – box files are rigid and protect the contents from dust and rough treatment;

(c) vertical – confidential information like this should be kept in a *locked* filing cabinet.

ANSWER 2

(a) concertina file;

(b) lever arch file;

(c) manila file;

(d) box file.

ANSWER 3

The five-figure number is similar to the number used for purchase invoices and may lead to confusion.

Similar lines of stock are not linked in any way.

A better system would be to give stock items a number based on their type. For example:

01 02 1123

01	Clothes
02	Men
1123	Unique reference for this stock line

AAT UNIT 20

WORKING WITH
INFORMATION TECHNOLOGY

TEXTBOOK

CHAPTER 8

Introduction to computer systems

ASSESSMENT FOCUS

This chapter covers the following Knowledge and Understanding and Performance Criteria of the AAT Syllabus.

♦ The organisation's computer software, systems and networking (*Knowledge and Understanding elements 20.1 and 20.2*)

♦ The relationship between different software packages (*Knowledge and Understanding element 20.1*)

♦ The purpose and application of different software packages: accountancy packages; spreadsheets; databases; and word processors (*Knowledge and Understanding element 20.1*)

♦ Relevant security and legal regulations: data protection legislation, copyright, VDU legislation, health and safety, retention of documents (*Knowledge and Understanding element 20.1 and 20.2*)

♦ The purpose of passwords (*Knowledge and Understanding element 20.2*)

♦ Organisational security policies (*Knowledge and Understanding elements 20.1 and 20.2*)

♦ Data to be input into the computer system is clarified with the appropriate person (*Performance Criteria element 20.1*)

In order to cover these, the following topics are considered:

♦ Overview of computer systems

♦ Hardware

♦ Software

♦ Application packages

♦ The relationship between different software packages

♦ Typical system, organisational and legislative requirements to run the packages - passwords, copyright, Data Protection Act, health and safety at work, etc

Introduction

This course is about using computers to process accounting information. You will use your chosen software packages to learn more about this area. Remember that this unit is particularly relevant to work as most businesses use computers as part of their accounting systems.

Before starting this course it is important to identify why you are going to process accounting information by electronic means. What do *you* think the advantages of processing information by computer are?

You may be able to:

♦ process data more quickly than by manual methods;

♦ process data more accurately;

♦ analyse information more efficiently and effectively;

♦ generate reports more efficiently and effectively.

It is important to remember that computers cannot replace all parts of a manual accounting system. It is also important to remember that the quality of the *analysis* and *report-generation* performed by the computer will depend very much upon the *quality* of the information input by the operator.

This chapter gives you an overview of computer systems, ie the hardware and software. The software includes the various applications and the relationship between different software packages. It also covers a checklist of typical system, organisational and legislative requirements you need to be aware of before you get started, eg passwords, copyright, Data Protection Act, health and safety at work, etc.

1 Computer systems

1.1 Introduction

Computer systems are composed of two integrated parts - hardware and software.

Hardware is the term given for equipment, circuits and machinery, which come in boxes and containers, ie the physical components of the system.

Software is the term used for the instructions, represented or stored electronically in the machine itself. The software controls and co-ordinates the operations of the components in the system and the instructions give the machinery the ability to process data. For example, the accounting system records a large number of facts (data) about materials, times, expenses and other transactions. These facts are then classified and summarised (processed) to produce accounts. Then they are organised into reports (output) which are used to plan and control the organisation's activities.

All data processing consists of the computer reading in data (input), processing that data (central processing unit), often with reference to other data (back-up store) and producing results (output).

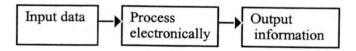

All information for this AAT unit is contained within these three data processing functions.

1.2 Hardware

The basic components of the computer's hardware, whether a portable, a PC or a mainframe, comprise input devices, a central processing unit, external storage equipment and output devices.

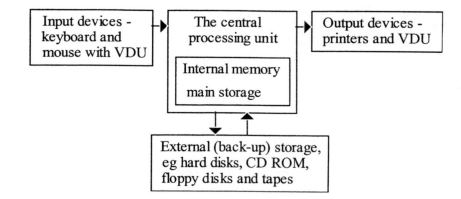

- The input can be from a variety of sources. In modern systems, much of the input will be directly from other computers. The most common input devices are the VDU with a keyboard and mouse, but scanned input is increasingly used (eg bar-code readers, swipe cards, touch screens and document scanners) and voice input is now possible.

- The processor is a collection of electronic circuits that may be condensed into a single silicon chip like the Pentium.

- Because the computer's main memory is very fast and expensive, as well as being volatile, it is necessary to have an auxiliary memory known as back-up storage. This is where data and programs that are not in use can be held until required.

- Disk drives provide a computer with additional memory and millions of bits of storage that can be accessed in a fraction of a second. Disks store programs, data and directories. The programs may be those you write or buy in order to perform some useful function (application programs) or those used by the computer to run other programs (system programs). The data stored on disk is used by the programs as input data, which the program may change and write back on the disk as new data or as an update of previously stored data.

- Output devices include VDUs and printers, which can be used to obtain information that has been retrieved from a file.

Activity 1 *(The answer is in the final chapter of this book)*

What sort of input device would be used to gain access to a building or car park?

It is going to be assumed that you will be working on an individual PC (standalone) or on a PC linked to other computers in a network. This can be via a server or as a terminal for a mainframe. Your system probably consists of the following units:

- the processor

- the workspace

- a minimum of one floppy disk drive (sometimes two)

- a hard disk

- possibly a CD ROM drive

- keyboard

- mouse

- monitor

- printer

Although you will not be asked specific details of the system you are working on, it is still a good idea to check out the type of hardware that your organisation has invested in.

The diagram below shows a typical PC configuration with each of the computers linked to their neighbour and sharing the same files, printers and other peripherals.

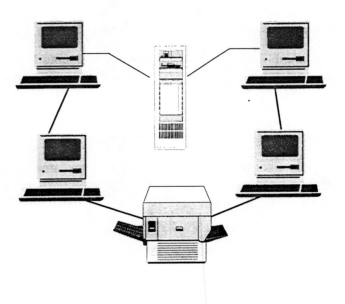

 Activity 2 *(The answer is in the final chapter of this book)*

List the hardware components in your system. Include details of the specifications of components (eg type and size of hard disks and data entry devices) where you can.

1.3 Software

Whichever type of hardware you are using, they all have one thing in common. The processes carried out by the computer are dependent upon the *software* in use. Let us assume you are using a PC with a *hard disk*. The PC needs two types of software to run:

- the operating system; and

- the application programs.

The operating system is a series of programs which form a link between the hardware and the application programs and which provide the user with certain basic functions. PCs use a different operating system from a mainframe. You will be more familiar with the Microsoft Windows NT, Windows 95 or Windows 98 operating system in your PC. These all offer a Graphical User Interface (GUI), which is a user-friendly tool consisting of a work area with menus, icons and windows. An icon is a small picture used for the selection of a software tool or function, eg the icon to save a file is a picture of a floppy disk.

A Window is an area of the screen in which an application or task may be performed.

The operating system makes it easier for the user to use the system. For example, before an application program can be run, it must be loaded into the computer's main memory. This is a complex task, but the user is generally unaware of this as it is carried out by the operating system. Other functions include allowing the user to *back-up* files or to *copy* files.

Activity 3 *(The answer is in the final chapter of this book)*

What does this icon represent?

---

2   Application programs

2.1   Introduction

Many computer users have the same applications. For example, any business has to have systems for payroll, sales ledger, bought ledger and stock control. Very often the requirements for these applications are similar for a wide range of companies.

An application program is a standard program, or suite of programs, designed to perform a specific task. It saves users from having to develop application programs that are essentially the same as those already developed. Some examples of the more common types are:

- Financial modelling (spreadsheet)

- Word processing

- Information retrieval

- Nominal ledger

- Payroll

- Production control

- Sales ledger

- Bought ledger

- Stock control

- Transportation

- Audit packages (which carry out audit tests on files)

Some of these packages can be used on their own or linked together as part of a larger integrated system that brings varied tasks together, eg office administration packages that comprise word processing, creating and using a database, spreadsheets and business graphics (Office 2000).

2.2   Integrated systems

Many integrated packages now exist and organisations will use an integrated applications package as an alternative to buying in a number of dedicated application packages.

They have a number of different modules, which usually consist of a spreadsheet, word-processor, communications package, graphics package, and database.

Integrated packages have certain advantages and disadvantages. The advantages include:

♦   Compatibility between the separate modules.

♦   Efficiency - there is no need to quit one application to access another.

♦   User friendly - there is only one set of Function Keys to learn because they have the same function in each of the modules.

Disadvantages:

♦   The memory size required might be more than that required by a dedicated package.

♦   The modules contained in the package would not have as many features as in a dedicated application.

♦   There may be more modules contained in it than those required by the user.

The essential concept of an integrated system is that programs communicate with each other inside the computer instead of outside it.

♦   The single input principle is used. When a transaction is input to the system, it results in all the relevant files being updated.

♦   Output is produced for communication to the user, not to communicate with another system.

♦   All files can be accessed by programs as needed; a program is not limited to access to a single file.

Integrated systems are usually, but not inevitably, associated with the use of databases.

EXAMPLE

Three systems that are often integrated are order processing, sales accounting and stock control.

1.   A customer order is input, and is checked against the customer file (for credit) and the stock file (for availability).

2.   The stock file is updated. If meeting the order causes the stock to fall below reorder level, an exception report is produced.

3.   Prices are obtained from the stock file and details of discounts from the customer file, which is then updated with details of the invoice.

From a single input (customer order), two files (customer and stock) are updated. The outputs produced (exception report, invoice set) are for communication to users and not between systems.

Further systems may be added to the integrated system:

1.   Where the order cannot be met from stock, but has to be manufactured, the production planning system can be activated to schedule the manufacturing processes.

2.   The production planning system would then update the stock file as materials were allocated for the manufacture. The stock control system would in turn be activated to replenish stocks if necessary.

3.   At the proper time, the order would be placed in a work-in-progress file and processed by the production control system.

2.3   Fully integrated accounting systems

At their simplest level, accounts packages can be considered as electronic ledgers, with the routine transactions recorded on a computer system, rather than on paper, and the general principles of double entry bookkeeping being incorporated in the software.

There are many advantages in computerising an accounts system using a software package. Most accounting packages include sales invoicing, stock control and report generation, as well as the basic sales, purchase and nominal ledgers. The user can set the format of the invoices as pre-printed forms. Other features that can be expected from even the simplest packages would include some form of security and auditing controls. More advanced, and more expensive packages would be expected to provide such options as payroll, multiple currency accounts, and cheque production facilities with integrated word processors and spreadsheets so that information can be used anywhere in the system and incorporated into financial modelling routines and reports or letters as required.

Pegasus Capital Gold and Sage Line 50 are typical of the integrated packages that you will use when completing the performance criteria for this unit. Most accounting packages are *menu-driven*. This means that they guide you through the various parts of the program by presenting you with options from which you must choose where you want to go.

Activity 4 *(The answer is in the final chapter of this book)*

What packages do you think would make up the integrated accounting system?

2.4   Databases

A database is used to store data. A card index system is a database, the files containing individual records. Think of these as individual card files listing all the data related to one item (eg a customer's details). If you were using a card-file system you would have to choose how to order and store the cards (eg *alphabetical order*), although you could use *cross-referencing cards* for certain entries. This would mean that you could only look up information easily if you knew the name of the customer. It would be possible, but time-consuming and inefficient, to extract any other information (eg all customers within a certain town).

A computerised database, however, allows the storage of data, which may be accessed in some systematic way to retrieve the data for further processing at a later date. The main features of database packages include:

♦ The ability to store numeric or textual data for subsequent use.

♦ The ability to add to or delete records.

♦ The ability to retrieve data previously stored and transfer it to another system for further processing.

♦ The ability to search for specific data.

♦ The ability to view the data in different formats.

♦ The ability to design or format input/output screens.

♦ The ability to interface with other applications.

♦ The ability to print out user-defined reports.

Information is added through *forms* displayed on the screen. Some databases are set up in advance and therefore are not expected to be modified (see *accounting packages* below), others are blank shells to be customised by the individual user.

Examples of database packages include Microsoft Access and Paradox.

2.5 Spreadsheets

A spreadsheet is a framework that is used to handle numbers with ease. Each cell in the spreadsheet is identified by being given a unique row (labelled 1, 2, 3, etc) and column identification (labelled A, B, C, etc). A cell entry can have a value or an instruction put into it.

Any numerical data entered into cells can be manipulated and arithmetic operations can be carried out on it as well as more complex operations. The cells can be referenced in the spreadsheet and linked together in performing the necessary operations required by the model. These operations can be done very quickly. Graphs can be drawn and plotted from data within the spreadsheet model.

Different spreadsheet packages contain different facilities, but almost all offer the facility to copy one or more cells, to set cell display characteristics, to produce graphs, to save and retrieve a spreadsheet, and to write programs (macros).

Activity 5 *(The answer is in the final chapter of this book)*

Can you give any examples of spreadsheet packages?

2.6 Word processing packages

Word-processing involves the generation, manipulation, modification, storage and communication of data in the form of text. The main packages on the market have the following features:

- Text can be entered, edited, moved, retrieved, stored and printed in large volumes very easily.

- Produce standard letters, which can be typed, stored and used over and over again. This saves time and allows for higher productivity.

- Document checking - a dictionary and a Thesaurus are standard facilities in most word-processing packages. Documents and letters can therefore be quickly checked for typographical errors. Word count facilities are also available so that the length of the document can be checked to see if it is on target or needs to be amended.

- Text can be combined from many sources to form a new document.

- Special layouts can be generated to improve the appearance of text and give a 'corporate image'.

- Diagrams, graphs and other graphic features can be incorporated into documents.

- Mail-merging - standard letters are merged with names and addresses on an automated mailing list (this could be a file created in a database program). Mail merging allows for standard letters to be personalised by using the details stored on the mailing list.

- File merging - standard paragraphs or clauses can be stored on a separate file and then incorporated into letters or documents.

- Document printing - the software generally provides a number of print options, including a choice of fonts and line spacing options, the ability to justify the text and the facility of headers and footers to add chapter headings or page numbers to the document. Contents tables and indexes can also be generated.

The only way to learn how to use these programs is to practise. You should read the manual before starting and refer to it if you have any problems. This Study text is not designed to tell you which buttons to push. It is designed to help you 'explore' your chosen application package through a series of case studies and assignments.

Activity 6 *(The answer is in the final chapter of this book)*

List the names of the operating systems and applications software to which you have access.

---

3   Basic requirements

3.1   Keyboard

Whatever type of computer system you are using you will need certain basic skills to be able to use it to its full potential. You will need to be able to:

- input information using the *keyboard*;

- interpret information shown on the *screen*; and

- print out reports using a *printer*.

You can see that these skills also refer to the three areas of data processing (input, processing and output) that we referred to earlier in this chapter.

Let us look first at the keyboard.

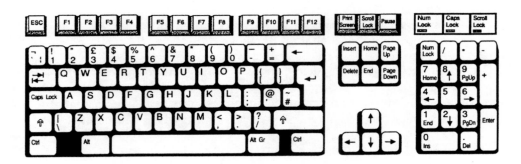

The keyboard to your computer is based on a typewriter keyboard. It has the same basic layout of keys as a typewriter. The main difference is that it has extra keys. The main additional keys may include:

♦ Backspace key - used to erase the character to the left of the cursor.

♦ Function keys - extra keys, which have different uses depending on the software you are using, eg pressing F5 while in Microsoft Word brings up the following:

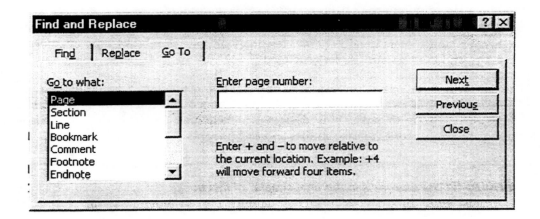

♦ Return key - like the return on a typewriter, it is sometimes used to move to the next line. It is also used to mark the end of an entry.

♦ Direction/calculator keys - these keys have two functions depending upon whether or not the *number lock* is used. With number lock on, the keys can be used as a calculator but *without* it they are used to move the cursor around the screen.

♦ Direction keys - some keyboards have an additional set of direction keys.

♦ Escape key - used in certain programs to move between different levels of the program.

3.2 WIMP

Interpreting information on the screen is very easy when using a graphical user interface. WIMP is an acronym for Windows, Icons, Mouse and Pointer. Windows allow the screen to be divided into a number of areas, each of which can display information from a different file or area, eg to view different documents simultaneously.

Each window has similar features, eg in the Microsoft Word window shown above you can see:

♦ The title bar showing the file name at the top left hand corner;

♦ The tool bars with pull down menus;

♦ The icons showing the various functions.

Icons are sometimes used instead of numbers, letters or words to identify and describe the various functions available for selection, or files to access. For example, in Word these icons represent **B** *I* <u>U</u> Bold, Italic and Underline.

The mouse moves the pointer (cursor) around the screen. Clicking on the left button once will select the icon or other option required. Clicking on it twice will execute the current command.

The pointer changes depending on the application and the contents of the window. It can be an arrow or like a capital 'I'. Its movement mimics that of the mouse and helps you navigate around the screen. If you point to one of the icons and hold the arrow in place it will highlight an explanation of the function. For example, positioning the arrow over the icon that looks like a floppy disk will highlight the box that tells you it is the Save function.

3.3   Printing

The quickest way to print something from a Windows environment is to press the print button. However, there are a few checks that you will have to remember, especially when you are demonstrating your knowledge and understanding when using the printer.

The printer needs to be switched on and ready to print (on line). The paper needs to be aligned properly, with continuous stationery positioned at the top of the page. If a single printed page is spread across two pages of continuous stationery, due to faulty alignment, it could mean that you would have to print all the output again.

To save time and money, you should only print what is necessary. When specifying the parameters for printing a document, you can choose to exclude information that is not needed. Most application packages will give you clear instructions about printing selected output via prompts on the screen, eg print range to specify the invoice numbers to print.

When you are demonstrating your ability to print reports, it is important that you show that you are considering the time and money aspect of your organisation's resources.

3.4   Shutting down

If you want to close the current Window and you have saved your work, then you can click on the X button in the right hand top corner of the Window. Alternatively, you can select the *File* menu and then *Close*.

When you are ready to shut down the computer, click on the Start button at the bottom left corner and then select *Shut Down*. Clicking on the *Yes* button will close down the computer. Clicking on the *No* button will take you back to the previous window.

Activity 7 *(The answer is in the final chapter of this book)*

What do the three icons at the top right hand corner of the Window represent?

4 System and organisational requirements

4.1 System requirements

Let us look at certain areas, which you should be aware of *before* you start to use your chosen packages. These are:

♦ care of disks and CDs;

♦ using write-protect;

♦ making back-up copies.

Care of disks and CDs - if you are using floppy disks, you must store them in a clean, dry place, such as a disk box (a specially designed plastic tray). If you leave them lying on your desk they may have something put on top of them or have coffee spilt on them. Keep the disks away from electrical equipment as this may scramble the information on the disk and do not write on labels that are already stuck to the disks as the pressure from the pen may damage the disk.

CDs are a bit more robust and not prone to damage from magnetic fields. However, they should not be left in direct sunlight and they can get scratched if they are not put back into their sleeves.

Using write-protect - disks are like cassette tapes or videotapes, they can be bought for what is recorded on them, or you can use them to record something of your choice. Also, like tapes, you may want to avoid losing something by recording over it. Cassette tapes and videotapes allow you to stop this from happening and so do disks. This is vital if you want to protect programs that you have bought or data that you cannot recreate.

Making back-up copies - if you are using a *twin-floppy* you will have to store all your data on disk and re-input it next time you want to run your program again. If you damage these disks you will have lost all your work; therefore you should make extra back-up copies on different disks each time you leave the system. Even if you are using a machine with a hard disk, the hard disk may sometimes develop a fault. You should make regular back-up copies even if you are using a hard disk.

4.2 Organisational requirements

There are two areas to be aware of when starting up an application:

♦ security and confidentiality; and

♦ maintenance.

Security and confidentiality - the system that you are using (particularly if you are one of many users on a *network* or *mainframe*) may contain confidential information. Think of it as a filing cabinet full of documents. If it were a filing cabinet you would want to lock it. The computer equivalents of locking the cabinet include:

♦ using passwords to restrict access;

♦ restricting user access to certain parts of the system only;

♦ storing confidential information in a particular directory (a directory is like a drawer in the filing cabinet);

Maintenance - it is important to keep your computer clean if it is to work properly. There are special products available to clean the machine. *Never* use ordinary household cleaning products. The screen should be wiped with a special anti-static screen-wipe. The keyboard should be kept free from dust with a keyboard brush. Any marks on the computer casing should be removed with a special cleaner.

5   Legislative requirements

5.1   Health and safety

You will have covered health and safety in another part of the course, but it is worth repeating the main points relating to the use of computers and VDUs (*Visual Display Units*).

Remember that like any other piece of electrical equipment you should observe basic safety, eg do not leave trailing flexes or overload plugs. Remember that only a qualified electrical technician should carry out repairs on electrical equipment.

Certain aspects of data processing present a particular risk to the health of individuals. If you spend a large part of your working day working at a VDU you risk various problems including eye strain, back problems and RSI (*Repetitive Strain Injury*). RSI appears to arise from making the same movements over and over again, and affects hands and arms. If you ever suffer any pain or discomfort while working at a VDU then you must take a break. It would also help if you could move on to a task not involving the VDU.

If you work at a VDU there are certain things you can do to reduce the risk of problems.

♦ Use a five-leg swivel chair (preferably with an adjustable back rest) set at the correct height.

♦ Sit with the keyboard and monitor *directly* in front of you. (Do not sit in a position that means you have to turn your head to see the screen.)

♦ Adjust the monitor so that it is on the same level as your eyes.

♦ Avoid a position which means there is light reflected directly from windows.

♦ Sit with your feet slightly raised on a support or book.

♦ Use the keyboard in its *flat* position. Your forearms should be level with the work surface and your wrists should rest on the work surface.

♦ Make sure you have enough space in your work area for books and papers you are working on. Tidy away any other items that you are not actually using.

♦ Take regular breaks and avoid looking at the screen continuously for long periods of time.

5.2   *Data Protection Act 1984*

The increasing use of computers in all aspects of business has meant that increasingly large amounts of information about individuals are now kept by various organisations.

There is a risk that some of this information is *inaccurate* which could cause serious problems for the individual concerned (eg they may be refused a loan if they have the wrong credit rating). To help reduce this risk, the Data Protection Act was introduced.

The *Data Protection Registrar* keeps a register of companies who hold information on computer. Each company which falls into this category must register of its own accord. A copy of the Data Protection Register is held in all major libraries.

Any unregistered data user who holds personal data which is not exempt commits a criminal offence; the maximum penalty for which is an unlimited fine.

The Act covers the following issues:

♦   Any information held must have been obtained by *legal* methods and must not be held for any longer than necessary.

♦   People can find out what information is held about them by writing to the organisation and asking for a copy.

♦   Personal data must not be disclosed to others for any reason other than the reason for which it is held.

♦   Data must be up-to-date and not excessive considering the purpose for which it is held.

♦   Proper security precautions must be taken to stop unauthorised access to data.

5.3   *Patent and copyright infringement*

An integral part of the data processing standards must be to comply with the Data Protection Act and with the copyright laws, and to avoid any action that might reflect badly on the reputation of the company.

Copyright law covers books of all kinds, sound recordings, film and broadcasts, computer programs, dramatic and musical works.

Modern software packages are complex and costly to produce, but are often easy to copy and distribute. Manufacturers are increasingly bringing prosecutions to try to reduce the number of pirate copies of their software. Staff should be made aware of this. Master and back-up copies of packages (usually on diskette or CD-ROM) should be kept in a locked safe. Programs on LAN servers should be given 'execute only' protection to prevent them being copied, and physical access to the server should be restricted. Regular and automatic audits should be made of personal computers to check that they only contain authorised programs.

The **Copyright Designs and Patents Act 1988** states that the copyright holder (usually the software publisher) has the exclusive right to make and distribute copies. An amendment made in 1992 allows you to make a copy for back-up purposes. Application packages will always contain an embedded serial number. If a pirate copy is found, the original purchaser can usually be determined. There are steep penalties for companies prosecuted for software theft - unlimited damages, legal costs and the cost of legitimising the software. However, most breaches of copyright law happen because business users do not know what the law is.

Where a package is intended for use by more than one person, for instance on a network, then a multi-user licence is normally purchased, and this sets a limit on the total number of users.

An alternative to this is a site licence, but this can be restrictive if, say, a travelling salesperson or someone working from home connects to the network.

The Federation Against Software Theft (FAST) organises awareness campaigns and assists companies in carrying out software audits. The Business Software Alliance (BSA), which comprises several major US software houses, is active in organising corporate 'raids' and bringing prosecutions.

Activity 8 *(The answer is in the final chapter of this book)*

Copyright law covers:

(a)   Reference books, sound recordings, film and broadcasts, computer programs, dramatic and musical works

(b)   Books of all kinds, sound recordings, film and broadcasts, computer programs, dramatic and musical works

(c)   Books of all kinds, sound recordings, film and broadcasts, computer programs written in the UK, dramatic and musical works

(d)   Books of all kinds, sound recordings on CD, film and broadcasts, computer programs, dramatic and musical works

Which one is correct?

5.4   *Enforcement of standards*

Observance of standards is more a matter of attitude than policing. When people are aware of the purposes of standards, they are more likely to follow them than if they are just threatened. Training is the main element of enforcement.

There are some cases where ignoring standards should automatically lead to disciplinary action:

♦   any standards to do with safety, eg dangerous positioning of cables, particularly power cables, or working alone in an electrically hazardous environment;

♦   standards with legal implications, eg ignoring a requirement of the Data Protection Act or using an illegal copy of a program;

♦   actions which may affect a number of other people, eg running a program which might introduce a virus into a network;

♦   attempted unauthorised entry, eg trying to find someone else's password or unauthorised copying of confidential files (eg salaries).

Activity 9 *(The answer is in the final chapter of this book)*

DF Ltd have just purchased a number of microcomputers for use in administrative tasks. They are intending to buy spreadsheet, word-processing and database packages to help with these tasks.

Describe the main features of each of these three packages.

6   Summary

After reading this chapter, you should have a better idea of how the various parts of the computer system fit together. We will build on this basic understanding and explore some of the areas in much more detail.

CHAPTER 9

Data input

ASSESSMENT FOCUS

This chapter covers the following Knowledge and Understanding and Performance Criteria of the AAT Syllabus.

♦ Types of data held on a computer system *(Knowledge and Understanding element 20.1 and 20.2)*

♦ Location of information sources *(Knowledge and Understanding element 20.1)*

♦ Data is input and stored in the appropriate location *(Performance Criteria element 20.1)*

♦ All vital fields are completed *(Performance Criteria element 20.1)*

♦ New unique codes are generated as necessary *(Performance Criteria element 20.1)*

♦ Work carried out on a computer is saved on a regular basis *(Performance Criteria element 20.2)*

♦ Passwords are used where limitations on access to data are required *(Performance Criteria element 20.2)*

♦ Passwords are kept secret and are discreetly changed at appropriate times *(Performance Criteria element 20.2)*

In order to cover these, the following topics are considered:

♦ User interface - Windows and Icons

♦ Methods of input

♦ Types of source documents - complete and incomplete

♦ Modification of existing information

♦ Deletion/cancellation of existing information

♦ Data v Information

♦ Types of processing

♦ Problems associated with input

♦ Data validation/verification

Introduction

In this chapter we will be looking at the first part of data processing - that of data input. The design of the input sub-system covers the following:

♦ Data collection

The mode and method of data collection/capture must be determined.

♦ Batching/on-line entry

It should be decided whether to batch input documents, or to enter them on line. If the source documents are to be batched, then the frequency and controls must be determined.

♦ Entry of code numbers

Wherever possible code numbers should be pre-printed on documents. Where this is possible, the code should be kept as simple as possible. Also checks (eg check digits) should be built into the input system as far as is practicable.

♦ Error messages

Where errors are detected, error messages should be printed or displayed. The recipients of error messages should understand their meaning. Procedures must be established for error correction and re-inputting.

1   Data collection

1.1   Authorisation

In this section, we will look at the different types of data collected by an organisation, and outline where that data comes from.

Data is a collection of raw facts such as words, numbers and pictures, in the form in which it is collected. It relates to facts, events and transactions, and is the raw material for data processing.

The data might be used to update or amend other data held on disk, eg the record of a supplier could be updated upon payment of their invoice. The term 'data input' also applies to an enquiry, eg retrieving an item of data already held on file.

Before accessing the system and inputting to or retrieving from certain files, you must have the required level of authority and check that the organisation's policies are being met. Some programs have built-in controls to limit the access to certain files, eg a pre-set list of log-in names may be able to process certain transaction files.

1.2   Data sources

Information can either be collected as data and processed into information, or it can be collected as information that has already been processed by someone else.

In the same way, information can arise from sources both within and outside the organisation. For example, in making 'selling price decisions', information about production possibilities and costs will arise from within the organisation, whereas information about potential demand for the products will be found by market research, which is an external source. Information concerning competitors' pricing policies and other aspects of 'market intelligence' is also external.

Internal data - this data will be associated with activities or transactions performed within the organisation, such as administrative tasks, the production of products and services, or the sale of those products. Often these activities generate costs and revenues and much of the internal data collected will be quantitative.

The data may be written on a paper document and used when keying into the computer systems. For example a customer order is generally recorded on a sales order form. This is used as a source document for input to the sales order processing within the accounting package.

Gathering data/information from inside the organisation involves:

♦ establishing a system for collecting or measuring data, eg measuring output, sales, costs, cash receipts and payments, asset purchases, stock turnover, etc. In other words, there must be established procedures for what data is collected, how frequently, by whom and by what method - and how it is processed, filed and communicated;

♦ relying to some extent on the informal communication lines between managers and staff, eg word of mouth and conversations at meetings.

External data - organisations need to collect data relating to the outside world or the 'environment' of the organisation.

Data relating to the environment of an organisation might be classified under the following headings:

♦ Political (such as Government policy)

♦ Economic (such as inflation or exchange rates)

♦ Social (such as buying patterns or fashion)

♦ Technological (such as materials and production methods)

♦ Competitive (such as the behaviour of customers, suppliers and rivals)

Activity 1 *(The answer is in the final chapter of this book)*

A goods received note and the supplier's purchase invoice are used for input to which system?

1.3   Source documents

It is important for you to be able to give plenty of examples of the types of source documents used in your organisation.

Typical source documents used as input to a computer system include:

♦ Goods received notes (GRN).

♦ Stores requisition forms.

♦ Purchase order forms.

♦ Purchase and sales invoices.

♦ Time sheets.

♦ Cheque books to record payments.

♦ Bank statements.

◆ Cash receipts.

◆ Petty cash books.

Goods received notes (GRN) - are used to record the arrival of material from suppliers. They are supplied pre-numbered in triplicate, and all copies should be eventually entered into the computer system with a report of missing serial numbers. There are three main areas on the form: - receiving, details of material received and inspection.

The source of most of the data for the GRN is from the supplier's delivery note. It provides the following:

◆ Supplier's name and address and delivery note number

◆ The quantity, unit of measure, supplier's part number and description for each item received.

The inspection procedure will generate more information to input into the system, eg quantity rejected, discrepancy between quantity shipped and quantity received.

A **stores requisition** is the authority to draw material from stores for use in production. Some small companies will use manually prepared stores requisitions. Larger manufacturing companies are more likely to have a computer-based production control system where the system produces stores requisitions.

The source of most of the information on a stores requisition will come from the production schedules. The information that you might have to input includes:

◆ Requisition number

◆ Quantity required

◆ Quantity issued

◆ Part number

◆ Description

A **purchase order** gives authority to the supplier to supply. A copy is given to the receiving department, so that they know what material to expect. It also helps them identify it when it arrives.

The function of the purchase order, in the inventory control system, is to compare the total of the quantity in stock and on order with future requirements. This will determine whether further supplies are ordered. The data for the purchase order comes from a few sources - purchasing records, quotations and releases provide most of the information on the order.

As the purchase order constitutes a contract, it is important to see that the company name and address and the purchase conditions are set out.

1.4　*Formatted data*

Formatted data includes numerical or alphabetical characters or groups of characters, which are arranged in a predefined format in which the meaning of each item has been previously defined. For example:

Part number	Quantity in stock	Quantity on order	Cost price each (£)
A22945	1953	2500	0.13
R64983	140	1500	0.67
P33454	2981	0	0.83
S46855	3843	1000	0.16

In this illustration, the data is organised in a predefined format where the part number is presented first followed by the quantity in stock, quantity on order and finally cost price each. The meaning of each item is predefined and explained by the headings to each column. This kind of data is processed and stored in transaction processing systems.

2 Input using a keyboard

2.1 Concerns

When choosing input methods and media, most users are concerned with the following:

♦ how to economise on the use of manpower;

♦ how to prevent or detect errors in the source data;

♦ how to achieve data capture at the lowest possible cost;

♦ how to achieve input sufficiently quickly.

Input devices can be divided into two main categories:

♦ those using a keyboard;

♦ those using direct input of the data.

2.2 Keyboard devices

These devices have keyboards similar to that of a normal typewriter and they usually have some sort of visual display unit or VDU (like a television monitor) attached so that the operator can see what has been typed.

Data may go directly from the keyboard to the computer where it is processed immediately (on-line input), or it can first be recorded on an intermediate medium which is later read into the computer (off-line input). The advantage of the latter method is that many keyboard devices can be made available at relatively low cost, allowing many operators to record the data. This can then be input at high speed so that the computer is not forced to slow down to operator input speeds.

Examples of intermediate input methods include:

♦ Key-to-disk systems - when data is entered via the keyboard, it is held in temporary storage allocated to each workstation. A program carries out logical checks on the data. If the data is accepted, it is written onto a designated area on the disk for later input to the computer.

The supervisor can allocate disk areas to key stations and can also choose the validation and control programs relevant to each key station.

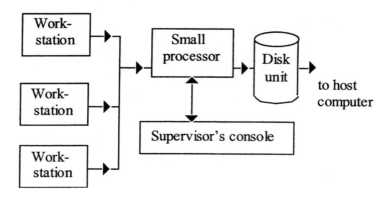

♦ Key-to-diskette (floppy disk) - after being recorded, the data on the diskettes can be input to the computer.

2.3 Input on screen

Most of the input for accounting applications will be via a keyboard or mouse attached to a VDU screen.

There is a two-way communication between the user and the computer program. The screen displays messages or information asking users to give information or input data into a field outlined by a pointer or cursor. The screen also prompts users on what to do next from a selection of different options. The screen displays the data that has been keyed in by the user so that it can be checked prior to entering it into the system. Incorrect data can be amended or abandoned before it is entered.

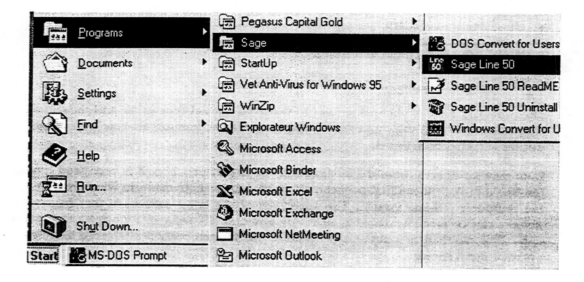

Microsoft Windows uses a hierarchy of menus for inputting data. It starts with a main menu and works down to sub-menus.

The screen shown above starts from the main menu (obtained by clicking on Start). 'Programs' is selected and then Sage and then the Sage Line 50 software.

Once you have gained access to the package, the Sage screen has another menu bar - File, Edit, View, Settings, etc. Further options are shown as icons - Customers, Suppliers, Nominal, Bank, etc.

Activity 2 *(The answer is in the final chapter of this book)*

What type of an application is Excel?

Assuming that you are working in a Windows environment, all the menus will have the main functions on the top menu, eg programs, settings and shut down. The rest of the menus available to you will not look like the illustration because of the different choices of software used by different people.

Some packages have screens that look like index cards. The one shown below has the general details of a supplier. When entering data about a new supplier, the ID is the unique identifier. From this entry, the user is stepped through the other fields to fill in the rest of the details. By clicking on the "financial details" or "comments" tab the user can enter more information about this supplier. If you try to enter the wrong type of data, some applications will not let you proceed. They just beep to alert you to your mistake.

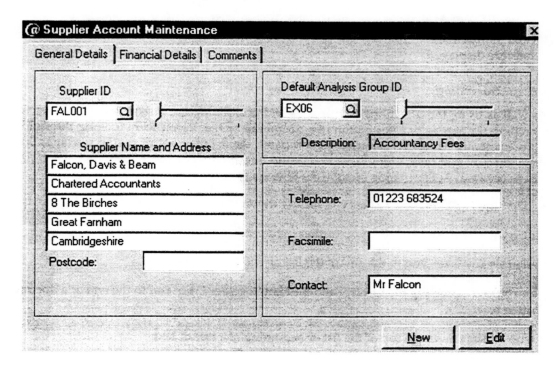

Navigating around the screen is similar in most applications - you use the direction arrow key to move the cursor to the menu item required.

The **Enter** key (also called the **Return** key) has various uses:

♦   it is used to select a chosen option

♦   with some packages it is used to enter the data fully into the system

♦   when using packages such as word processing, it is used to move down from one line of text to the next - returning to the beginning of the next line.

The **Tab** key (on the left-hand side of the keypad with bi-directional arrows on it) is also used to step through the various fields, such as the one shown above. If you were asked to change the contact name at the Chartered Accountants to Mr Beam, you would access the file by keying in the supplier ID (a unique code), then press the Edit button and tab key until it reached the contact field. Alternatively, you could just use the mouse to position the pointer or cursor over the required field and then click the left-hand button on the mouse.

To change the data, you could position the cursor at the beginning of the surname and then press the delete button until all the letters of Falcon were deleted and then key in the replacement. Another way is to position the cursor at the beginning of the word or section that you want to delete, then keep the left hand button of the mouse depressed whilst dragging the mouse across the area that is going to be deleted. This highlights the area and allows you to check that it is OK to delete before pressing the **Enter** key.

2.4   Codes

We will be looking at codes in more detail in a later chapter because they are very important when inputting data to a computer system. They are widely used because they save time and storage space on the files. The accounting system will use codes to identify suppliers and customers. Typically, as soon as the first few letters of the code are keyed in, the full details will be displayed on the screen. If it is the wrong customer or supplier, eg where there are several similar names, you can tab to the next Smith or Jones, etc in the file until the correct details are displayed.

2.5   Searching

As well as using the directional arrow keys and positioning the cursor, there are other ways of searching for entries or information in a document or file. If you were looking through a long list of customer names for a particular company, the list may not fit on the screen at the same time and it would take a long time to find the information by using the cursor direction keys. Alternative ways of searching include the following:

Pg Dn - the page down key takes you further down the list

Pg Up - the page up key takes you further up the list

End - this key takes you to the end of the list or end of a line of text

Control/End - pressing the Control and End key together takes you to the end of a document of written text.

Home - takes you to the top of the list or beginning of a line of text

Control/Home - pressing the Control and Home key together takes you to the start of a document of written text.

Find - Control +F allows you to specify what you are looking for:

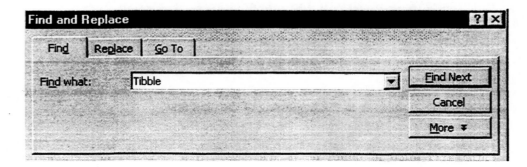

Go To - Control + G gives you the opportunity to specify more options:

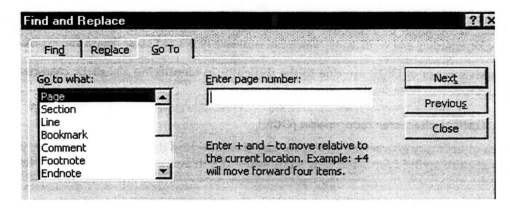

Using the Edit pull-down menu and selecting the option you want can also access both the **Find** and the **Go To** functions.

Activity 3 *(The answer is in the final chapter of this book)*

What happens when you press the Control and Home keys together?

3   Direct input devices

3.1   Data capture

Input via a keyboard, whether on-line or using key to disk/tape requires the original information to be transcribed via machines. However this:

♦   is costly as someone has to be employed to operate the machines;

♦   introduces delays in processing data;

♦   introduces errors to the system.

You should be able to explain why direct input to the computer may be more beneficial to an organisation.

The following input devices all allow direct input to the computer allowing much greater efficiency. The term used to describe this activity is data capture.

3.2   Optical mark reading (OMR)

Standard pre-printed documents are used on which horizontal marks are made with a black marker (pencil, ballpoint pen, typewriter) in predetermined positions. The positioning of each mark is determined by dividing the form into areas or boxes printed in a distinctive colour. Each mark has a meaning, which is dependent upon its position. OMR is used widely by the following:

♦   Some utility companies, such as the gas and electricity boards, use OMR forms for meter reading purposes. Each numeric digit on the meter is represented by a mark on the form.

♦ Certain educational establishments use OMR to evaluate multiple-choice examination papers.

The main advantages of OMR are that it is simple to use and data is captured without labour intensive keyboarding and verification, which can introduce errors and cause delays and expense.

The disadvantages of OMR are due to the difficulty in identifying alphabetic characters and the expense of specialist form design.

3.3 Optical character recognition (OCR)

The idea of ordinary characters, which are also machine-readable, is obviously attractive. OCR used to require stylised fonts but now some systems will accept a wide range of ordinary type faces.

The machine must recognise not just the presence or absence of a mark, as with OMR, but the particular character shape. For example OCR techniques are used for public utilities' remittance advice slips, eg by the gas and electricity boards. The consumer's cheque is despatched with the remittance advice when the bill is paid. The remittance advice provides computer-readable input as the consumer's code number and amount are both scanned by an optical reader.

The benefits of OCR include the input being both human and machine-readable and no labour-intensive keyboard preparation.

The disadvantages of OCR are mainly that the form design, stationery and printing costs are high and the specialist hardware and software required can be expensive.

3.4 Magnetic ink character recognition (MICR)

As with optical methods, a special typeface is used, but the printing ink contains a metallic substance, which enables the characters to be magnetised. They are recognised by the particular magnetic field pattern that they produce. The MICR technique is widely used by banks for the encoding of cheques where the sheer volume of documents would present an enormous input problem if done via a keyboard. Certain information (branch code, account number, cheque serial number) on each cheque has already been printed in magnetic ink. When you issue a cheque and it is returned to the banking system for clearing, the amount of the cheque is encoded in the same way. The cheque can be read by computer, which automatically updates your account balance.

MICR is useful where the original documents are handled frequently before they reach the computer and can become dirty, crumpled or scribbled upon. The dirt and marks are not magnetic, so the underlying magnetic characters are clear to the reading device.

3.5 Kimball tags

These are small tickets having pre-printed numerical information and pin-sized punched holes. The tickets are used as identification tags on goods, particularly in the retail clothing business, and are removed at the point of sale. They can be processed through a special converter and the coded information transferred to magnetic tape or disk for subsequent computer input. Transcription from manually raised sales dockets is eliminated, reducing error in subsequent computer-produced sales analysis and providing it more quickly.

3.6 Voice data entry

Recently, methods have been developed which allow simple spoken information to be understood by a computer. The words must be spoken with care and vocabulary is limited but commercial applications include stock-taking. A part number and quantity can be dictated on to a recorder which is then played back when attached to the computer. Some micros now accept a spoken vocabulary of several thousand words.

3.7 Point-of-sale (POS) systems

A point-of-sale system is a generic term for various types of devices used in retailing businesses. At their simplest they consist of cash registers, which store data in computer-sensible form. They also provide a printout/add-list and display the details of each transaction, the change required, and a total. The use of POS systems is widespread in chains of supermarkets or cash and carry warehouses, which need regular information on stock positions and receipts.

Data can be entered via a keyboard or when a sensor or light pen is passed over a bar-coded label.

Bar codes are used in libraries to record the lending of books.

3.8 Badge readers

These devices are used in a variety of applications. The badge is a plastic card with a magnetic strip for data. The card is also embossed with data such as holder's name and number, expiry date, etc. Badge readers can be used, for example:

♦ to record times of production workers;

♦ as part of cash-dispensing systems to holders of credit cards, where the card acts as the badge;

♦ in electronic funds transfer (EFT), where a card may be used to debit the customer's bank account and credit the retailer's account;

♦ as credit cards.

The badges can also be embossed with an OCR character set for impressing documents and creating machine sensible inputs.

3.9 Other input methods

Other methods, such as light pens, touch-sensitive screens and the mouse, are not very useful for inputting new data, eg hours worked. They are largely confined to systems where the operator can choose from pre-set options (or menus) presented by the computer, for example using icons - a diagrammatic representation on the VDU of the function to be carried out (for example, a picture of a filing cabinet indicates a filing option, and a picture of a dustbin indicates the option to scrap or erase data).

(a) *Light pens* - a pen-like device, attached to the computer by a cable, is place on the screen and the computer detects its touch. For example, a list of prices is displayed on the screen and the operator selects one by touching the pen against that item. Light pens are also used in computer-aided design (CAD) where they can draw lines on the screen or select parts of a drawing for modification. Light pens do not emit a beam of light, they detect light from the screen.

(b) *Touch-sensitive screens* - similar in operation to a light pen except that the operator can use a finger or ordinary pencil to indicate choices. Often used in cash dispensers.

(c) *The mouse* - this is a small box attached to the computer by a cable. When used with appropriate software, the act of moving the mouse over a surface causes a pointer to move similarly on the computer screen. By positioning the pointer over an icon or a particular menu choice, then pressing a button on the mouse, specific action may be initiated. A mouse can also be used to highlight easily a block of information on screen which can then be copied, moved, deleted, or subjected to some other editing function. Systems that use Windows, Icons, a Mouse and pull-down menus are known as **WIMP systems.**

4 Data processing

4.1 Transformation process

In general, data may be transformed into information by any of the following processes:

◆ bringing related pieces of data together;

◆ summarising data;

◆ basic processing of data;

◆ tabulation and diagrammatic techniques;

◆ statistical analysis;

◆ financial analysis.

The value of information may be affected by the quality of the data on which it is based. If source data is flawed then information can be worthless and any decisions made on the basis of that information could be incorrect. However, the way in which data is processed can make it more valuable to users by giving it certain qualities.

4.2 Transaction processing

Most of the everyday work in accounting systems is transaction processing. Examples include:

◆ processing customer order

◆ payroll

◆ purchases and creditors ledger

◆ cost analysis.

Every organisation documents and controls such transactions to do their necessary tasks or to assist management in their decision-making.

Data is input to the system during the transaction, eg to amend or update existing records. In a supermarket, for instance, transaction processing would entail recording the sale and the sum involved, maintaining a continuing total of incoming payments and updating stock levels.

There are generally three types of files of records found in this type of system.

◆ The master files, which are like ledgers, eg the sales ledger master file, the stock records master file, etc. Each master file contains many similar **records**. For example, the Sales Ledger master file contains one record for each customer. Each of these records contains a certain amount of permanent data (or 'standing data'), eg name, address, bankers details. It also contains transaction data (ie numerical records of transactions, balance outstanding, etc).

♦ The transaction files - on these files there is one record for each recent transaction of a particular type. An example would be a file of issues from stores. This file is used to update the stock records master file.

♦ The reference files - these are files of data that are referenced during processing for example a price list of the company's products that is referred to when computing the value of a customer's order.

There are different processing approaches. The data might be processed immediately and the results either output from the system or transferred to another file (on-line processing) or it may be processed on demand. Alternatively, the data might be held in a file for processing at a future time (batch processing). In many applications it is common to collect several source documents of a single type and input the data for all of them at the same time as a 'batch'.

The approach chosen depends firstly on management requirements. These may be:

♦ Routine recording of accounts data, eg purchase ledger, sales ledger, payroll.

♦ Preparation of regular 'packages' of management information, eg monthly reports.

♦ Fact retrieval for decision-making, eg can company Y exceed its credit limit?

The processing system must also take into account:

♦ input volumes;

♦ management priorities;

♦ the purpose of the information processed;

♦ response-time (ie the time between the collection of the source data and the processing results).

4.3   Batch processing

With batch processing, a group of similar (routine) transactions are processed in the same processing run. The data may accumulate over a given time resulting in a delay before it is all processed at once, eg when purchase invoices are processed and paid on a monthly basis. This mode was formerly the major form of processing. It is still the most logical method of dealing with large transaction volumes at a specific time.

A classic example of batch processing is an organisation's payroll. Typically, the wages section segments transaction records into small batches (eg one per department). In this way, most input data is in smaller collections.

4.4   Demand processing

Demand processing is undertaken when a transaction must be processed straightaway. Examples include:

♦ a request for information, eg the amount owed by a customer;

♦ the decision to pay a large account immediately, eg where previously delayed because of an error;

♦ recording an infrequent or special activity.

4.5   On-line processing

A system is referred to as 'on-line' when the data is input directly to the computer from the point of origination, and where the output is transmitted to the user's location. Good examples of such a system are ground-to-air missile control, or a bank's cashpoint dispenser.

Activity 4 *(The answer is in the final chapter of this book)*

Your job probably involves processing data most of the time. List the processing activities required to convert the input received into the output required in your office.

---

5   Input errors

5.1   Passwords

Passwords may be built into a system to limit access to certain areas and prevent accidental or deliberate changes to data. They can operate at a variety of levels to prevent people from getting beyond an initial screen or to prevent them accessing specific confidential parts of the system.

Certain procedures may require users to have authorisation attached to their user name when logging onto a system. This type of control is used to prevent junior staff from performing tasks where they have insufficient experience to work unsupervised.

5.2   Classification of errors

Input data can get lost or can contain errors. It is important to identify how errors might occur during the operation of a system other than as a result of failing to establish proper administrative controls. Errors will fall into the following classes:

Data capture/classification errors - these occur before data is ready for input to a system and arise because of:

♦   incorrect classification of data, eg allocating a production cost as an administrative cost;

♦   assessment/measuring mistakes, eg recording the arrival of ten tons of raw material when only nine tons was delivered;

♦   incorrect spelling, eg of a customer's name;

♦   transposition, eg recording a manual receipt of money as £50,690 instead of the actual figure of £90,650.

Transcription errors - these arise during the preparation of data for processing where data, which has been written down previously or which is passed on orally, may be incorrectly recorded on data input forms.

Depending on the method used to process the input data and the cost of making an error, integrity controls ought to be applied to reduce the risk.

5.3   Data validation

Methods to validate input data and processing of data include authorisation and scrutiny of input and output by responsible officials. Certain transactions should not be processed unless they have been properly authorised. For example, a supplier's invoice must not be posted to the purchase ledger unless a signature of an authorised person has been added to either the invoice or the goods received note. This signature or initials will confirm that the goods have been received or the services provided and the amount on the invoice is correct.

 In a situation where an input document has not been properly authorised, or is missing some important details, you should ask your supervisor for instructions before you continue with the processing of the transaction.

Validation of input includes checks on the correct file being processed, character checks, check digits, format checks for completeness and checks on the reasonableness of data.

♦   *Type checks* - every entry must comply with the prescribed format. For example, dates may be defined as consisting of 2 digits, 3 alphabetic characters and 2 further digits such as 04APR93. Any other form of input will result in an error.

♦   *Non-existence checks* - data fields requiring entry may have a separate validation table behind them such that the data being input must exist on that table. For example, a supplier account number must exist already before the system will accept that number on an invoice.

♦   *Checks for consistency* - where data is originally entered and does not require on-going maintenance, the fact that it is still consistent with the original data input should be checked within an appropriate time-scale. For example, batch totals should not be altered once input, and payee codes for suppliers paid by BACS should be confirmed by printout against source data on a half-yearly basis.

♦   *Duplication/repetition checks* - for example, the system may check that only one invoice has been received from a supplier with the supplier's invoice number currently being input.

♦   *Range checks* - a minimum and maximum value could be established against which input is checked.

5.4   Data verification

Data verification controls check to ensure that the data being presented to the system comes from a verified source. The types of verification include:

♦   *Batch total preparation* - the people that prepare the data for input may submit their own batch totals separately to the system administrator for input so that any discrepancies with the data processed can be identified immediately. The failure to present these batch totals would prevent any data being processed.

♦   *Separate validation run* - before being processed, batch files uploaded via a network can have hash totals built in to the file header along with special passwords, all of which are checked by the application before processing can commence. The Banks Automated Clearing Service system (BACS), which allows payments to be made directly from one bank account to another, operates on this basis.

6   Summary

There are three basic transaction-processing modes. Batch processing is used for similar, routine transactions that are processed in the same processing run, eg an organisation's payroll. Demand processing is used when a transaction must be processed straight away. On-line processing is the input of transactions while the input device is connected directly to the main CPU of the system.

It is important to identify how errors might occur during processing. We have identified two types - transcription errors and data capture/classification errors. Integrity controls are normally classified as verification or validation. Verification is a procedure to check the completeness and accuracy of data. Validation is a series of rules to check the reasonableness of the data.

CHAPTER 10

Reference codes

ASSESSMENT FOCUS

This chapter covers the following Knowledge and Understanding and Performance Criteria of the AAT Syllabus.

◆ Types of data held on a computer system (*Knowledge and Understanding elements 20.1 and 20.2*)

◆ Organisational security policies (*Knowledge and Understanding elements 20.1 and 20.2*)

◆ Data is input and stored in the appropriate location (*Performance Criteria element 20.1*)

◆ New unique codes are generated as necessary (*Performance Criteria element 20.1*)

◆ Errors in inputting and coding are identified and corrected (*Performance Criteria element 20.1*)

In order to cover these, the following topics are considered:

◆ Types of inputting: addition of new information, some of which require the generation of unique reference codes, modification of existing information, deletion/cancelling of existing information

◆ Examples of unique reference codes are stock codes, customer references, invoice numbers, employee numbers

◆ Methods of requesting items: specification of unique reference codes, specification of details

◆ Methods of locating details: automatic searching, manual searching (browsing)

Introduction

In this chapter we will continue to look at data input but will also include the methods of searching for and retrieving information.

◆ Entry of code numbers - wherever possible code numbers should be pre-printed on documents. Where this is possible, the code should be kept as simple as possible. Also checks (eg check digits) should be built into the input system as far as is practicable.

◆ Error messages - where errors are detected, error messages should be printed or displayed. The recipients of error messages should understand their meaning. Procedures must be established for error correction and re-inputting.

1 Reference codes

1.1 Coding manuals

Coding manuals giving the details of the codes allocated to each area within the system should be distributed to all personnel who are likely to be involved in recording or processing data.

Whilst many frequently used codes will quickly be memorised, it is important that easy access to codes be made available to encourage correct allocation when basic records are prepared.

For example, at the checkout of the supermarket the assistant will have a list of codes to allocate to fresh fruit and vegetables.

1.2 Coding systems

Examples of reference codes in everyday use are bar code numbers on consumer goods, post codes for addresses and account numbers for bank accounts. In accounting systems coding systems are used for:

♦ customer and supplier accounts;

♦ personnel and departments;

♦ finished products, raw materials and jobs.

Computer systems need strict discipline with all code numbers used. There is a conflict of requirements between people, who prefer an alphabetical narrative, and the computer, which works more efficiently with concise numerical codes. For example narrative descriptions that use a string of alphabetic characters (eg Alec Guinness reading 'A positively final appearance' on tapes) are preferable as far as people are concerned but they take far longer to be processed by a computer than a more concise numerical code. It takes a computer a great deal longer to sort descriptions into alphabetical order than it does to sort codes into numerical order. It also takes extra time for input preparation because alphabetical descriptions are generally very long.

1.3 Code design

Code design is closely linked with the design of documents. The purpose of a code is to identify an item more precisely and concisely than a written description. In a computer-based system a code may also:

♦ Save storage space. For instance, a product code can be kept on a record which if necessary can be cross-referenced to a more detailed description of the item held as standing data on a master file. There is no need for a detailed description to be included in each record.

♦ Save input time. The time and cost of data preparation can be reduced. There will need to be some controls to ensure that the code used is correct, eg by using check digits.

The general features to remember when designing a code system are:

♦ It must be precise, concise and unique.

♦ It should be easy to use. It is particularly important to avoid a situation when a computer-generated code is so long that it becomes cumbersome for people to use.

♦ It must be designed to avoid errors, such as the duplication of code numbers for different items.

- It should be flexible enough to cope with minor systems changes without a complete alteration of the coding system.

- It must allow for expansion unless it is absolutely certain that there will be no additions to the items to be coded.

- It should preferably be easy for users to remember and easy to communicate by both speech and writing. In this context descriptive codes are particularly useful.

- It is important for codes to be capable of validation by the computer so that errors of transposition can then be avoided. Check digits (see later) can be used for this purpose.

1.4   Unique codes

You should be aware that there are some records or files that must have a unique identification code or reference code.

For example, in a sales ledger system there must be a unique code to identify each customer because the same code must not be allocated to two different customers. This field in a record that contains a unique reference code is called the 'key field'.

Other records that require a unique reference code include:

- stock items in a stock control system;

- personnel in an organisation's payroll system;

- suppliers in a purchase ledger system.

Activity 1 *(The answer is in the final chapter of this book)*

Give examples of codes used in everyday life.

---

2   Main types of coding systems

2.1   Numerical coding systems

There are many different types of coding system, from the very simple to the sophisticated. They include the following:

- Sequence codes

- Group classification codes

- Faceted codes

- Significant digit codes

- Hierarchical codes

- Mnemonic codes

2.2 Sequence codes

These entail the allocation of numbers of items in a straightforward numerical sequence. There is no obvious connection between an item and its code, eg

0001	bolts
0002	washers
0003	screws
0004	nuts

Sequence codes allow for simple file design but they are rarely used when large numbers of items are involved because they do not readily allow for the classification of items. However, there are some exceptions such as order numbers and invoice numbers.

2.3 Group classification codes

These are sometimes known as *block codes* and they extend the simple sequential codes by providing a separate sequence for each group of items, eg

1000 - 1999	different types of bolts
2000 - 2999	different types of washers
3000 - 3999	different types of screws
4000 - 4999	different types of nuts

In effect the prefix signifies the group to which the item belongs. The code is sequential within each group so that this is only a very limited advance on sequential coding. For example a nominal ledger is set up in sections. Each section has a unique block code as follows:

100	Fixed assets
200	Current assets excluding stocks
300	Stocks
400	Fixed liabilities
500	Current liabilities
600	Income
700	Expenditure

Subsequent digits would act in the fashion of a sequence code. Code 101 might therefore signify 'Freehold land', 102 'Freehold buildings', 103 'Machinery' and so on.

2.4 Faceted codes

Faceted codes extend the principle of group classification by having each digit (which may include letters) or perhaps several digits representing some facet or characteristic of the item. For example, the first digit could be the nature of the item and the second digit could be the material from which it is made and so on.

1 = bolt	1 = steel
2 = washers	2 = brass
3 = screws	3 = zinc

In the following example, the first three digits indicate the type of good, its classification and its product area (eg 412 - 125 is Food Processor No 125) classified as kitchen equipment in the product area of electrical goods. Further elements could be added to the code to indicate the manufacturer and the storage location in the warehouse.

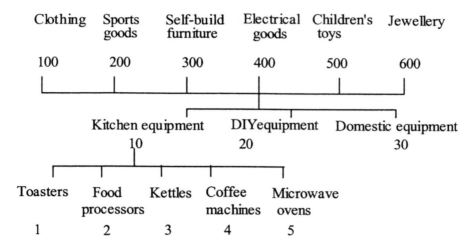

Another example of a faceted code is the European Article Number used to code products in retailing businesses and supermarkets. This enables automated data capture at point of sale.

2.5   *Significant digits codes*

Significant digits codes extend the concept of faceted codes by using digits in the code to directly represent a feature of the item, eg

> 3203   a brass screw 3 centimetres long
>
> 3204   a brass screw 4 centimetres long

As another example, a producer or supplier of shoes might have the last two digits specifying shoe size, so that 987611 would represent a pair of size 11 shoes (in some style and colour).

2.6   *Hierarchical codes*

A hierarchical code is a type of faceted code in which each digit represents a classification. A primary digit identifies the main entity and successive digits explain its attributes.

1	Ladies wear
11	Lingerie
112	Nightwear
112.1	Pyjamas

The digits to the right represent sub-sets of the digits to the left. Decimal points may be used to break up the code number into its main parts. The best known example is the universal decimal code used by libraries. For example;

60	signifies management accounting
60.0	USA publication
60.0.3	programmed learning text
60.0.3.056	standard costing and variance analysis.

2.7 Mnemonic codes

These use a mixture of alphabetical and numerical characters to signify characteristics of the items, eg

MT/FA/HW6/2 stands for

♦ Mid-term course

♦ Financial accounting

♦ Homework question 6

♦ Page 2

Mnemonic codes are often more easily recognisable to people but there is the possibility of numbers being mistaken for letters or vice versa (eg 1 instead of l). It may be less clear how many items there are in the group than a block code (eg how many pages make up HW6?).

Airlines use mnemonic codes in booking systems, eg LDN for London, HNLU for Honolulu and KL for Kuala Lumpur.

3 Error checking

3.1 Control totals

These are still used to check data entry when items are batched before being input into the system - especially the accounts system. For example, a batch of invoices will have its total calculated manually, the invoice details will then be entered and the computer will check the total of the invoices that have been entered. The control totals will then be compared.

3.2 Self-checking codes

A common problem in coding systems is that errors may be made in preparing the data. It is relatively easy to make transposition errors when writing down a number. For example 181418794 could be wrongly transcribed as 181481794. Worse may follow; the number might be written down as 181481974.

In the first case there was an error caused by a single transposition of numbers; in the second case there was double transposition of numbers. There are several ways in which errors can be reduced:

♦ Split the code into sub-groups divided by a space or stroke, eg it is easier to read 23/0570/16 than 23057016.

♦ Use an alpha-numeric code, eg it is easier to read and remember OHP 364P than 615 3645.

However, these methods may well escape detection before input to a computer system and so a system of self-checking numbers is often used. The most common is the use of the *check digit*. This generally takes the form of an extra numeric digit added to the right hand side of the number. The purpose of this check digit is to detect either transposition errors or random errors in the transcription of code numbers.

The use of integrated accounting systems has reduced the scope for many types of input errors. For example, on entering an account code in an integrated system, the customer's name will appear. This can be checked before continuing with the transaction.

3.3 *Check digits*

A *check digit* is a validation character, which is normally appended to a code number to give the whole code (including the check digit) some special mathematical property. Check digits may be calculated by various formulae and this calculation is carried out each time the code is entered into the system. A common model is the one where each digit in the code number is assigned a rank or position, and a prime number is used to calculate a check digit, which is placed on the right hand side of the code.

The check digit is devised so that when the computer performs a processing routine on the whole code, it will yield a number which is exactly divisible by the prime number chosen, ie there is no remainder. If the calculated digit and the entered check digit do not correspond (ie there is a remainder from the calculation), then it is likely that an error has been made in entering either the code number or the check digit; the system will inform the user accordingly. If there is a remainder from the calculation, the code number used is invalid.

To determine a check digit two things are needed:

♦   a modulus;

♦   weights.

As an example we will use the common Modulus 11 system. This means that the prime number used in the calculation is eleven.

We wish to calculate a check digit for the reference number 6312. After we have calculated the check digit the code number will be 6312n where n is the check digit.

Step 1   Assign a weight to each digit using 2 for the digit on the right hand side:

Number/Code	6	3	1	2	
Weights	5	4	3	2	

Step 2   Multiply each number by the weight and add the totals:

Number/Code	6	3	1	2	
Weights	5	4	3	2	
	30	12	3	4	Total = 49

Step 3   Divide the total by the modulus and find the remainder:

49 ÷ 11 = 4 remainder 5

Step 4   Subtract the remainder from the modulus to find the check digit:

11 - 5 = 6

Step 5   Append this to the previous code to give the full code number:

63126

We could now test the code by assuming that the operator accidentally enters the code number 63216:

Number/Code	6	3	2	1	6
Weights	5	4	3	2	1
	30	12	6	2	6

The total = 56

$56 \div 11 = 5$ remainder 1

The fact that there is a remainder shows that the code number is invalid.

This type of check digit has been shown to detect all transposition errors and a high percentage of random errors.

It should be noted that if the check digit works out to be 10 then the Roman Numeral for 10 (X) is sometimes used.

Sometimes different weights and a more complex procedure are used to calculate the check digit. This is often done when there is a need for security or confidentiality. An example of this is for validating credit card numbers.

Activity 2 *(The answer is in the final chapter of this book)*

The number 416792 is validated using a Modulus 11 check digit. Is this number valid?

3.4 Error correcting

Because it is easy to make errors when inputting data, the system should allow for their correction. If an error is identified as it is being typed, the user will be able to delete it with the delete key (DEL) or the backspace [←] key.

There is often an opportunity to confirm that data is correct before being entered into the system. Messages appear such as 'Are you sure? (Y/N)'. Where the error is detected by the machine, eg the wrong code or date is entered, an error message will be shown, identifying the problem and the action needed by the user to correct it.

Activity 3 *(The answer is in the final chapter of this book)*

Calculate the Modulus 11 check digit for the food processor coded 412 – 125.

---

4   Data retrieval

4.1   Search facilities

After data has been input to a computer system and the source documents have been filed, there will still be many occasions when you want to look up an item of information for example to answer queries from staff about their pay, or to respond to customer queries about their accounts.

The first step is to access the appropriate applications package. Click on **Start** in the bottom left hand corner of your Window, then slide the pointer up to **Programs**, and then select the required application.

Using typical Windows applications:

♦   for queries on letters or other written documents select the **Word for Windows** application;

♦   for queries on a spreadsheet worksheet, such as a budgeted cashflow amount, select the **Excel** application;

♦   for queries on a database, such as the holiday allowance for an employee, select the **Access** application;

♦   for queries on customer accounts, select the accounting package used, eg Sage Line 50 or Pegasus Capital Gold.

Once you have accessed the package, then you must identify the file you need. By clicking on **File** (top left in Window), then **Open**, you can search for the file that you need.

EXAMPLE

A customer, Mr M G Jones of 14 Ash Way, Chester, has a code number 1048972. He is complaining that his son, also Mr M G Jones, is receiving communications that are not his, even though he is also a customer. His son's number is 1048973.

If you wanted to find all the entries throughout your system for Mr M G Jones - letters, sales, receipts - you could do a search using the customer code and also a search using his name. Doing two searches would eliminate the chances of missing an entry and also identify mistakes that may have been made.

For this search you would look through all the files for Mr M G Jones and then compare them with all the entries under his code number 1048972. From the Start button, go to the Find and then the Files or Folders.

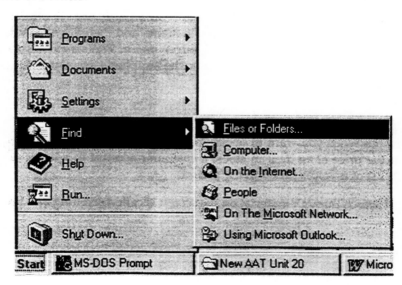

This will bring up the Find box where you can specify the location, the type of file or folder and the text.

When you click on **Find Now**, the computer will search through the specified files for the entries that you need and display the file names where there are entries that match your requirements.

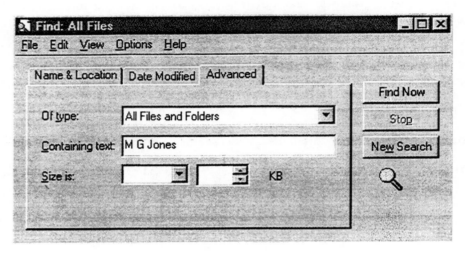

4.2 Data retrieval

Retrieval of the data required, so that you can display it on screen or print it out, varies with different packages.

Automatic search facilities are provided by most commercial application packages, eg clicking on **Edit** and **Find** in Word will give you a prompt to type in the name or word you are looking for. The finder will highlight each entry of your item in turn or display a message if it is unable to find the entry.

In a typical accounts package, you could check an item in a particular supplier's account by first selecting the **Purchase Ledger** option on the main menu, and then the **Accounts Enquiries** or **Transactions History** option on the Purchase Ledger menu. The screen display will then prompt you to specify the unique reference code for the supplier's account before displaying the details on the screen.

4.3 Using manual search facilities

There may be occasions when you want to search manually through records. For example, you might wish to find the price of an item in stock, a customer account in a list of accounts or a specific invoice in a list of invoices raised in the period.

This type of manual search through material on the screen is called scrolling and browsing.

There are different ways of moving about the screen. You can scroll up and down through material on screen by using the arrow keys or the PgUp (page up) and PgDn (page down) buttons on the keyboard.

A faster way is to point to and move the scroll bar in the middle on the right side of the screen. Alternatively, you can move one of the directional triangles or double arrows, also on the right side of the screen.

5   *Summary*

In this chapter we have looked at some unique identification/reference codes. The main types of code are sequence, faceted, group, classification and hierarchical.

Because the inputting of data is prone to error, some codes are self-checking. A check digit is a validation character, which is added to a code to identify specific types of error.

CHAPTER 11

Data storage

ASSESSMENT FOCUS

This chapter covers the following Knowledge and Understanding and Performance Criteria of the AAT Syllabus.

◆ Relevant security and legal regulations: data protection legislation, copyright, VDU legislation, health and safety, retention of documents, security policies *(Knowledge and Understanding elements 20.1 and 20.2)*

◆ Organisation procedures for changing passwords and making back-ups *(Knowledge and Understanding element 20.2)*

◆ Location of hardware, software and back-up copies *(Knowledge and Understanding element 20.2)*

◆ Data to be input into the computer system is clarified with the appropriate person *(Performance Criteria element 20.1)*

◆ Confidentiality of data is maintained at all times *(Performance Criteria element 20.1)*

◆ Back-ups of work are made in accordance with organisational procedures *(Performance Criteria element 20.2)*

◆ Passwords are used where limitations on access to data are required *(Performance Criteria element 20.2)*

◆ Work carried out on a computer is saved on a regular basis *(Performance Criteria element 20.2)*

◆ The computer is closed down in a way so as not to cause loss of information or damage to the computer system or storage media *(Performance Criteria element 20.2)*

In order to cover these, the following topics are considered:

◆ Types of storage media

◆ Backing up - Grandfather, father and son storage of files

◆ Hardware security

◆ File security - care of disks and back-up

◆ Access control - Passwords

◆ Closing down

Introduction

The central processing unit (CPU) of a computer has a certain amount of internal storage, but generally the business computer files are larger than the internal storage can handle, so there has to be a method of holding data on file when it is not required inside the CPU. These files must be able to hold the data in a machine-sensible form until it is needed for further processing.

Good file management on a personal computer may seem a very minor issue, but the risk of loss of important data from poor file management is significant. This chapter describes the way in which files can be and should be organised on a personal computer. It also examines some of the regular 'housekeeping' that is necessary to keep data files organised effectively.

1 Data storage

1.1 Memory systems

Computers use two kinds of memory systems. Main memory contains data and programs for immediate processing. Storage devices provide long-term storage for data and programs. Main memory is much more expensive than the equivalent amount of storage, so computer systems include only enough main memory to contain the data and programs that must be processed concurrently. Storage space is provided for all the data and programs that will be processed at various times.

The most commonly used storage devices are magnetic disk and magnetic tape, although CD-ROM is becoming more prevalent as the price of CD-ROM writers has fallen.

1.2 Storage requirements and characteristics

Before looking at the media used for the storage of data, it is useful to consider the requirements of any large-scale storage system.

- *Low access time* - the average time needed for gaining access to the stored records must be low enough to enable the processing of the data to be accomplished within an acceptable time.

- *Storage capacity* - this must be sufficient to hold all the data needed during any processing run.

- *Security* - the storage media must hold the data without fear of loss, damage or deterioration over long periods whether it is in use or not.

- *Transfer rate* - the data has to be transferred to and from the storage media at a high enough rate to meet the time restrictions on the work.

- *Cost* - the cost per unit of stored data must be low enough to make the system economical.

The above requirements have resulted in a variety of storage media being developed. As with most decisions, when deciding which method is most suitable it is a matter of balancing one characteristic against another whilst keeping within the acceptable cost.

1.3 Storage size

One major factor governing the processing capability of a computer is the size of its internal storage. The number of addressable storage locations that it contains measures this.

Various terms are used to describe how much data can be stored in a storage device (whether internal or external). The most common terms are bit (binary digit), byte, kilobyte, megabyte, and gigabyte.

The internal storage must be big enough to provide space to accommodate:

♦   The data being processed.

♦   A work area to hold intermediate results of processing.

♦   A buffer area to either hold data which has been input, prior to processing, or has been processed and is waiting to be output.

♦   The program currently in use.

♦   The operating system, which is a collection of programs controlling the whole configuration.

1.4   Storage devices

Memory chips - can be used as a storage medium. There are various kinds of chips used, eg ROM cards, EPROM cards, Static RAM cards, EEPROM cards (electronically erasable programmable read only memory) and RAM disks.

Magnetic tape - a very versatile recording medium; used for input and output as well as storage. Tape is said to be bulk non-addressable storage. It is a serial device, which means that file organisation and access must be serial or sequential. Tape can be used to take fast back-up of the contents of the hard disk on a PC. The device used to do this is a tape streamer.

Magnetic disks - the main form of mass storage. Disks hold information on both surfaces and information is recorded in a series of concentric circles or tracks. Their use has provided a reasonably efficient back-up storage facility. However, the disk technology still has its problems. Dust particles can be a problem and if a particle does interfere, a head may 'crash' (ie hit the surface of the disk), obliterating data and ruining the magnetic coating.

Different types of disk unit include:

(a)   fixed disks - hard disks are mostly found in PCs. They work like a rigid assembly of floppy disks with several disk surfaces available, each one having its own read/write head. The disk rotates continuously while the machine is switched on and is fixed permanently in the processor. When you switch the computer off, the data on the hard disk remains intact. However, if anything should go wrong mechanically with the hard disk and the contents of the disk have not been backed up elsewhere, it could mean a substantial loss of information. The close positioning of the read/write enables a high density of data to be stored. Even small units typically hold from 40 million characters (megabytes) up to 20 thousand million characters (gigabytes).

(b)   floppy disks - are widely used as back-up storage for PCs. They have much slower access times than hard disks. Addresses on floppy disks refer to a head number, track number and sector number. Typically a 3.5" disk stores 1.44 MB.

(c)   video or optical disks - look like an audio compact disk and data is recorded as minute patterns along each track. Reading is carried out by shining a laser on to the disk and capturing reflections of the patterns, which are then translated by logic circuitry into a binary code. Unlike the traditional magnetic disk that records data in consecutive tracks, the recording groove on an optical disk is one continuous spiral, which on some systems is around 45,000 tracks. Each track is sub-divided into sectors. An important feature to note here is that unlike the conventional magnetic disk, data once recorded cannot be erased; they are usually read-only devices (although they can be written to using a special CD writer machine).

To access the disk, the laser unit is moved across its surface, counting the number of tracks scanned. The relevant sector is found by reading the pre-recorded numbers of the tracks and sectors.

These disks are cheap, durable, of high capacity and robust. They are covered with a plastic coating so that they can be handled without the risks associated with the conventional magnetic disk.

1.5 Types of optical disk

There are three basic types of optical disk commonly used to store data:

♦ A **CD-ROM** disk is a read-only device, with data stored on the disk at manufacture. It is often used to distribute large quantities of centrally produced or published data. Another common use for CD-ROM is in educational software - an entire encyclopaedia can be stored on one disk. Multi-media software, which makes extensive use of sound and graphics, often uses CD-ROM to store data.

♦ **WORM** - the acronym stands for Write Once Read Many times. These devices are used for archiving large quantities of data.

♦ **Magneto-optical disks** are re-usable. Lasers are used to read the data and to erase it prior to writing new data, but the data is written magnetically.

1.6 Using floppies

♦ Always label disks with details including the name of the owner, roughly what is on the disk, when it was first used and whether it is a back-up (copy) of another disk. If you are going to use a lot of disks then set up a list or book.

♦ Do not leave disks lying around. They might get lost, stolen or damaged and also they might contain confidential information not meant for anyone else to see.

♦ Whenever possible use the write-protect facility. Disks should be write-protected when:

- they have critically important data recorded on them;

- they are being copied;

- they are used to provide programs for formatting another disk (formatting destroys any files which may be on disk).

♦ It is a good idea to buy a storage box with a lock on it.

♦ Always make back-up copies of important files on a separate disk.

In all of these cases inadvertent errors can cause loss of valuable data. Write protection is easy; the 3½" disk has a sliding write-protect mechanism.

Activity 1 *(The answer is in the final chapter of this book)*

What is the capacity of the average floppy disk?

---

2   Files and directories

2.1   Storage areas of files

Storage areas on disks are usually divided into directories or folders, depending on the type of machine you are working on.

Because folders are used in a Windows environment or on Apple computers, we will only use this term to save repetition. However, anything said about a folder would also apply to a directory.

Each folder will normally hold a number of files and it makes sense to put related files or applications into one folder. Think of the example of a filing cabinet. The whole cabinet represents the whole storage medium - the disk. A drawer of the cabinet represents a folder and within each drawer there are files holding information.

Most people would organise their filing cabinets so that all customer records were in one drawer and all personnel records in another. This makes specific files easier to find. It also means that a whole group of files can be dealt with at one time as they are all in one place and can all be processed as a group.

The folders are usually arranged into a tree structure or hierarchy. This should have a logical structure.

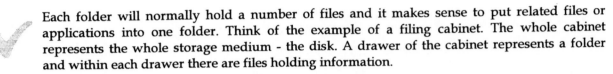

Activity 2 *(The answer is in the final chapter of this book)*

Arrange the following into increasing levels of detail: files, disks and folders.

2.2   Methods of filing

There are five methods of filing documents and files:

- **Alphabetical** - knowing how to deal with certain exceptions is the problem with this type of filing. There are certain rules that must be followed.

- Numbers are treated like words, eg, 7 Stars is filed as if it were Seven Stars *or* (in the telephone directory) they come before the As.

- The word 'The' is ignored.

- Where two businesses have the same name, the address is used.

- Public bodies (eg local authorities) are filed under the name or the town or district, eg Oldham (Metropolitan Borough Council), Social Security (Department of).

- Letters come first, eg M1 Cash and Carry comes *before* all the other Ms.

- Saint and St are all filed as Saint.

- People's names are filed by *surname*.

- Shorter names come first (eg Brown before Browne).

- For the same surname use first names or initials (eg. J Brown before M Brown).

- Initials come before full first names, (eg M Brown before Mary Brown).

♦   All Macs and Mcs are treated as Mac and come before all the Ms (but *after* the letters).

♦   Apostrophes are ignored (eg O'Leary would come between Oldman and Oliver).

♦   D', de, etc are also ignored (eg De'Ath would be found in the As).   Note that in telephone directories they may come under D.

Note: if the name of an organisation contains a person's name but only their initial (eg H Goodman Supplies) it is normally filed under the surname (ie G). If an organisation's name contains the full first name (eg Henry Goodman Supplies) it may be filed under either initial (ie H or G).

Activity 3 *(The answer is in the final chapter of this book)*

Put these customer names into alphabetical order - C Browne, J Brown, Mary Brown and M Brown.

♦   **Chronological** - used where the order of events is important, eg filing of birth certificates at a Register Office or correspondence. Correspondence is normally filed chronologically by client/customer. The customer/client file is then filed as part of an alphabetical or numerical system. In an accounts department chronological order may be used for petty cash vouchers.

♦   **Numerical** - This method is very widely used in accounts departments, eg filing of purchase invoices received and sales invoices sent out. The only drawback of a numerical system is that it requires forward-planning if it is to be easily expanded. One of the most famous numerical systems is the *Dewey Decimal System* used in libraries.

♦   **By subject** - this system is not really practical for large filing systems, but it can be used in parts of a system. For instance all correspondence, documents and invoices relating to the letting maintenance of a particular building may be kept in one file. This is the system that you are most likely to use in your own notes.

♦   **Geographical** - this method is used by organisations that divide their operations up into areas.

Activity 4 *(The answer is in the final chapter of this book)*

Avon and Walker Ltd trades under the name of Cut Price Stores. They have a number of retail outlets selling clothes, toys and fancy goods.

The purchasing department processes all purchase invoices received from suppliers. These are given a consecutive number on receipt. On the 7 July 20X5 the last number used was 33566. Invoices are filed in number order.

The warehouse deals with the recording of all stock items received. Each new line is given a new number. The last number used was 66388.

What are the disadvantages of using this numbering system for stock? Suggest a better method of numbering stock items.

2.3   *Housekeeping*

With Windows, there are many facilities that are available:

◆ To create a new folder or file select the drive that will be used and click on File, then on the choice of file that is required:

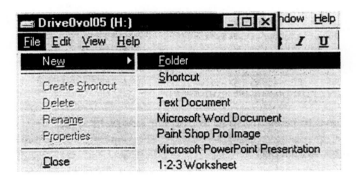

The new file or folder will then be ready to be named.

◆ Files and folders can be renamed by highlighting the file to be renamed, selecting 'Rename' from the File menu and entering the new file or folder name.

◆ To move a file or folder, place the mouse pointer over it and drag it to where you want it to be.

◆ Copies can be made from folder to folder or from disk to disk, but you will not be allowed two files with the same name in the same folder. To copy, place the mouse pointer over the file or folder you want to copy. Click on the Edit menu and choose Copy.

Go to the folder or disk where you want to put the copy and then use the Paste option on the Edit menu.

◆ Deleting - before files or folders are deleted you must be very certain that they are not needed, either by you or someone else. Because hard disks eventually fill up, it usually becomes necessary to delete files and folders at some point. Many of the files will be unused and may represent earlier versions of current files. If you are going to delete files you should carefully consider whether it might not be a good idea to take archive copies so that files could be retrieved again in the future.

◆ Files and folders can be deleted by highlighting the file and selecting 'Delete' from the File menu. You will be asked to confirm deletion.

◆ Retrieving - under Windows 95, when you delete a file it is sent to the 'Recycle Bin'. This is the equivalent of placing a piece of paper in a waste-bin, from where it can be retrieved so long as the waste-bin has not been emptied. To retrieve the file, open the recycle bin, highlight the file to be restored and access the Restore command from the File menu.

3   File security

3.1   Safeguards

Because vital records are stored on magnetic media, if files are lost or damaged it may leave an organisation in a serious position. All computer storage media are highly vulnerable to a number of dangers, eg:

- operator mishandling;

- machine malfunction;

- incorrect environmental conditions (dust, humidity).

Consequently, safeguards have to be established to prevent loss of files, eg:

- standards and procedures for users;

- standby facilities to use another computer or alternative facilities in the event of a breakdown;

- temperature and humidity controls.

3.2   Care of disks and CDs

Whether you are using floppy disks or compact disks, you must store them in a clean, dry place, such as a disk box (a specially designed plastic tray). If you leave them lying on your desk they may have something put on top of them or have coffee spilt on them.

Keep the disks away from electrical equipment as this may scramble the information on the disk.

If you are using floppy disks, do not write on labels that are already stuck to the disks as the pressure from the pen may damage the disk.

Precautions can be taken to ensure that you do not lose the material on disks, eg software that has been purchased, or data that you cannot recreate.

Floppy disks have a small tab in one corner that slides across. The machine will check the tab before over-writing the contents of the disk.

3.3   Making back-up copies

The medium on which data is stored for everyday use can be subject to failure and it is important that controls are put in place to ensure that the risks of that loss are minimised.

If any of the disks that you are working on are damaged, it could mean that you have lost all your work. Even if you are using a machine with a hard disk and floppy disks, the hard disk can sometimes develop a fault, so you should make extra back-up copies on different disks each time you leave the system.

However, even if you do this, the worst may happen and a file may be destroyed.

The standard way of coping with this potential problem is to maintain proper back-up procedures. Copies of files are kept in a 'security store', together with necessary update transactions, so that copies can be recreated.

The method of creating security back-up files and programs depends on the storage medium:

♦   Where the data is maintained on-line, data will be backed up each day along with separate audit printouts so that, if the normal storage medium fails, the information is available by which the system can be restored to the last point of data entry prior to the back-up being taken.

♦   Where the data is maintained by batch processing, the Grandfather/Father/Son method of backing-up will be used. The principle of this method is that, at any point in time, the last two back-ups made should be available plus all of the batches that have been processed since the older of the back-ups was made.

3.4   *Grandfather /father /son*

It is standard practice to keep at least three generations of a file or database, the third providing a further level of security in the event that restoration is not achieved using the first back-up copy.

The principle can be explained using the 'grandfather', 'father' and 'son' method.

When an updating run occurs a new disk is written, combining the previous master disk and any updates and leaving the previous master disk unchanged. Both the previous master (now the 'father') and the new master (now the 'son') are retained, together with the actual transactions processed. In the next updating run, the 'son' disk is used as the master and a new (blank) disk is used to become the new master. At the completion of the second run the 'father' becomes the 'grandfather', the 'son' becomes the 'father' and the new disk becomes the 'son'.

Activity 5 *(The answer is in the final chapter of this book)*

To demonstrate that you understand how it works, draw a diagram to show the grandfather/father/ son method of backing up files.

3.5   *Periodic dumping of data*

It is standard in most IT installations at regular intervals to 'dump' data held on-line to floppy disk (small amounts) or to magnetic tape or removable hard disks. There are also methods of increasing the data on floppy disks (eg optical tracking) which make them more suitable as a back-up medium. The purpose of the dump is to have a basis from which to begin restoration work in the event of failure or loss. It is vital to record exactly when the dump was taken, and the information retained must include all the files and data required to restore the situation to the point immediately prior to the failure.

A log of the data input to the computer since the last dump may be kept. After a failure, data can be restored from the dump and then completely reconstructed by reprocessing the logged input data. The data that is backed up is often held in a compressed form and special software is required to store and retrieve it. Ensure that such software is backed up separately (in non-compressed form).

3.6   *Back-ups*

For most of the applications used in current practice, disk files are usually overwritten during updating and the technique of grandfather/father/son does not apply. Instead the disk file is copied and dumped on to a back-up file.

There are two types of back-up:

♦   **full** - all the data is stored (done, for example, weekly);

◆   **incremental** - only the files that have changed are stored (done, for example, daily).

Given that one of the risks that we are trying to counteract is the physical destruction of the installation, it is sensible to put in place controls to ensure that back-up data is stored in a fireproof environment on-site. Occasionally, some form of master back-up is removed completely from the installation site.

4   Safeguarding your files

4.1   Virus-checking

A virus is a piece of data which infects the PC and causes it to behave in an undesirable manner. Viruses are spread by software that is most likely to be copied, eg free software, pirated software, games and e-mail attachments. They can affect floppy disks, networks and the Internet.

It is extremely important that a policy for preventing the spread of a virus is adopted. This may take the form of individual measures but should ideally be adopted by the organisation as a whole.

Procedures should be adopted to check floppy disks that have been out of the department for viruses. Periodic checking of the hard disks for viruses should also be standard practice. It is not wise to keep back-ups of important files on the same hard disk occupied by the originals. If the disk crashes or gets infected with a virus, the back ups will be corrupted along with the originals.

Virus-checking software is readily available and should be installed on all computers. It can be installed in such a way that, as soon as an infected disk is inserted into the disk drive, the machine displays a warning or even 'freezes'. It is of particular importance in situations where employees use several different machines, or share disks, as this aids the spread of the virus.

The procedure once a virus has been discovered on a disk is as follows:

◆   the disk is disinfected if possible;

◆   any important files are transferred to a 'clean' disk;

◆   the previously infected disk is reformatted or, ideally, destroyed.

4.2   Damaged disks

Disks may become damaged in other ways. If this happens copy all files to another location (eg a hard disk). Only when this has been done should you attempt to rectify the damage. There are numerous utilities available to do this, but if the files themselves have been salvaged, it is often more time-efficient to discard the disk (unless, of course, it is a hard disk!).

4.3   Recovering deleted or damaged files

On discovering that you have inadvertently deleted a file, or an important file has become damaged, seek assistance immediately. You may find that the situation is recoverable, but the chances of a successful outcome will be enhanced if you do not delay.

5   Data controls

5.1   Procedures

Data control procedures must be designed to make sure that data integrity and data confidentiality are maintained.

In any organisation, data is a vital resource, the loss of which may result in financial loss. The loss may arise directly (eg as a result of theft) or indirectly (eg where a competitor gains access to sensitive marketing data).

5.2   Access control

Access control is generally one of the data processing security measures that is applied as part of the organisation's regular operations.

It is a way of imposing limitations on the number of individuals who may freely enter the computer room and other sensitive areas such as the back-up library. Access control may be enforced by special door locks and limiting the issue of keys to those who need to enter the room.

5.3   Physical security

In parallel with the development of sophisticated hardware and software, many comprehensive techniques have evolved to minimise the risks to data maintained at an installation.

The broad principles that should be applied to ensure that physical security is maintained over access to data files and the underlying programs which can manipulate that data include the following:

(a)   Where possible, PCs/terminals should be physically locked using the keyboard lock keys and these keys should only be given to authorised personnel.

(b)   Password controls should control initial access to the system.

(c)   Programs should have their own password controls to cover access to applications.

(d)   In particular circumstances, some form of separate, personal identification of the user should be required (eg by using fingerprints or eye retina 'prints').

(e)   Where data is transmitted over some form of network, the data should not be transmitted in 'raw' format but should be encrypted (encryption).

5.4   Passwords

The British Computer Society's definition of a **password** is 'a sequence of characters that must be presented to a computer system before it will allow access to the system or parts of that system'.

Passwords are effectively software 'keys'. They consist of a short combination of alphabetic and/or numeric characters which the terminal user must enter into the computer and have verified by it (against a central file of valid passwords) before he or she is permitted access to specific data or programs.

If there is a network that staff can call into with a user ID and a password then it is not advisable to allow the welcome screen to identify which - the ID or the password - is wrong, in the event of a mistake. That way an unauthorised user has a more difficult task to figure out a way in.

 To be effective, the password needs to keep out unauthorised access. There are problems with password confidentiality:

(a)   An authorised user may divulge their password to an unauthorised user possibly to bypass the administrative 'hassle' of getting new identities on the system.

(b)   Most passwords chosen by authorised users have some form of association for them or are extremely simple to form and can be discovered by intelligent experimentation.

(c)   If you assign people random combinations of letters and numbers, which are far more difficult to crack, you come up against the problem that they are also far more difficult to remember. Most users will write their password down either on the terminal itself or nearby, making the task of discovering it easy.

The system administrator needs to provide a number of options by which the end-user can generate their own password such that it will be easily remembered but difficult for anyone, even personal colleagues of the end-user, to decipher from their knowledge of the end-user. Examples might include dates of birthdays plus personal initials of some sort.

Some systems include an automatic password generator, but experience has shown that, where these are used, users tend to write them down as they are virtually impossible to remember.

In any event, all passwords should be changed on a regular basis (eg quarterly). Repeated attempts to log in using incorrect passwords should be noted and reported on the system so that users who have problems in this area can be given specific assistance.

Consider the data processing security measures in place in your organisation.

♦   What measures do you take to prevent the spread of viruses?

♦   Does your organisation have a strategy to tackle this threat?

5.5   *Personal identification*

The most common form of personal identification is the **PIN** (personal identification number) which acts as a form of password. Other, more sophisticated techniques that are coming into use include fingerprint recognition where the user's palm print is recorded using an optical scanner and then compared with the user's every time access is requested. Eye retina 'prints' and voice 'prints' are being investigated and it is likely that these forms of checking will be the normal security control mechanism in addition to, or in place of, password controls.

5.6   *Encryption*

Where data is transmitted by any means other than fibre-optic cable, a determined eavesdropper can easily gain access to the data using modern 'bugging' equipment. Encrypting data to be transmitted, even across a simple office LAN, is the only way to reduce significantly the risk of such unauthorised access. However, it should be stressed that there are very few completely secure encryption schemes.

Encryption is the use of a cipher code to transform original data so that, when transmitted, the data appears to be nonsense until the 'key' code is applied to the data.

Most methods require that both the sender and receiver know the same 'key', which immediately increases the likelihood that it will be disclosed to an unauthorised user. Current scientific development is looking at what are known as 'public keys'. With these, the sender of the data uses a cipher which can be made available to the public at large, but the 'key' to the data is known only by the receiver and is the only way of deciphering data. Using 'public' keys removes the security risk of more that one individual knowing the deciphering key to the data.

5.7   *Closing down*

For systems that use passwords and logging on techniques, the workstation should not be left in the middle of editing. A screensaver with password control can be used for short absences, which saves closing down the machine. At the end of the day there should be procedures for closing down the system in such a way so as not to cause loss of information or damage to the computer system or the storage media.

♦   How would you normally leave your computer when you go for a coffee break?

♦   Is it different when you leave the office for a long meeting?

6   *Summary*

Storage devices provide long term storage for data and programs. The most commonly used storage devices are magnetic disk and magnetic tape.

This chapter has described magnetic disks and how files are organised on disks. It has also looked at how the files can be managed: creating directories, moving files, deleting files. You should be aware of the importance of taking regular back-up copies of data, keeping confidential data secure, minimising risks and seeking assistance if something appears to have gone wrong.

CHAPTER 12

Output

ASSESSMENT FOCUS

This chapter covers the following Knowledge and Understanding and Performance Criteria of the AAT Syllabus.

- Causes of difficulties: printer problems (*Knowledge and Understanding element 20.2*)

- How to save, transfer and print documents (*Knowledge and Understanding element 20.1*)

- House style for the presentation of documents (*Knowledge and Understanding element 20.1*)

- Data required from computer system is clarified with the appropriate person (*Performance Criteria element 20.1*)

- Effective use is made of available search facilities (*Performance Criteria element 20.1*)

- Confidentiality of data is maintained at all times (*Performance Criteria element 20.1*)

- Data is output as required in line with agreed deadlines (*Performance Criteria element 20.1*)

In order to cover these, the following topics are considered:

- Examples of recorded details of requested items are: cost codes for a cost heading, type of payment of an order, progress and status of an order, credit limit/status/worthiness of a customer, employee details and grant codes for courses

- Examples of standard database reports are: invoices, payments, pay runs, statements of accounts, infringement reports and flexitime reports

- Generation: specification of the start and finish of the range and selection of the required report

- Standard reports: bar charts, pie charts, histograms, standard database reports (some of which require special stationery)

- Types of problems associated with output

Introduction

As with choosing an input medium, choosing a suitable output medium depends on a number of factors, which you should bear in mind when discussing the subject.

In this chapter, we will be discussing the output required, the volume of the information produced, the speed at which output is required, the suitability of the output medium to the application and the cost of the medium.

You might be required to select the most suitable medium in a particular situation so you should formulate your own ideas on the advantages and disadvantages associated with them.

1 Information output

1.1 Routine reports

Most output is the result of processing in the data processing cycle. Some type of information must be produced. A sales order system is of no use if it does not produce invoices.

Transaction documents or routine reports are required to conform to business conventions, eg invoices sent to customers, purchase orders sent to suppliers, day book listings, payslips and standard letters. There is not much scope within these conventions to vary the contents or format of these routine reports. As you are probably aware, many of these documents are produced in the day-to-day running of the enterprise. They may be produced in electronic form and displayed on the screen or alternatively in paper form.

1.2 Management reports

Summaries or extracts of the routine reports or data that has been processed will form the basis of the management information system. For example, the labour cost analysis, sales analysis and stock report will summarise many individual transactions into a few key figures that give management an overall picture of the organisation's performance.

Relatively few management reports are produced compared to transaction documents but they do provide the feedback that management use to exercise control.

2 Output methods and media

2.1 Categories

Output can be divided broadly into two categories:

♦ Machine readable

♦ Human readable

Machine readable data can be output to magnetic tape, disk, CD ROM or modem by writing the data on to it. The output can only be viewed after having been re-processed via a computer.

A modem converts the output from a computer into a form suitable for transmission down conventional telephone lines. However, its use is declining as more users take advantage of digital telephone lines that do not require modems.

Human readable data can be permanent (hard) or transient (soft) output:

(a) **soft output** is the term given to output of an impermanent type, such as voice simulation or visual displays;

(b) **hard output** is the term given to output of a permanent type, such as printed paper or microfiche.

2.2 Choosing the output method

The following factors need to be considered when making a choice of output method.

♦ **Suitability** of the medium to the application, ie the purpose of the output, eg:

♦ a VDU is well-suited to interactive processing with a computer

♦   large volumes of reference information for people to hold in a library might be held on microfiche or microfilm

♦   output onto a disk, tape or CD would be a good choice if the data is for further processing.

♦   The **VDU** screen can only hold a certain amount of data and it becomes more difficult to read when information goes off-screen and can only be read a bit at a time. Questions to ask include:

   ♦   Is the display suitable for long periods of continuous use and can the brightness and position of the screen be adjusted?

   ♦   Is the feel of the keyboard acceptable to the staff?

   ♦   How many lines can be simultaneously displayed?

   ♦   How many characters per line can be displayed?

   ♦   Is the size and resolution of the screen sufficient to display the required graphical detail?

♦   **Quality** of hard output - if the output includes documents that are going to be used for OCR turnround, the quality of the printing must be good. If the information is used as a working document with a short life, eg a copy of text for type checking, then a low quality output might suffice.

♦   **Cost and volumes** - some output devices would not be worth having because their advantages would not justify their cost, eg a small business producing 100 invoices a day and processing payroll once a week is likely to want a relatively small, cheap printer to service this modest workload. A credit company producing 15,000 statements a month, together with reminder letters and default notices, will require a fast printer capable of producing multi-part documents of good quality at speed, as well as visual displays for quick and easy reference.

♦   **Handling requirements** - some output is long-lived and required for reference, eg the balances in the nominal ledger. Other output is required to be multi-part for legal reasons, eg invoices for VAT purposes and credit arrangements (under current consumer credit legislation). Certain output needs to be printed but is used only for a limited period of time, eg the daily balance listings prepared by a clearing bank in the High street.

♦   **Speed of system response** - a customer interrogating his or her bank's computer requires a swift response. A telephone clerk employed by a credit card company wants to be able to give an instant validation or rejection of a transaction. An aged list of balances for control purposes does not have the same degree of urgency.

2.3   Soft copy output

Soft copy is computer output on a display screen, which is sometimes called a computer monitor or a visual display unit (VDU). The VDU screen lets the user review an individual record or a small part of a file at any time. Screen output is for immediate viewing and is lost when the user moves onto another page or file.

Various video technologies are employed to produce soft copy, but essentially they all accomplish the same thing: they display output (numbers, text, graphs and pictures) on a screen.

Text displays - the standard display of text on most screens is a total of 2,000 characters in an arrangement of 25 rows by 80 columns. Displays can be designed to incorporate:

(i)   reverse video, ie black on green;

(ii)   colours;

(iii)   blinking displays; and

(iv)   graphics.

Graphics are a feature of many business applications. The component parts of the display are formatted by means of special software into a number of individual picture cells (pixels) in order to produce the required pattern, for example pie or bar charts.

Graphics possess the following advantages:

(i)   they emphasise relationships;

(ii)   they uncover previously hidden facts;

(iii)   they focus interest;

(iv)   they save time in analysing data;

(v)   they help recall.

EXAMPLE

The monthly sales of £1,465.24 of a company are attributed to the following customers:

AB Plastics Ltd £14.57

F Browns Ltd   £29.38

J Cables Ltd   £122.44

J Hoggs Ltd   £246.75

DC Covers Ltd   £53.35

L Quick Ltd   £998.75

This can be shown graphically, eg as a bar chart or as a pie chart.

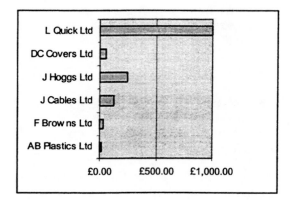

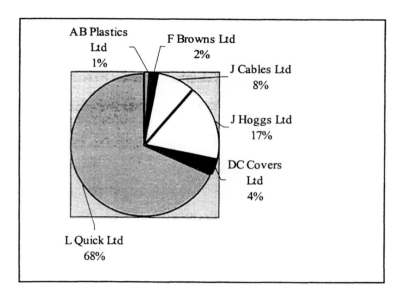

Voice systems are growing in popularity and are used in a variety of ways from the 'speaking clock' to the voice synthesisers in certain makes of car. They are not yet of great importance in accounting systems.

2.4   Hard copy output

Hard copy is computer output on paper. Devices that produce hard copy include printers and plotters.

Graph plotters - allow the output to be produced in graphic form. They can draw graphs, charts, plans and maps. Since output is produced via pens drawing on paper, output can be in full colour. There are also plotters that can handle very large sheets of paper, eg for production drawings and building plans.

Printers record information on paper in a variety of ways. For convenience we can divide them into two categories as follows.

(a)   **Impact printers,** as their name suggests, are those that produce output by the pressure of print characters on paper. They are, therefore, suitable for the production of multi-part output such as invoices or payroll/payslip preparation.

(b)   **Non-impact printers** are only suitable for the production of single part output. For large volumes of output optical printers or xerographic printers are used. There are no type bars or devices to be impressed against the paper. Instead, an image is produced using a cathode ray tube or laser and a xerographic copy is made (as in a photocopier). A complete page of output can be captured at a single operation and the process is fast and silent. Desktop laser printers are popular for printing straightforward letters and reports. They are especially useful in desktop publishing (DTP) where a wide range of type fonts, graphics and pictures are used together.

The selection of printer depends upon the needs of the user. The sort of factors to consider are indicated below:

♦   What is the printed output to be used for? Is the print of an acceptable quality for internal or external use?

♦   Is the printer speed acceptable?

- Is there a wide choice of typefaces?

- Is it necessary to use more than one typeface in the same document?

- Is the paper width compatible with the characters displayed on the VDU?

- Are supplies of stationery, ribbons, print heads readily available and reasonably priced? Is it easy to replace the consumables in the printer?

- How noisy is the printer?

- What maintenance contracts are available?

Inevitably, if the organisation is looking for better quality, design and flexibility of its equipment, this may be more expensive. There is a continuous play-off between costs of those features and the benefits of them.

2.5   *Specialised output methods*

Computer output on microfilm (COM). In certain business situations there is a need for high volumes of hard copy output at frequent intervals. An example of this type of application is that of the UK clearing banks who require a list of customers' balances on a daily basis for monitoring purposes. Formerly this information was provided by a bulky paper tabulation, which required storage and, ultimately, destruction because of its sensitive nature.

Nowadays the information is prepared on microfiche, which can be scanned with a microfilm reader. The microfiche is not bulky to store and preserves confidentiality as well. This advance is made possible by the technique of computer output on microfilm (COM) in which the microfilm or fiche is produced directly from the computer without the need for a conventionally printed intermediate copy.

Many libraries also use microfiche for the storage of reference material.

The COM method is becoming increasingly popular. Its advantages are:

- Stationery costs are reduced: reproductions made from a master microfiche are quite inexpensive.

- Transport is simple and cheap.

- Retrieval of information is easier. A reel of film can be coded and an automatic search facility provided in the viewer.

- Processor time is saved because the primary output medium (magnetic tape) can be produced more quickly than print.

The disadvantages are:

- Special equipment is needed to view the film (an enlarged image has to be projected onto a screen) and to provide a full size hard copy if required.

- COM production equipment is expensive (many organisations use a bureau service instead of buying their own).

- Microfilm can only be used internally because of the need to provide viewers.

3   *Printing and distributing reports*

3.1   *Navigating parts of the file menu*

Before printing any reports, you should check with your supervisor that the correct layout and format is set up on your computer.

Clicking on **File** in Microsoft Word gives you the following printing and distributing options:

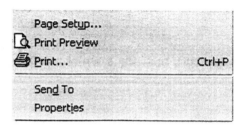

The **Page Setup** allows you to select from the following options and shows a preview of your choice:

The **Print Preview** gives you a view of the contents of the page that would be printed.

Clicking on **Print** allows you to choose the range and the number of copies.

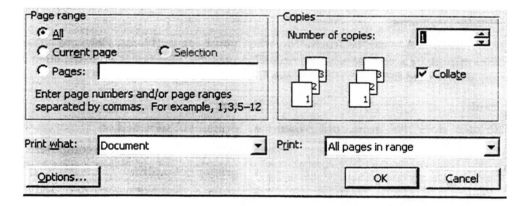

The **Properties** button gives you the chance to choose the paper size, the orientation of the sheet (the option of having the print in landscape or portrait mode) and the resolution of the graphics.

The **Send To** option (depending on the version of Word you are working with) will allow you to route the selected document to everyone on a mailing list, a fax list or an e-mail list. This could be over the organisation's LAN, via a fax modem or over the Internet.

You can select an **Exchange Folder** to copy the file to. This allows you to use Exchange or Microsoft Outlook to view, group, categorise, or sort files by their properties.

By clicking on **Microsoft PowerPoint**, the package assumes that the selected document will form part of a presentation.

3.2 *Using the printer*

Before using your printer (as with all electrical equipment), read the manual carefully. Look out for these procedures in particular:

♦ Connecting the printer to the computer.

♦ Switching the printer on.

♦ Checking that the printer is *on-line* (ie ready to print).

♦ Aligning the paper.

♦ Advancing the paper to the top of the next page.

♦ Stopping the printer safely (eg to unblock a paper jam).

Before you can print out your first report you will probably have to select the type of printer used from a list provided by the package.

The **Print** command will normally be part of the package you are using.

3.3 *Printer problems*

When using the printer it can be frustrating when you have problems. Here are some of the more common problems with some of the possible reasons. This is not an exhaustive list and you should always read the manual before dealing with a fault.

Fault	Reason
Printer does not print out when command is given	♦ printer not switched on ♦ printer not connected to computer ♦ printer not on-line ♦ wrong command used
Output is not as expected (eg characters used, characters wrong size, spacing incorrect)	♦ wrong printer type selected ♦ printer incompatible with software ♦ printer cable faulty ♦ printer using incorrect fonts ♦ fonts have not been downloaded correctly from computer to printer
Quality poor, characters faint	♦ ribbon or cartridge needs replacing
Paper jam	♦ wrong paper used ♦ paper damaged
Printed crooked on paper	♦ paper not aligned properly

3.4   *Types of paper*

The type of printer that you are using will dictate which type of paper you can use.

The two types of paper available are:

♦   continuous stationery; and

♦   single sheet paper.

Continuous stationery tends to be a sandwich of several copies, which are printed simultaneously. The paper feeds through as one continuous sheet with individual pages marked by perforations. The length of page must be set (usually through the software) so that the printer starts each page of text at the top of a new page of paper.

There is a lot of handling required to prepare documents for distribution and filing. The paper sandwich is held together by side strips which have holes which fit over the sprockets on the printer. These strips must be torn off to separate the copies (decollating). The individual pages must also be separated for distribution (bursting).

This type of stationery is obviously suitable for producing multiple copies of documents such as delivery notes, invoices and purchase orders. For these standard documents the business would possibly have its own pre-printed stationery, although most accounting packages do have accompanying standard forms.

Some businesses also use computer cheques. These are supplied by the bank and are customised for the particular business. They are used in conjunction with the creditors' ledger (and payroll) programs. Invoices for payment are identified and cheques are automatically produced during a cheque run. A remittance advice is usually printed at the same time.

Single sheet paper - is usually placed in a special tray or feeder. The printer takes a fresh page when it requires one.

3.5   *Distributing reports*

Before distributing reports or any other printed documents you should check the quality carefully. This will save time in the long run because you will not have to answer any queries or re-print reports (and this may be impossible anyway).

Remember that when you send a report or document internally you should always include at least a compliment slip with your name and the identity of the report on it.

If the report is confidential put it in a suitable envelope, seal the envelope and mark it *private and confidential*.

When sending documents to customers or suppliers follow the procedures of your organisation.

3.6   *Fax*

The Fax - short for facsimile transmission - permits identical copies of drawings, hand-written messages and so forth to be reproduced. An optical scanner reads the document and converts the data into binary digits which are transmitted over the phone line, the process being reversed at the receiving end. Fax requires more storage capacity and data transmission time than e-mail, and the results cannot be fed into a word processor for later use or modification. It is, however, popular and easy to use.

A PC can be fitted with a fax modem that allows data to be transmitted directly from the PC without going through a separate fax machine.

Activity 1 *(The answer is in the final chapter of this book)*

Can you think of a problem associated with a PC fitted with a fax modem?

3.7   Electronic mail (E-mail)

E-mail allows letters and documents typed in one office to be delivered instantaneously to another place in the world without physically delivering pieces of paper. The transmission is via a telephone or data network and a computer.

The sender of a report can format it and attach to it the address code of the recipient, which ensures that the document is delivered along the right routes. Intermediate recipients can add to the text if appropriate or confidential information can be screened from other users by means of a special password code.

E-mail can be used to send documents and reports by attaching a file.

4   Summary

Computer output can be used immediately or stored for later use. Output devices include soft copy devices and hard copy devices. Various video technologies are employed to produce soft copy but they all display output on a screen. Hard copy output devices include printers and plotters.

CHAPTER 13

Risks

ASSESSMENT FOCUS

This chapter covers the following Knowledge and Understanding and Performance Criteria of the AAT Syllabus.

♦ Different types of risks: viruses, confidentiality; hardware; software (*Knowledge and Understanding element 20.2)*

♦ Causes of difficulties - necessary files which have been damaged or deleted and hardware problems(*Knowledge and Understanding element 20.2)*

♦ Organisational security policies (*Knowledge and Understanding elements 20.1 and 20.2)*

♦ Data to be input into the computer system is clarified with, and authorised by, the appropriate person (*Performance Criteria element 20.1)*

♦ Potential risks to data from different sources are identified and the appropriate person is promptly notified (*Performance Criteria element 20.2)*

♦ Hardware and software are securely located (*Performance Criteria element 20.2)*

♦ The computer is closed down in a way so as not to cause loss of information or damage to the computer system or storage media (*Performance Criteria element 20.2)*

♦ Work carried out on a computer is saved on a regular basis (*Performance Criteria element 20.2)*

In order to cover these, the following topics are considered:

♦ Identify the risks to hardware, software

♦ Physical, human and systems security risks

♦ Managing the risks:

    ♦ assessment

    ♦ management

    ♦ transference

♦ Controls

♦ Standards

Introduction

Data processing and computing, as with other areas of an organisation, must be subject to various controls in the interests of confidentiality and security. Although a computer should be accurate, reliable and consistent, the lack of adequate security and control over computer systems has threatened the existence of some organisations.

Mistakes do happen and a mistake on a computer system can be costly. A customer who is mistakenly overcharged will usually complain whilst the same customer, if undercharged, will probably quietly hope that the mistake is not discovered.

Other privacy and confidentiality issues can arise including a system being broken into and access being gained to sensitive information.

This chapter identifies some of the major risks to the security of computer systems and discusses some controls available to reduce or eliminate those risks.

1 Risks to the system environment

1.1 Security risks

Security is defined by the British Computer Society as 'the establishment and application of safeguards to protect data, software and computer hardware from accidental or malicious modification, destruction or disclosure'.

The factors that affect the security of an organisation's computer system can be divided into three groups: physical, human and system.

Physical - computer systems consist of a mixture of electronic and mechanical devices. The operation of these devices can be severely impaired where they are subject to events such as fire, flooding, or improper environmental conditions such as heat, dust, etc. A fire could destroy not just the computer hardware (which is presumably insured and can easily be replaced), but the company's programs and data files, which may be irreplaceable. Consideration of physical security encompasses also the prevention of theft and accidental or malicious damage caused by external parties or internal staff.

Human - while computer systems are made up of physical items, the input of data and the output of information is designed for the benefit of human beings and is subject to their interpretation. Security risks arise where input and output occurs. The risks may arise due to innocent events such as running the wrong program, or inadvertently deleting data that is still of value to the organisation. More importantly, as more and more systems consist of networks of computers, the risks of unauthorised users getting access to those systems increases significantly. This type of activity is referred to as 'hacking' and encompasses anything from the unauthorised accessing of personnel details to the manipulation of important accounting or other financial information.

Systems - there is always the risk that a computer system will suffer a malfunction of one of its parts. Unfortunately, data may be lost or physical damage may occur that is virtually impossible to guard against.

1.2   *Physical damage*

Valuable records are contained on computer files and it is essential that they are properly controlled and secured. Poor security may result in physical damage, both accidental and deliberate, to the installation. The effects of poor security could be:

♦   Loss of records/hardware due to fire, floods or riots - the loss of accounting records could be sufficient to cause the company to fail.

♦   Loss of records due to incorrect physical environment - dust and magnetic fields can cause damage to files and delicate hardware.

♦   Deliberate physical attacks, including theft or damage to installation in general - files being misappropriated.

♦   Fraudulent attacks by employees or management or fraudulent transactions by altering programs.

♦   Loss of confidentiality - sensitive information obtained by outsiders or non-related employees.

1.3   *Security procedures*

Physical security includes protection against natural and man-made disasters, eg fire, flood, etc. Examples of measures to avoid physical damage to the system include:

♦   Fire precautions, eg smoke and heat detectors, training for staff in observing safety procedures and alarms.

♦   Devices to protect against power surges.

Physical security also includes protection against intruders and theft. As computers and other hardware become smaller and portable, they are more likely to be taken from the organisation. Burglar alarms should be installed and a log of all equipment maintained. People with official access to the equipment who are taking it off-site should book it out with the appropriate authorisation.

Access to the building may be controlled by security guards, closed circuit TV monitoring access, other mechanical devices such as door locks and electronic devices, eg badge readers and card entry systems.

Guidelines for data security include keeping files in fireproof cabinets, shredding computer printout if it includes confidential information, controlling access to the data, (eg passwords and physical access controls) and taking back-ups of data to minimise the risks of destruction or alteration.

To offset the risk of fraudulent attacks there must be: adequate controls over input/processing/programs; strict division of duties; and regular internal audit review of systems and controls.

To prevent loss of confidentiality, there should be controls over input and output. With on-line systems there should be passwords issued only to authorised personnel, restricted access to files at the terminals and a computer log of attempted violations.

Contingency plans for a disaster should include standby facilities, with a similar computer user or a bureau, being available to allow processing to continue.

Master file copies should be taken at regular intervals and kept at locations away from the main computer installation.

Activity 1 *(The answer is in the final chapter of this book)*

What measures can an organisation take to reduce the risk of equipment being stolen?

1.4   *Confidentiality and hacking*

Organisations often require that the contents of certain files (eg payroll) remain confidential and only available to authorised staff. Managers can manage this by keeping tapes or removable disks containing the files in a locked cabinet, and issuing them only for authorised use. However, the problem is rather more difficult when on-line files can be inspected via terminals. Security at the terminal should be adequate; the terminal can be locked and/or kept in a locked room. Access and use should be properly recorded and controlled.

As organisations have grown to depend more and more on systems and the data stored on them, individuals and other organisations have become increasingly interested in gaining access to those systems and the data.

Since the 1980s there has been a growth of an underclass of highly intelligent individuals who, using their knowledge of systems, have gained unauthorised access to systems for their own purposes. This form of activity is called 'hacking' and the perpetrators 'hackers'.

The consequences of such activities can be very serious and there are a number of specific areas that need to be addressed. Currently, beyond simple snooping, such hacking activities can:

♦   generate information which is of potential use to a competitor organisation;

♦   provide the basis for fraudulent activity;

♦   cause data corruption by the introduction of unauthorised computer programs and processing onto the system, otherwise known as 'computer viruses';

♦   alter or delete the files.

By specifically identifying the risks that the hacker represents, controls can be designed that will help prevent such activity occurring. Examples include:

Physical security– checking that terminals and PCs are locked and, where dial-in communication links are in place, a 'call-back' facility is used, ie the person dialling in must request that the system calls them back to make the connection. The system will only make a call to a pre-defined telephone number that is assigned to that specific user. This is a way of stopping unauthorised users from using a modem attached to the system to log in from an unidentified location.

Passwords - the controls over passwords must be stringently enforced and their misuse should represent a serious disciplinary offence within an organisation. Linked to the password, the computer will store a list of files that the user is allowed to inspect. Access to unauthorised files or data will be denied by the operating system and attempting to access them will be reported at the central computer.

Data encryption - files can be scrambled so as to be unintelligible unless a decoding password is supplied.

System logs - every activity on a system should be logged and be subject to some form of exception reporting, eg unusual times of access could be reported.

Audit trails – sensitive data, eg payee codes, should be subject to a separate audit report showing when the data was read, written to or updated. It should show also the before and after state and the data causing the change.

Sensitive users – every facility must be accessible by at least one person. This should not mean that the same person has access to every facility. The system should allow a different user to be assigned to specific facilities as a form of segregation of duties so that at least some form of collusion would be required, eg to generate an automatic payment on a non-existent supplier account.

Random checks - the 'constable on the beat' approach which checks who is doing what at random intervals on the system and ensures that they are authorised for those activities.

1.5   *Malicious damage*

Access to the system to steal data is not the only crime that can be perpetrated on a computer system. There is potential for malicious damage and possibly bribery. There are many instances of disaffected employees destroying data or software. Systems programmers can include 'trap doors' in their programs to allow future penetration. They can also include a 'logic bomb', which is a section of code that does something unexpected as a result of some criteria being met. For example if a specific date is entered into the system all the files on the system are deleted.

A further security and control issue, which has been highlighted in recent years, is the growth of computer viruses. A virus is a program that can attach itself to other programs and modify or destroy them. As the name suggests, they have the ability to infect a whole computer system. The infected programs may then act as carriers for the computer virus with the result that the infection process can have a spiralling effect. Given the mobility between computerised systems and the sharing of resources and data, the threat posed by a viral attack is considerable. Although much research has been carried out to prevent the unauthorised access and dissemination of information, and many security measures are now available, very little has been done to safeguard against the entry into a system of potentially damaging information.

2   *Fraudulent activities*

2.1   *Introduction*

Fraudulent use of computer facilities is becoming more common. Data can be tampered with; files can be destroyed by accident or by malicious acts. Fraudsters can divert funds from an enterprise to their own pockets or can attempt to hold employing companies to ransom by the threat of sabotage to vital computer systems. No information processing system can afford not to install rigorous systems of control and security.

2.2   *Fraud*

Computer frauds come from disgruntled employees, organised crime and hackers.

Distributed processing, allowing many employees access to the system, makes certain types of fraud easier. Fraud normally involves staff removing money from the company but other methods of fraud that might affect the data held on a computer system include:

♦   the creation of fictitious supplier accounts and submission of false invoices, usually for services rather than goods, so that payments are sent to the fictitious supplier.

♦   misappropriation of incoming cheques from bona fide customers.

♦   giving unauthorised discounts to customers.

- stock losses, including short deliveries by drivers.

- fictitious staff on the payroll. This was reported as prevalent in newspaper publishing a few years ago.

Activity 2 *(The answer is in the final chapter of this book)*

Give examples of the type of fraud that might be perpetrated?

---

3 Controls

3.1 Objectives

The overall objectives of control are:

(a)   to provide a framework within which performance standards can be established;

(b)   assess to what extent those standards are achieved;

(c)   correct any failures to achieve the standards required; and

(d)   adjust the standards to take account of changing conditions.

All information systems should have some form of internally designed controls, irrespective of whether they are based on computers or not. All controls have both a development cost and an ongoing operational cost. As part of the risk management process, their cost-effectiveness must be continually reviewed and their relevance considered.

Failing to design the right controls for a particular system, failing to ensure that they remain relevant and failing to adjust them to take account of changes underlie nearly all of the damage that arises when risk turns to reality. Standards are important in this area.

3.2 Standards

The purposes of any standard are:

- to provide a method of working which, if used, is likely to result in a quality outcome; and

- to provide a means of measuring the outcome against the standard expected.

With respect to computer systems, the adoption of standards reduces the likelihood of errors and misunderstandings during the development and operation of computer systems.

When standards are adopted as part of the establishment and operation of controls, the **benefits** that arise include:

(a)   realistic, attainable systems requirements leading to optimum resource utilisation;

(b)   more effective monitoring of progress;

(c)   a higher quality result;

(d)   simplified procedures during development;

(e)   fewer problems arising from staff absences;

(f)   a wider understanding of the problems which can occur and the ways of circumventing them by staff.

Bodies within the UK and elsewhere which continually publish standards specifically designed for the IT world, as well as for society at large, include:

(a)   the British Standards Institution (BSI);

(b)   the National Computing Centre (NCC);

(c)   the International Standards Organisation (ISO), authors of Open Systems Interconnection (OSI);

(d)   the American National Standards Institute (ANSI);

(e)   IBM, Digital, Hewlett Packard, Compaq and other computer suppliers.

4   Control over processing

4.1   Introduction

The objectives of processing controls are:

- To make sure all the data is processed

- To detect and correct errors

- To detect and correct fraud

The four main areas of control are:

- Input

- Processing

- Output

- Master files

4.2   Input controls

Validation of input includes checks on the correct file being processed, character checks, check digits to confirm account numbers, format checks for completeness and checks on the reasonableness of data. Control totals and items over accepted parameters should be logged and followed up.

The key words to remember for input controls are completeness, accuracy and authorisation.

Completeness - means that all of the data that should be processed is actually processed. Typical completeness controls are pre-numbering documents and performing sequence checks, document counts in batch techniques and performance of a one-for-one check, ie checking each processed document against the input forms.

Accuracy - means that all data that is processed is processed accurately. Typical controls for accuracy are rigorous data validation and verification routines, comprehensive batch techniques and/or one-for-one checking.

Authorisation - means that approval for processing is enforced. This can be either manual (ie somebody checks the document and signs it approving it for processing) or computerised (ie a data validation program vets the information to ensure that it is valid and therefore approved for further processing).

 It is essential that the input controls are performed over the significant data field on the input, eg hours for clock card input, value for purchase invoices, quantity for stock orders, etc.

4.3 Processing controls

Measures to validate data for processing include:

Batch total agreement. The computer checks the details of the batch documents and agrees the information with the batch header form.

Check digit verification. Check digits are a way of using an arithmetical relationship between the last digit of a number and the other digits of the number to safeguard against transposition and transcription errors.

Master file matching. This is a check on the validity of the account number, etc by matching it against the particular account on the master file.

Sequence number. The computer can report on the documents in a sequence not yet processed.

Reasonableness. Pre-defined constraints can be programmed into the computer to make sure that data is valid, eg purchases in excess of £500 may have to be listed for manual approval at a higher level.

Range check. Involves the pre-definition of valid parameters, eg discount rates in the range 20% to 30%.

Format. Where the computer is programmed to accept data in a pre-defined format,, eg account number, name, address, discount rate, etc, then the input should be in that format and will be rejected if it fails to conform.

Run-to-run control. When a file of data passes from one routine to another, run-to-run control totals are maintained on the header and trailer labels to ensure that no data is lost at the transfer stage.

Rejections. The computer can be programmed to accumulate details of rejected transactions that are awaiting correction and re-submission.

4.4 Output controls

Typical output controls are:

♦ Batch totals - is a control on the total of accepted and rejected data.

♦ Completeness of output reports - are made either by summaries of control totals at the end of the report or by printing 'END OF REPORT' on the last line of the report. In this way, the user knows the report is complete.

♦ Distribution of output - ensures that the correct users get the proper reports.

♦ Exception reporting - involves informing management of transactions that are abnormal in some way (though *not* invalid or rejected). Management can be more efficient if informed of data that warrants further investigation (eg cheques drawn greater than £500) rather than being inundated with all cheques. Exception reports are therefore very important to ensure proper management controls.

5 Managing the risks

5.1 Introduction

As with all **risk management**, the key objective is to introduce measures that cost less over the life of the system than the potential damage that might arise if the risks identified actually occurred.

Specifically, risk management of the security threats to systems involves three steps: **risk assessment, risk management and risk transference**.

5.2 Risk assessment

All potential risks that can be thought of should be listed and categorised under the headings of physical, human and systems. The types of risk are likely to depend on both the nature of the computers involved - mainframe or PC - and on the extent to which the computers are connected via some form of network.

These risks should then be assessed for the impact and damage they would cause to the business if they occurred. The risk should be quantified as far as possible; for example the failure of a particular computer on the network might result in the loss of half a day's sales and the time involved in re-keying information. The qualitative nature of the risk needs to be noted as well (effect on morale, customer loyalty, etc).

5.3 Risk management

Once the potential damage has been assessed, the steps that are put into place to minimise the damage fall under the heading of risk management. It is a vital element of risk management that the cost of the steps taken must be commensurate with the damage avoided.

5.4 Risk transference

Ultimately, there are some areas where the risk is small in terms of probability but high in terms of damage that would be incurred. An example might be earthquake damage in most of the UK, or losses arising due to fire, etc. Whilst steps can be taken to ensure the integrity of data, the risk that systems may not be operational for a significant period of time is such that the most sensible way of dealing with the risk is to transfer or share the cost. This could be via insurance or some other form of contingency plan covering the area of 'disaster recovery'.

Activity 3 *(Note: there is no printed answer for this activity.)*

Consider the system at your place of work and list all the security threats to hardware and software. Indicate those risks that might be accidental and those that could be malicious.

What steps can you take to minimise these risks? Consider procedural steps, such as back-up routines, job specifications, physical locations, extra hardware, passwords, etc.

Explore your back-up procedures.

---

6   *Summary*

This chapter looked at the factors which most affect the security of a computer system within an organisation: physical risks, human risks and system risks.

This was followed by a discussion of the process of managing risk and the need to establish controls as a way to minimise the risks.

Adopting control procedures, for input of data, data processing and output of information from the system, helps to make sure all the data is processed and both errors and fraud are detected and corrected.

CHAPTER 14

Spreadsheets

ASSESSMENT FOCUS

This chapter covers the following Knowledge and Understanding and Performance Criteria of the AAT Syllabus.

♦   The purpose and application of spreadsheets *(Knowledge and Understanding element 20.1)*

♦   How to save, transfer and print documents *(Knowledge and Understanding element 20.1)*

♦   House style for the presentation of documents *(Knowledge and Understanding element 20.1)*

♦   Data required from computer system is clarified with the appropriate person*(Performance Criteria element 20.1)*

♦   Effective use is made of available search facilities*(Performance Criteria element 20.1)*

♦   Confidentiality of data is maintained at all times *(Performance Criteria element 20.1)*

♦   Data is output as required in line with agreed deadlines*(Performance Criteria element 20.1)*

In order to cover these, the following topics are considered:

♦   Generation: specification of the start and finish of the range and selection of the required report

♦   Standard reports: bar charts, pie charts, histograms, standard database reports (some of which require special stationery)

♦   Using examples to show:

   ♦   using correct part of system

   ♦   using search facilities

   ♦   identifying and correcting errors

   ♦   retrieving correct details

   ♦   printing required report

   ♦   checking information is correct and complete

   ♦   documents collated and distributed as directed

   ♦   hard copy is clean, clearly printed and aligned correctly

♦   Efforts are made to minimise the wastage of paper

Introduction

This chapter and the rest of the Textbook introduces you to those aspects of Unit 20, Working with Information Technology, that can only be effectively taught and learnt whilst sitting in front of a computer.

For those unfamiliar with spreadsheet packages, this chapter will provide the basic introduction needed to feel confident to 'get into' Microsoft Excel and carry out the simple tasks required in the Performance Criteria. This package has been chosen because it is the most popular and therefore the most likely to be used in your college or work environment. The editions and programs that you are using may not be the same as those used in this text. In that case, the screens you produce will not be identical to those shown here. However, all spreadsheet packages will perform the basic functions covered in this chapter and access to a different package will not cause too many problems.

If you are at all unsure, you should read the manual that accompanies your chosen spreadsheet.

1 The use of spreadsheets

1.1 Introduction

Two aspects of computerised management information systems that are available to organisations are **financial modelling** and **databases**. There are readily available integrated packages which allow data to be transferred from the spreadsheet to the database, word-processors and so on, and *vice versa*.

The following section deals with the **basics of spreadsheets**, using Microsoft Excel as an example.

1.2 What is a spreadsheet used for?

Much of the data of a company is likely to be held on a number of spreadsheets. They are a convenient way of setting up all sorts of charts, records and tables, including:

♦ profit and loss accounts

♦ sales forecasting

♦ budgeting charts

♦ breakeven point analysis

♦ mortgage payments

♦ stock valuation

♦ exchange rate charts.

Anything with a **rows and columns format** can be used.

1.3 Spreadsheets

A spreadsheet is used to manipulate data. You could define it as a table of rows and columns that intersect to form cells. Each row is identified by a number and each column by a letter (or letters). Each cell has a unique identifier formed by a letter (or letters) and a number.

In its simplest form the computer spreadsheet is a representation of the enterprise in financial terms; it is designed to aid the planning and forecasting processes. There are two and three-dimensional **spreadsheets**, which can be used to illustrate the behaviour of various financial variables over time.

The word **spreadsheet** has its origins in the large sheets of paper used by accountants, over which they spread their figures and calculations in neat rows and columns. The little boxes made by the horizontal and vertical lines have their counterpart in the PC's spreadsheet and are called **cells**.

Into these cells may be entered numbers and text. Besides data a cell can contain a programming statement or formula. These are not visible when you are entering data but reside in the background. A formula normally involves a mathematical calculation on the content of other cells, the result being inserted in the cell containing the formula.

The size of spreadsheets, in terms of the number of columns and rows, varies greatly between packages. Spreadsheets with millions of cells are possible.

Because most business worksheets are quite large, extending beyond the edge of the computer screen, the screen is in effect a 'window' into the worksheet.

In addition the 'paper' can be 'cut and pasted' together in different ways as appropriate.

Some or all of the spreadsheet can be printed out directly or saved on disk for insertion into reports or other documents using a word processing package. The power of these systems is that the data held in any one cell on the 'paper' can be made dependent on that held in other cells, so changing a value in one cell can set off a chain reaction of changes through other related cells. This means that a model can be built in which the effect of changing key parameters may be observed.

Three-dimensional spreadsheets have the advantage of consolidation that the two dimensional ones do not have. An example to highlight this facility might be sales figures by region, where the top sheet (All products) might be a total of the sales of all the products that the company has (whilst Products 1 to 4 have separate sheets behind).

1.4 Building a worksheet

Electronic worksheet - spreadsheet packages tend to offer more than just a spreadsheet; they usually include a database and the option to create graphics.

A spreadsheet is a working area made up of columns and rows. An accountant's ledger is a manual equivalent. Once the worksheet data has been entered, it can be manipulated. You can carry out arithmetic and logical operations on it, change it, move it, store it, and graph it.

Database - some spreadsheets have commands that organise information in a way most useful to you. This information becomes a database that can make accessing information, and making decisions based on this information, a much easier task.

Graphics - 'a picture is worth a thousand words' is especially true when it comes to numbers; a spreadsheet is no exception. Since a column of numbers can be difficult to interpret, a graphical representation can help decipher the information. Spreadsheets give you the ability to choose the part of the worksheet that you want to illustrate, and will graph the figures to your specification or represent them in some other graphical form such as a pie chart.

2 Accessing a spreadsheet

2.1 Excel

In the instructions that follow you will be using the Excel for Windows (or similar) package to create a worksheet, make calculations, enter formulae and copy data.

The following should be read and attempted in full if you are unfamiliar with the use of spreadsheets. If you are confident using spreadsheets check through the notes and exercises for any areas you may not have covered previously.

If you do not have access to Excel it will be assumed that you can use a similar package and you should refer to your manual for the basic mouse clicks.

As you are introduced to more commands, the worksheet will provide more information and give you a way to make business forecasts, called the 'What if' analysis. When you have completed your report, you will print out a copy to present to your manager.

2.2 Running the program

The way to gain access to the spreadsheet package depends upon the type of computer system in use. A **menu** may be available to allow access to the chosen software by entering a single number or letter or by use of a cursor or mouse.

If you are using the spreadsheet at work, you must check first with your supervisor that it is allowed and that you are using the right version of the software.

If you are working in a **Windows** environment, you will access the spreadsheet package using the mouse. Click on the Start button in the bottom left hand corner of the Window. Keeping the mouse button depressed move to highlight the 'Programs' and then to the package that you want to use. Click on the icon.

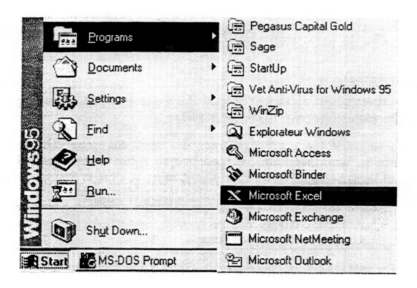

The opening screen in Microsoft Excel might look like this:

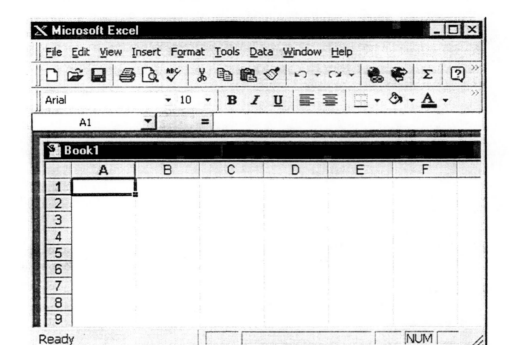

On the screen you will see the **title bar**, the **menu bar, the function tool bar** and in the top right corner the buttons to **minimise, maximise**/restore and close the worksheet. As with most Windows you can change the size and move the Excel Window.

If your screen does not have a formula bar, a formatting bar or a toolbar you can show these by accessing **View** and then Toolbars from the menu at the top of the screen. You can then select (or deselect) what you want to show on the screen. A tick signifies that it is switched on.

The toolbars are below the menu bar. Clicking on any of these buttons provides a shortcut to selecting options from the menu bar. If you pause the pointer over a button a label will appear and, in the **status bar**, Excel will tell you what that button does.

The formula bar is between the spreadsheet and the toolbar. This provides you with information about the contents of the active cell. The co-ordinates of the active cell are displayed on the left-hand side of the formula bar.

The status bar is at the bottom of the screen. It gives you information about your spreadsheet, such as when you are opening or saving a file and whether you have CAPS LOCK, NUM LOCK or SCROLL LOCK on.

Scroll bars are used to move your spreadsheet both up and down and left to right. The vertical scroll bar (on the right hand side of the spreadsheet) is used to move up and down. The horizontal scroll bar (below the spreadsheet and above the status bar) is used to move left and right.

2.3   *Vocabulary*

The spreadsheet is now ready to go to work, but first you will need to know some basic terms and some spreadsheet vocabulary, so that you can give instructions.

♦   Worksheet: a worksheet or spreadsheet (as shown above) is the basis of all the work you do. It could be considered to be the electronic equivalent of an accountant's ledger.

◆ Workbook: is a collection of worksheets. The workbook is simply a folder that binds together your worksheets. When you open a new workbook, it automatically contains 16 worksheets.

◆ Cells: the worksheet is divided into columns and rows. The intersection of a column and a row is known as a 'cell'. To refer to a particular cell, use its column and row location. This is called a 'cell address', for example A1, B22, etc.

◆ Columns: each column is referenced by one or two letters in the column heading. The whole worksheet consists of 256 columns, labelled A through IV.

◆ Rows: each row is referenced by the row number shown in the row heading to the left of a row. There are 65,536 rows in Excel.

◆ Sheet tabs: these are between the worksheet and the status bar and are used to move between worksheets in your workbook.

◆ Window: you can only see part of the worksheet at any time; you could consider the screen to be a window onto the worksheet. You have the facility to move this window, so that you can view any part of the spreadsheet.

◆ Cell pointer: look at the cell that is highlighted; this highlighted area is known as the cell pointer. It indicates the cell in which you are currently working. The current cell location is also displayed on the edit line above the spreadsheet.

2.4   Creating and saving a new file

When you first open Excel, a blank spreadsheet appears on the screen and you can start typing straight away. At this point you can work on an established spreadsheet or start on a new one by creating a file as described below.

From the file menu choose the NEW option, and a new Excel workbook will appear on the screen. Once you have created a document, you must save it if you wish to use it in the future. To save a file:

◆ From the **FILE** menu choose the **SAVE AS** option.

◆ A dialogue box will appear.

◆ If necessary, use the DRIVE drop down menu to select the relevant drive; if you are saving to floppy disk, it is generally the 'a:' or 'b:' drive.

◆ In the **FILE NAME** text box type in the name you wish to use (up to 8 characters). All spreadsheet packages automatically add a three-digit extension to your filename. In Lotus it will begin with wk and in Excel it will begin with xl.

◆ Click on the **OK** button.

When you have saved a file once, you do not need to choose the **SAVE AS** option again, but simply choose **SAVE** from the **FILE** menu or click on the icon on the tool bar (picture of a floppy disk).

2.5   Closing a file/Quitting

When you have finished working on a spreadsheet and you have saved it, you will need to close it down. You can do this by either pressing the button at the top right hand side of the worksheet with a cross on it or by choosing the CLOSE or EXIT option from the FILE menu.

If you only want to exit Excel briefly and prefer not to close down the whole package you can switch to another application or back to the Windows Program Manager by pressing <Alt><Tab> repeatedly. This allows you to step through all the opened packages in rotation.

If you have changed the file, Excel will ask if you wish to save the changes you made before closing. Click on the appropriate button.

3 Moving around the spreadsheet

3.1 Cell pointer

The whole worksheet consists of many columns and rows. On opening the spreadsheet, you can only see a small part of it - generally columns A to H and rows 1 to 16. The screen is like a window onto the worksheet and you have the facility to move this window so that you can view any part of the worksheet. The cell pointer highlights the cell you are currently in.

By moving the cell pointer you are able to enter information into any cell of the worksheet. There are a number of ways of moving the cell pointer, but the easiest way is to use the mouse. You can move around the spreadsheet by positioning the **mouse pointer** over the appropriate cell and clicking to select that cell. If the cell address you want is outside the range shown in the current window, it is possible to move down or across the spreadsheet by clicking on the scroll bars to the side or below the Window. Alternatively, you can use the arrow keys on the keyboard.

3.2 Moving directly to a cell: the GOTO command

Sometimes we want to move to a specific address in the spreadsheet that is too far from our present position to warrant using the arrow keys to get there. On the top of the keyboard you can see a row of keys labelled F1 through to F12; these are known as 'function keys'. When these keys are pressed, a special function is invoked. For the moment we will explore the F5 key. This is the **GOTO key** in both Excel and Lotus 123.

Let us assume you wished to go to D19. Press F5 and a dialogue box appears. You are prompted to enter an address or range. Enter D19 and the cell pointer will go directly to cell D19.

Try moving around your worksheet now. You can find where the end is because the spreadsheet will beep whenever you attempt to go beyond the worksheet boundaries.

Activity 1 *(The answer is in the final chapter of this book)*

What is the biggest co-ordinate in your worksheet?

3.3 The help facility

Excel has a comprehensive help facility, which provides both **general** help and **context sensitive** help.

To invoke the help command type <Alt> Help Contents or alternatively the shortcut key F1. To obtain information on any particular subject shown, move the mouse pointer over the required topic and click.

Context sensitive help is available either when a help button is displayed in a dialogue box or when an error message is flashed onto the screen. Asking for help at this stage by either clicking on the help button, ? box or by pressing F1 will result in the help window appearing at the topic relevant to the problem encountered.

If you wish to search through the help file alphabetically or by entering a specific topic, type <Alt> Help Contents and Index and fill in the search topic.

4   Entering data

4.1   Putting data onto the worksheet

Entering data on the worksheet is very easy. You simply type your entry at the keyboard, press return and whatever you typed will be placed in the current cell, ie where the cell pointer is.

As you type, each character will be displayed on the edit line at the top of the screen. The entry is not put onto the worksheet until you press the return key.

Move to cell A1. Type ABCDEF <Enter>

Now move to Cell A3. Type 123 <Enter>

When you have finished entering data you can either press the <Enter> key on the keyboard or click on the Enter Box (a tick) on the formula bar.

If you change your mind about entering the data then either press the <Esc> key on the keyboard or click on the Cancel Box (a cross) on the formula bar.

If you have made a mistake, you can press the 'backspace key' (the key above the ENTER key) to delete what you have done one character at a time. If you have already pressed the ENTER key, you can delete it by highlighting the cell or cells and pressing the Delete key.

There are three types of data that can be entered into your worksheet - text, numbers and formulae.

4.2   Entering text

Text is entered by simply typing into a cell. Typing any letter at the beginning of a cell entry causes it to be accepted as a 'label', rather than 'value'. If the text you enter is longer than the width of the cell then the text will 'run over' into the next cell. But if the next cell also contains data/information then you will only see part of the text you entered, ie the label will be truncated.

There will be times when you want the spreadsheet to treat a number or a formula as text. To do this you must type an apostrophe in front of the number or formula you are entering, eg '01707 320903 or '=A4+D5.

4.3   Entering numbers

Numbers can be entered on the spreadsheet by simply typing into a cell. If the space in the cell is insufficient, the number will be shown in an exponential form on the spreadsheet, but the number will still be retained in full in the formula bar. If you want to see the contents of cells in full, the columns can be widened to accommodate the number (or text)

It is not necessary to put the commas in manually when entering large numbers (1,000 or more), because it is easy to format the data to display commas and decimal places to make the data easier to understand.

4.4   *Entering formulae*

The arithmetic operations and method of writing the basic formulae are very similar in all packages.

The **BODMAS (Brackets, Of, Division, Multiplication, Addition, Subtraction) rule** must be used to evaluate an arithmetic problem:

◆ Use brackets to clarify the correct order of operation and evaluate expressions within the brackets first.

◆ Calculate "of" expressions (eg 20% of the total).

◆ Perform division and multiplication before addition and subtraction.

◆ Work from left to right if the expression contains only addition and subtraction.

The basic commands for **statistical functions** that calculate lists of values are also very similar throughout the range of spreadsheet packages. Examples of these are:

SUM	The sum of the values in list
AVG	The average of the values in list
COUNT	The number of non-blank entries in list
MAX	The maximum value in list
MIN	The minimum value in list

A formula always starts with an equal sign (=) in Excel. If you start it with an equal sign (=) in Lotus 123, it automatically converts it to a plus (+) sign. Formulae consist of numbers, cell co-ordinates (eg A2, F7), operators and functions. Operators perform actions on numbers and co-ordinates. Examples of operators are plus, minus, divide and multiply. Functions perform more advanced actions on numbers and co-ordinates.

To enter a formula:

◆ Select the cell where you want to enter the formula.

◆ Press the equal sign (=) on the keyboard or click on the sign in the formula bar.

◆ Key in the formula directly from the keyboard or use the mouse to select the cells you want in the formula. There are no spaces in a formula.

◆ Press the <Enter> key.

When you have entered a formula, the resulting value appears in that cell. The formula is only visible in the formula bar.

Typical formulae:

=(A6+C10)-E25	Adds A6 with C10 and subtracts E25
=(H19*A7)/3	Multiplies H19 with A7 and divides the total by 3
=SUM(L12:L14)	A quick way of adding L12 + L13 + L14

An even quicker way to add a row or column of numbers is to click the [+½/₃] button in the toolbar for Lotus 1-2-3. The equivalent button in MS Excel is the Greek symbol sigma. [Σ]

4.5 *What to do if you make a mistake*

If you enter data incorrectly and you notice the error before pressing the return key then you can use the backspace key, which deletes characters from the entry, working from right to left. For example, let us assume that you wanted to enter the label 'Costs' into cell C1, but instead typed 'Cists'.

♦ Move cell pointer to C1

♦ Type   Cists (do not press the return key)

♦ Press backspace key five times

♦ Type   Costs

♦ Press the return key and 'Costs' will now appear in C1

Another method you can use if you notice the error before pressing **Enter** is to press the **Esc** key. The program will cancel what you have entered and return you to the Ready mode. You then simply re-key.

If you spot the error after you have pressed the **Enter** key then you could simply retype the entry, press **Enter** and the current contents of the cell will be replaced with this entry. For example, if you wished to change the contents of cell C1 from 'Costs' to read 'Total', simply re-key the entry.

♦ Ensure the cell pointer is still at C1

♦ Type   Total

♦ Total will now appear in C1

It would be frustrating if you had completed a long entry, spotted an error, and had to re-key the whole entry again. The spreadsheet comes to your aid with F2 - the **Edit** key.

Move the cell pointer to the cell containing the error, press F2. You will be put into **Edit** mode. The contents of the cell will be displayed on the edit bar with the cursor placed after the last character of the entry. You may then use the following editing features.

♦ Arrow Left - will move the cursor one character to the left

♦ Arrow Right - will move the cursor one character to the right

♦ Home - will move the cursor to the first character of the entry

♦ End - will move the cursor to the last character of the entry

To Insert/Overwrite/Delete a character:

♦ **Insert** <Ins> - will allow you to insert a character where the cursor is placed. The characters to the right of the cursor are moved to the right. It is a toggle key; you press once to go into overtype mode and press again to return to **Insert** mode. When in overtype mode, the cursor is replaced by the letter being highlighted.

♦ **Delete** <Del> - will delete the character under the cursor.

4.6   Selecting a range in Excel

When you select items to cut or copy it is usual to select a large range rather than a specific word or cell. This can be done in the following way.

Keyboard - move to the first cell (usually top left hand corner of selection) and hold down the shift key. Use your other hand to move to the last cell (bottom right) using the arrow keys. You will notice the selection expanding on the screen. Once you have covered the cell intended you can release both keys and proceed.

Mouse - using the mouse pointer move to the first cell in the selection, press the left hand mouse button and hold down. Move the mouse pointer to the last cell and then release the button.

If you are copying a range of cells to a new location then you will be asked to specify their new position. This can be done by clicking in the cell that you wish to be the first cell (ie the top left).

4.7   Exercise 1 - Basic data entry

In Excel, open a new blank worksheet and enter the following data. Leave plenty of space so that the titles are distinct. You will probably be putting the first invoice number in row 6.

Sales Invoices	August 20X0		
Invoice	Firm	Items	Price
1001	AB Plastics Ltd	10	0.2
1002	J Cables Ltd	21	0.2
1003	DC Covers Ltd	45	0.2
1004	DC Covers Ltd	42	0.2
1005	J Cables Ltd	500	0.2
1006	AB Plastics Ltd	25	0.2
1007	J Hoggs Ltd	300	0.2
1008	L Quick Ltd	1000	0.2
1009	DC Covers Ltd	50	0.2
1010	AB Plastics Ltd	12	0.2
1011	AB Plastics Ltd	15	0.2
1012	J Hoggs Ltd	350	0.2
1013	L Quick Ltd	1500	0.2
1014	J Hoggs Ltd	400	0.2
1015	L Quick Ltd	1250	0.2
1016	DC Covers Ltd	90	0.2
1017	F Browns Ltd	48	0.2
1018	L Quick Ltd	500	0.2
1019	F Browns Ltd	52	0.2
1020	F Browns Ltd	25	0.2

4.8   Adding basic formulae

Excel allows you to build up mathematical formulae to perform many useful functions, eg add up data, find average values, produce variances, add or subtract VAT, etc.

It has the capability of producing complex analyses and as your experience grows you can pick up more of these using a manual or the on-screen help function.

We will look at building up some basic formulae, which are commonly used in financial spreadsheets. In this exercise, we are going to calculate the Net price, the VAT and the Gross. You need to add three more columns after Price and label them.

(a)   **Multiply** - in the 'Net' column we are going to put a formula to multiply the Items by the Price.

  ♦   Click on first entry in Net column (E6 probably)

  ♦   Type an = in the formula bar

  ♦   Click on first entry in the Items column (or type the address in - C6 probably)

  ♦   Type a * (to multiply)

  ♦   Click on first entry in the Price column (D6 probably)

  ♦   Press <Return> or OK

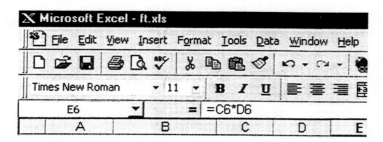

(b)   Using the same type of multiply formula in the VAT column (F6 probably), calculate the VAT on the Net figure: this will be =E6*0.175.

(c)   **Add** - we want to add the VAT to the Net to give us the Gross figure in G6

  ♦   Click on G6

  ♦   Type an = in the formula bar (or click on the = sign)

  ♦   Click on E6

  ♦   Type a +

  ♦   Click on F6

  ♦   Press <Return> or OK

(d)   Another useful function is SUM. This can be used to total a list of values in a row or column without specifying each one individually.

  We need to copy these formulae to the rest of the entries in the worksheet before we can total the columns.

4.9   *Copying*

Shown below are the Cut, Copy and Paste buttons toolbar at the top of the screen on both Excel (left) and Lotus

Cut then **paste** is used to move cells from one area of the spreadsheet to another.

Copy then **paste** is used to copy cells from one area to another.

Copying and pasting or cutting and pasting operations always have two parts:

♦   define the range you want to copy or cut **from**; then

♦   define the range that you want to copy or move **to.**

Click on cell D5 and key in '£, press Enter. Go back to D5 and click on the ≡ button to place the text in the centre of the cell.

This is the range you want to copy from. (Here the range is a single cell.)

Click the **copy** button on the toolbar (next to scissors). The border of D5 will start to shimmer.

Position the cursor over cell D5, hold down the mouse button and drag to the right until cells D5 to G5 have been highlighted (D5 will be white, E5 to G5 will be black). This is the range to copy to.

Click on the **paste** button on the toolbar. The '£' sign has been copied from D5 and should now appear in E5 to G5.

You can copy formulae to different cells by the same method. Try to copy the formula from E6 to E25. Then from F6 to F25 and G6 to G25.

4.10   *Illustration*

To give more practice with the important skill of copying, assume that we want to make a copy of the worksheet somewhere else on the spreadsheet. The part of the worksheet that will be copied is defined by the range A2..G28. These cells are the two diagonally opposite corners of the worksheet:

Place the cursor over cell A2. Hold down the mouse key and drag the cursor towards the bottom right of the screen until the area A2..G28 is highlighted. This defines the area that will be copied **from**.

Click on the **copy** button in the toolbar.

Click on cell N2. This defines where the **top left** cell of the copied range will go.

Click on the **paste** button in the toolbar. The copied area should now appear in cells N2..T28.

5 Improving the spreadsheet's appearance

5.1 Finishing the spreadsheet

We are going to tidy up the spreadsheet and finish with the totals in row 27 and the averages in row 29.

♦   In E27 we are going to total the column of values in cells E6 to E25.

♦   In E27 type =SUM.

♦   Click in E6 and look in the cell value bar. It should now read =SUM(E6

♦   Type : to indicate a range then click on cell E25

♦   Press <Return> or OK

The answer to the sum of the cell values should appear in cell E27. Label this row.

All formulae can be entered by a combination of typing and using the pointer.

♦   *Note.* A shortcut to summary values is to use the Σ symbol from the tool bar.

♦   Try this in columns F and G. In F27 click on Σ and press enter. Excel will automatically total the numbers in the cells above.

♦   Another useful function is =AVERAGE. This will average cell values in a range specified using the pointer as for =SUM.

♦   Try this in G28.

5.2 Rounding and truncation

Spreadsheet packages store numbers internally in several different ways, with varying effects on speed, storage space and accuracy. In some cases an exact representation of the required value may not be possible.

As well as this, multiplication and division will often result in a **small loss of accuracy**, as when a long division being done by hand is stopped after calculating several decimal places. In complex spreadsheets, these errors may accumulate and become significant.

In addition to the limitations of the computer, accuracy may be deliberately reduced to produce more credible reports. The space in a displayed cell or in a column of a printout may not be big enough for all the digits of the value that the computer holds.

(a)   If there is no room for even the digits before the decimal point (eg a value of 1,000 in a column width of three), then the display or printout will be some **warning code** (eg ###) if it is a calculated value.

(b)   Otherwise, the value is truncated (digits that will not fit are omitted) and should also be rounded to the nearest value that will fit (eg 3.666 is truncated to 3.67). If it is a keyed in number the program will calculate it as a power (eg 64587932156 in a width of 11 column points will be shown as 6.46E+10 in a column width of 8 points).

Even if the printed value is truncated, the value stored in the computer is not changed. This can lead to reports that appear to be incorrect, eg:

Values held in the computer	Truncated values printed (the total appears to be wrong)
1.006	1.01
2.007	2.01
3.013	3.01

To avoid this embarrassment, the values stored in the computer can be **truncated and rounded** using a function such as ROUNDDOWN or ROUNDUP in Excel.

ROUNDDOWN (x, 2) will give the value of x to not more than two decimal places and can be used in calculations, eg to keep monetary values as whole numbers of pence.

For example, if cell T1 contains the total value and cell N1 contains the number of items, then calculating the average value as T1/N1 will be accurate, but can lead to the problem above.

Calculating the value as ROUNDDOWN (T1/N1, 2) will avoid the problem, but will be less accurate and could be totally misleading for small values.

5.3   *General rules for rounding*

♦   For greater accuracy, only round those values that will be part of the final report.

♦   Avoid rounding values which will themselves be used with multiplication or division to generate further values.

♦   Do not round values which may be very small. Change to smaller units if necessary (eg pence instead of pounds).

♦   Increase the column width and allow more decimal places where possible (eg ROUNDDOWN (x, 5)).

♦   To work with whole numbers, use ROUND (x,0) or click Format, Cells, Number, General.

♦   Use the formatting tools in Format, Cells, Number to put currency, dates, etc into an appropriate form and to avoid data in adjacent columns overlapping.

5.4   *Formatting*

Making the spreadsheet look good is more than just a cosmetic exercise. Proper formatting, underlining and emboldening can make the spreadsheet easier to follow, draw attention to important figures and reduce the chance of errors.

To format the data you have entered and improve the appearance of the spreadsheet, we are going to do a number of things:

♦   Change the font to Times New Roman throughout. To do this click on the first cell with an entry in it and drag the mouse to the last cell with an entry in it. The area covered should go black. Then go to the Format menu and select Cells. Select the chosen style.

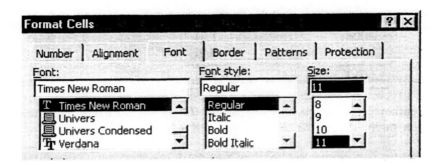

♦ The style format should be Times New Roman throughout with a font size of 14 for the titles and 11 for the main body of the text.

♦ Put the titles in bold. One way of doing this would be to activate the cells by clicking and dragging the cursor over them, then clicking on the **B** button (Bold) on the tool bar. Alternatively, all entries in a row or column can be selected by clicking on the letter at the head of the column or the number at the very left of the row.

♦ The Invoice column A and the Firm column B will not be wide enough initially to enter the full details. Change the column width of B to 15 characters by placing the mouse pointer in the column heading at the intersection between column B and C. A two headed arrow should appear. Drag this to the right until the column is wide enough. Adjust the width of the other columns to accommodate the entries comfortably.

♦ Align the column headings. If you look at your spreadsheet so far you will see that all the text is left justified in the cells (moved as far as possible to the left) and the numbers are all right justified (moved to the right in each cell). To adjust this use the align buttons on the formatting toolbar (to the right of the underline <u>U</u>).

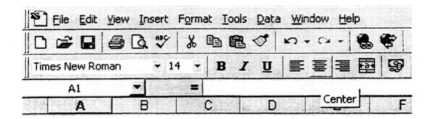

♦ Put the £ sign in the price column (Format, Cells, Currency)

♦ Underline the totals by outlining the cells containing the totals. Move the mouse pointer to Format on the menu bar right at the top of the spreadsheet. Click the mouse button, and a menu will appear. Click on 'Cells'... Ctrl+1 and a window similar to the following will appear. Click on 'Border'

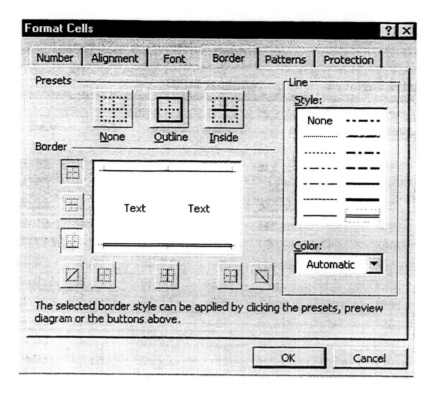

The box on the left shows the edges of the cell or selection of cells, which will have a border. The box on the right shows the types of lines that are available. Click on the top line on the left-hand list and then on the single, non-bold line (probably already selected) in the right hand options. The top of the 'totals' cells should now have a single underlining. Now click on the bottom line and then on the double under-lining style. Click on OK.

The finished spreadsheet should appear as follows:

	A	B	C	D	E	F	G
2	**Sales Invoices**		**August 20X0**				
3							
4	**Invoice**	**Firm**	**Items**	**Price**	**Net**	**VAT**	**Gross**
5				£	£	£	£
6	1001	AB Plastics Ltd	10	£0.20	£2.00	£0.35	£2.35
7	1002	J Cables Ltd	21	£0.20	£4.20	£0.74	£4.94
8	1003	DC Covers Ltd	45	£0.20	£9.00	£1.58	£10.58
9	1004	DC Covers Ltd	42	£0.20	£8.40	£1.47	£9.87
10	1005	J Cables Ltd	500	£0.20	£100.00	£17.50	£117.50
11	1006	AB Plastics Ltd	25	£0.20	£5.00	£0.88	£5.88
12	1007	J Hoggs Ltd	300	£0.20	£60.00	£10.50	£70.50
13	1008	L Quick Ltd	1000	£0.20	£200.00	£35.00	£235.00
14	1009	DC Covers Ltd	50	£0.20	£10.00	£1.75	£11.75
15	1010	AB Plastics Ltd	12	£0.20	£2.40	£0.42	£2.82
16	1011	AB Plastics Ltd	15	£0.20	£3.00	£0.53	£3.53
17	1012	J Hoggs Ltd	350	£0.20	£70.00	£12.25	£82.25
18	1013	L Quick Ltd	1500	£0.20	£300.00	£52.50	£352.50
19	1014	J Hoggs Ltd	400	£0.20	£80.00	£14.00	£94.00
20	1015	L Quick Ltd	1250	£0.20	£250.00	£43.75	£293.75
21	1016	DC Covers Ltd	90	£0.20	£18.00	£3.15	£21.15
22	1017	F Browns Ltd	48	£0.20	£9.60	£1.68	£11.28
23	1018	L Quick Ltd	500	£0.20	£100.00	£17.50	£117.50
24	1019	F Browns Ltd	52	£0.20	£10.40	£1.82	£12.22
25	1020	F Browns Ltd	25	£0.20	£5.00	£0.88	£5.88
26							
27		**Total**			£1,247.00	£218.23	£1,465.23
28							
29		**Average**			£62.35	£10.91	£73.26

Save your spreadsheet by clicking on the **Save** button on the toolbar (the picture of the disk). There is no need to enter a name this time, as it will be saved under the name you originally supplied.

6 Producing reports

6.1 Assumptions

Although the spreadsheet that you have completed is very simple, you still have the basis of a powerful planning and analysis tool. Assumptions and figures can be changed and the spreadsheet will automatically recalculate the results. The main benefit of the spreadsheet is the ability to do 'What if?' experiments.

This allows you to see what happens if, for example, the prices are raised with a subsequent reduction in sales. It can also be used to calculate the overdraft facility if different variables are changed in a cash flow calculation.

Another facility is 'goal seeking'. This is different from seeing what results you get from changing the variables. It gives you the opportunity to state the result you want and make changes until you get that result.

6.2   Changing the variables

In your spreadsheet, you are going to change some of the entries.

Activity 2 *(The answer is in the final chapter of this book)*

The price to all customers is going to be raised by 10%, but the organisation assumes that AB Plastics Ltd will use another supplier, so they will lose this business. Would the 10% rise be beneficial to the organisation?

6.3   Sorting the spreadsheet

Using the same reduced spreadsheet, you are now going to sort it into customer alphabetic order.

If you left gaps when you removed AB Plastics Ltd, you need to tidy up and remove them. Do this by clicking on the number of the row. This highlights the whole row and allows you to go to the Edit menu and click on Delete.

To sort the data you need to highlight the customer's column and then select **Data** from the toolbar and then **Sort**. You might get the following message, which will make sure that when you sort the data, the relevant orders go with the customers.

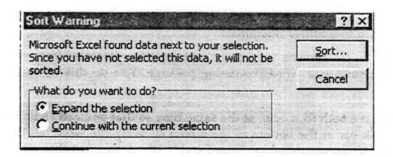

When the data is sorted, you can do a sub-total for each customer. Then reduce the number of entries to the following:

DC Covers Ltd	£58.68
F Browns Ltd	£32.31
J Cables Ltd	£134.68
J Hoggs Ltd	£271.43
L Quick Ltd	£1,098.63

6.4　Charts and graphs

Most spreadsheet packages make it easy to draw charts and graphs from the data in your worksheet. In Excel, the Chart Wizard is the icon that looks like a chart.

Make sure that your worksheet looks like the one shown above. If it does not, you need to select the areas by holding down the Control key while you do so. These two columns will form the basis of your chart.

With the two columns selected, click on the Chart Wizard. Select the type of chart or graph that you prefer and experiment with changing the data labels and percentages. Two examples are shown below.

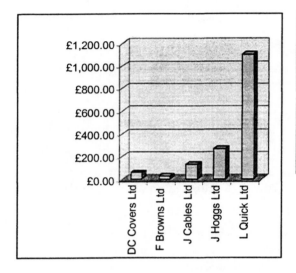
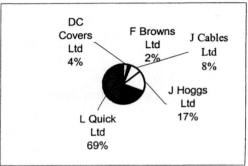

Not all types of graph are suitable for this data, as you will find if you experiment.

6.5　Transferring to another document

Under Windows, you can transfer (or copy) a chart or other diagrams from your worksheet to another document, such as a word processing package. You do this by using the copy and paste facilities.

It is easier if you have both files open at the same time so that you can switch from one to the other using the task bar at the bottom of the screen showing the windows that are currently open. For example, if you are switching from Excel to Word, you just click on the icon with the W on it. Vice versa, it has an X on it.

To copy a chart from Excel to a file in Word:

♦　Access the correct area of your worksheet

♦　Highlight the area you want to transfer or copy to another document

♦　Click on Copy (Control C)

♦ Switch to the other document by clicking onto it on the task bar

♦ Position the cursor where you want the chart to be and click on Paste (Control V). You can alter this position by grabbing the picture and dragging it to its position.

Activity 3 *(The answer is in the final chapter of this book)*

Set up a worksheet with the following headings and values:

Sales £m	20X0	20X4
Cat food	80	120
Dog food	80	100
Bird seed	25	20

Use your spreadsheet to draw two pie charts showing the percentage make up of the sales for both of the years. Copy both of them to a Word file.

6.6   Report design

Printed reports and the information that they contain are only as complete and accurate as the data that went into them. In the previous chapters, various checks and procedures were mentioned that could improve the completeness and accuracy of reports and of the information stored on computer.

The appearance of reports is very important and the design should incorporate the following:

♦ A clear **heading** to indicate what the report is about.

♦ A **date** that the report relates to.

♦ A **date** that the report was **printed** (in case it is amended and printed again).

♦ **Page numbers** to help control large reports over several pages (possibly also the total number of pages).

♦ **Column headings** to explain what each column contains.

♦ **Units** for data to ensure that monetary amounts are clearly stated as being in £, £'000 or £m.

6.7   Printing a report

When you are required to produce a report, you should try to concentrate on important information, starting and stopping at relevant points. However, this need to limit the scope of a report should not be at the expense of accuracy, and items that are necessary should not be omitted.

The performance criteria for this course are that you ensure that the required range and report are correctly specified. You also need to demonstrate that printed information is correct and complete and that hard copy is clean, clearly printed and aligned correctly.

To print from your computer make sure that it is connected to a printer and that it is switched on and loaded with the correct paper.

The quickest way to print anything in a Windows environment is to press the **Print** icon on the toolbar. If you want to print more than one copy, specific pages or a highlighted area you must select the Print option from the File menu. If necessary, change the number of copies required or change the page range to specify which pages to print.

To print an area from your worksheet, highlight the area that you want to print. Select **Print Area** then **Print Preview**. This shows you what your print will look like on the page.

The worksheet might be compressed if the page is set up in Portrait. To change to Landscape, click on Page Set Up and change the orientation.

When you are ready to print, click the OK button.

7 Summary

You started by learning how to enter and exit the software package. Accessing any new software can be a daunting process for the novice, but with practise you will become very proficient in a short time. The main reason for accessing the package is to enter some data and process it somehow to produce the information required. This information should be produced in a format that is acceptable to the person who is to receive it.

You now understand how to improve the appearance of your spreadsheet by formatting individual cells. The examples given are only a few of the many ways in which the appearance of cells can be changed. You should experiment with others on a separate spreadsheet.

CHAPTER 15

Databases

ASSESSMENT FOCUS

This chapter covers the following Knowledge and Understanding and Performance Criteria of the AAT Syllabus.

♦ The purpose and application of databases *(Knowledge and Understanding element 20.1)*

♦ Types of data held on a computer system *(Knowledge and Understanding elements 20.1 and 20.2)*

♦ How to save, transfer and print documents *(Knowledge and Understanding element 20.1)*

♦ House style for the presentation of documents *(Knowledge and Understanding element 20.1)*

♦ Location of information sources *(Knowledge and Understanding element 20.1)*

♦ Data is input and stored in the appropriate location *(Performance Criteria element 20.1)*

In order to cover these, the following topics are considered:

♦ Generation: specification of the start and finish of the range and selection of the required report

♦ Standard reports: bar charts, pie charts, histograms, standard database reports (some of which require special stationery)

♦ Using examples to cover each of the following:

♦ using correct part of system

♦ using search facilities

♦ identifying and correcting errors

♦ retrieving correct details

♦ printing required report

Introduction

In the last chapter we looked at how to use spreadsheets to organise data and produce report information. We continue by explaining what a database is and how you can use your spreadsheet to build database applications. This chapter then looks at the features of a database applications package, using examples based on Microsoft Access. Because most other common packages work in a similar way, if you have access to a different database package you should be able to practice using it in line with the examples given.

1 Database applications

1.1 What is a database?

The term database, often shortened to DB, refers to the data and the way in which it is held, rather than the tools or package used to manage the data. It is important for you to realise that a database does not require a computer. We are surrounded by them, eg a telephone directory, a textbook or a filing cabinet. The only requirement for something to qualify as a database is that it should contain data and that it should have a logical structure to allow easy access to the data.

A database application package is a software package containing facilities that allow you to create and manage databases.

Some tasks can be carried out using either a spreadsheet or a database package, eg simple cashflows could be kept on either. However, there are differences between the two types of package. Spreadsheets provide a more flexible working environment that is not limited in its structure. They are particularly good at handling numerical data and calculating results, and so are appropriate for many financial applications. Database packages have sophisticated data retrieval and reporting facilities that are not normally found in spreadsheets. They are more appropriate for conventional record-keeping tasks where the main requirement is to retrieve information and produce transaction documents and reports.

A database management system (DBMS) is a far more complex set of tools than a database application package. They are used for big business applications such as transaction processing systems.

1.2 Record keeping

The purpose of record keeping is to store, retrieve and analyse data. Data stored in a database must be grouped together and given a structure. The terms used to refer to different collections of data include the following:

Data items - individual pieces of data stored within the database. Each item may be numeric (eg price of goods and quantities) alphabetic (eg names) or alphanumeric (eg postcodes).

Field - single item of data within a record. For example in a personnel database the information held on each person would constitute one *record* and this would comprise a number of *fields* such as surname, first name, works number, department, age, salary, etc. One of the fields in a record may be a key field, meaning that the data in this field uniquely identifies the record and distinguishes it from all other records in the file. In the case of an employee record, a personnel number or works number will be the key.

Record - a collection of fields, each containing a data item, relating to a specific entity. For example in a file of names and addresses, a record is the data relating to one individual. All the records in a file have an identical structure.

Table - a collection of records in two dimensions, with each row in the table normally relating to a different record, eg each department in the organisation.

File - the tables and records are held in a file, or files, for the purpose of storage. A record keeping package enables you to set up files and store data covering many topics. There could be files containing names and addresses, details of customers' orders and stock. Both the data and the way it is organised (structured) will be different in each of these files.

There are many different types of database structures, but when we think of a database, we tend to see the data being associated like a kind of upside-down tree. In this structure, each file is directly related to the file above it in the hierarchy. The invoice data shown below is an example of a hierarchical structure.

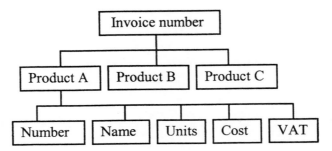

1.3   Using a database

There are four main operations in using a database:

♦   creating the structure of the files and records;

♦   entering data on to the database files, and amending or updating it;

♦   retrieving and manipulating the data; and

♦   producing reports.

2   Spreadsheets as databases

2.1   Building the database

A database is simply a file of data with a series of field names, each containing a number of records. We will be using the same data as we used in the last chapter.

Invoice number	Firm	Items	Price	Net	VAT	Gross
1001	AB Plastics Ltd	10	£0.20	£2.00	£0.35	£2.35
1002	J Cables Ltd	21	£0.20	£4.20	£0.74	£4.94
1003	DC Covers Ltd	45	£0.20	£9.00	£1.58	£10.58
1004	DC Covers Ltd	42	£0.20	£8.40	£1.47	£9.87
1005	J Cables Ltd	500	£0.20	£100.00	£17.50	£117.50
1006	AB Plastics Ltd	25	£0.20	£5.00	£0.88	£5.88
1007	J Hoggs Ltd	300	£0.20	£60.00	£10.50	£70.50
1008	L Quick Ltd	1000	£0.20	£200.00	£35.00	£235.00
1009	DC Covers Ltd	50	£0.20	£10.00	£1.75	£11.75
1010	AB Plastics Ltd	12	£0.20	£2.40	£0.42	£2.82
1011	AB Plastics Ltd	15	£0.20	£3.00	£0.53	£3.53
1012	J Hoggs Ltd	350	£0.20	£70.00	£12.25	£82.25
1013	L Quick Ltd	1500	£0.20	£300.00	£52.50	£352.50
1014	J Hoggs Ltd	400	£0.20	£80.00	£14.00	£94.00
1015	L Quick Ltd	1250	£0.20	£250.00	£43.75	£293.75
1016	DC Covers Ltd	90	£0.20	£18.00	£3.15	£21.15
1017	F Browns Ltd	48	£0.20	£9.60	£1.68	£11.28
1018	L Quick Ltd	500	£0.20	£100.00	£17.50	£117.50
1019	F Browns Ltd	52	£0.20	£10.40	£1.82	£12.22
1020	F Browns Ltd	25	£0.20	£5.00	£0.88	£5.88

Either retrieve this data from your Excel package or enter it again, creating a new file. Once data has been entered in this format Excel is a powerful tool to manipulate the data effectively.

Field names are simply column titles and records are the sets of data entered below these column titles. Entering consecutive data, eg numbers or dates, can be done very rapidly using the Edit Fill Series option from the menu bar.

To do this, enter the first number, eg in the first cell under Invoice number enter 1001. Highlight the range you wish to fill and select Edit Fill Series.

2.2 *Sorting the database*

Once databases are set up it is easy to re-sort the records using the Sort function in the Data menu.

Highlight the range of records (not the field names or titles) to be sorted and then click on Data Sort. Choose the sort keys you require. Alternatively, click on either the Sort Ascending or Sort Descending icon.

Activity 1 *(The answer is in the final chapter of this book)*

We sorted the initial database by invoice number. Can you re-sort this by firm name in alphabetical order and by gross invoice value?

2.3 *Extracting information from a database*

It is often useful to pull out specific records from a database to analyse further. For example we may wish to look at all the sales for a single firm or all invoices over a certain value.

Excel allows data to be selected and copied to another area of the spreadsheet using the advanced filter function.

To use this function, you must identify a series of ranges. The first range that must be identified is the original database. This is the source from which you will select your data. The next range is the criteria range. The final range is called the copy range and is the location where the selected records will be copied to.

We will go through this procedure step by step:

♦ Take out any blank rows between the titles and the data in the columns.

♦ Define and name the source database by highlighting the database including the field names. Click on Insert, Name, Define. The following screen will be shown:

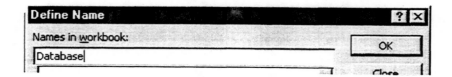

Type in **Database** in the dialogue box as above. Click on OK.

- ◆ Define the selection criteria. These are the field names of the records you wish to select from your database and the rules that you want Excel to follow when you are selecting the records on the next row. For example we may wish to extract all of one firm's (L Quick Ltd) records.

  Copy all the field names (the column titles) from the database to an empty section of the spreadsheet. Use the area to the right of your spreadsheet, I4 - O4. Directly under the Firm heading, copy L Quick Ltd.

Invoice	Firm	Items	Price	Net	VAT	Gross
	L Quick Ltd					

  This will tell Excel to extract all details for this firm.

- ◆ Perform the advanced filter. This is done by selecting Data Filter Advanced Filter from the menu bar.

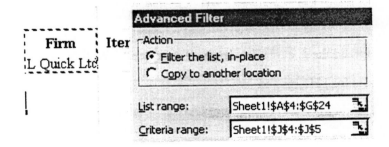

List range will initially be highlighted. Use your mouse to highlight the database range, including field names.

Next, click on the criteria range box and then highlight the criteria range:

We will copy our selected data to another location (I7 to O14). To do this click on **Copy to another location** in the dialogue box and the heading **Copy to** will now be visible in the dialogue box. Specify a range where the data can be copied to by highlighting it with the mouse. To perform the function, click on OK. The following data should be visible:

4	Invoice	Firm	Items	Price	Net	VAT	Gross
5		L Quick Ltd					
6							
7	Invoice	Firm	Items	Price	Net	VAT	Gross
8	1013	L Quick Ltd	1500	£0.20	£300.00	£52.50	£352.50
9	1015	L Quick Ltd	1250	£0.20	£250.00	£43.75	£293.75
10	1008	L Quick Ltd	1000	£0.20	£200.00	£35.00	£235.00
11	1018	L Quick Ltd	500	£0.20	£100.00	£17.50	£117.50

Next we could select all invoices with a gross value of more than £50.00. This is done as described previously. However, this time we remove L Quick Ltd from the criteria range under Firm and add >£50.00 under the field name Gross.

Specify all ranges as before and click OK to perform the function. The result should be as follows:

4	Invoice	Firm	Items	Price	Net	VAT	Gross
5							>£50.00
6							
7	Invoice	Firm	Items	Price	Net	VAT	Gross
8	1005	J Cables Ltd	500	£0.20	£100.00	£17.50	£117.50
9	1007	J Hoggs Ltd	300	£0.20	£60.00	£10.50	£70.50
10	1008	L Quick Ltd	1000	£0.20	£200.00	£35.00	£235.00
11	1012	J Hoggs Ltd	350	£0.20	£70.00	£12.25	£82.25
12	1013	L Quick Ltd	1500	£0.20	£300.00	£52.50	£352.50
13	1014	J Hoggs Ltd	400	£0.20	£80.00	£14.00	£94.00
14	1015	L Quick Ltd	1250	£0.20	£250.00	£43.75	£293.75
15	1018	L Quick Ltd	500	£0.20	£100.00	£17.50	£117.50

Activity 2 *(The answer is in the final chapter of this book)*

From the sales spreadsheet, name the database range and extract the following data:

(i)   All entries for J Hoggs Ltd

(ii)   Net invoice values of more than £25.00

2.4 Creating pivot tables

This function in Excel allows you to exchange rows and columns in a table to look at data in different ways. This can be very useful, for example to summarise a list of invoices and produce subtotals by firms or by month, etc.

Our sales data can be rearranged using a pivot table function to summarise sales by Firm.

This is done as follows:

First open the Data menu and choose Pivot Table. The Pivot Table Wizard dialogue box will appear, which will guide you through the process.

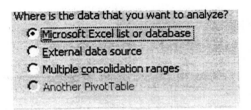

This is the first of four steps. Click on Next to enter the data range you wish to pivot. Highlight the range - this must include the data and column titles and must not include blank columns or rows.

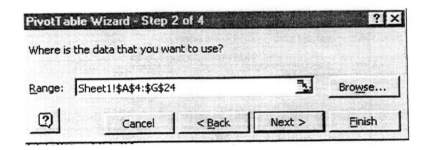

Click Next and the third pivot table wizard dialogue box will appear. Construct the Pivot Table by dragging the field buttons on the right to the diagram on the left as shown below:

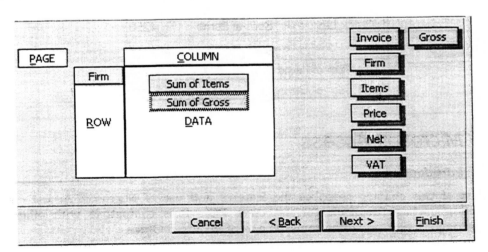

Click on Next for the final dialogue box. You can specify a New Worksheet to leave the original database intact and add the result of this pivot table to a new sheet. Alternatively, you can designate an area on the existing worksheet to carry out the function by highlighting it with the mouse.

Click Finish to create the pivot table.

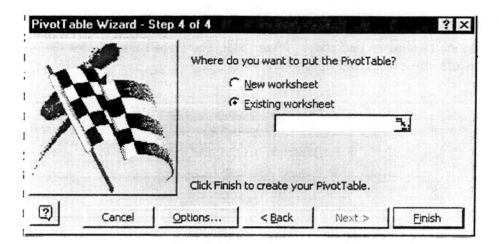

The final result will be as follows. Note some of the column widths have been adjusted to make the data easier to read.

Firm	Data	Total
AB Plastics Ltd	Sum of Items	62
	Sum of Gross	14.57
DC Covers Ltd	Sum of Items	227
	Sum of Gross	53.345
F Browns Ltd	Sum of Items	125
	Sum of Gross	29.375
J Cables Ltd	Sum of Items	521
	Sum of Gross	122.435
J Hoggs Ltd	Sum of Items	1050
	Sum of Gross	246.75
L Quick Ltd	Sum of Items	4250
	Sum of Gross	998.75
Total Sum of Items		6235
Total Sum of Gross		1465.225

3   Microsoft Access

3.1   Introduction

The rest of this chapter describes the features and use of Microsoft Access - a database application package available for use on a PC. It is compatible with other Windows application packages, and often comes as part of Microsoft Office.

Make sure that you are authorised to use the software by checking with your supervisor or tutor. During this tutorial there will be plenty of places where it would be convenient for you to quit the program, or leave it to go and have a break. Remember that it is advisable to take regular breaks from VDU-intensive work.

3.2   Opening and closing Access

To start Microsoft Access, Click the **Start** button in the bottom left hand corner of your desktop then click on **Programs** and select **Microsoft Access**.

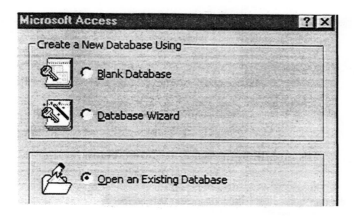

The opening screen invites you to create a new database or to open an existing one by selecting from a list. You can create a new database either from scratch, starting with a blank database, or by using the database 'Wizard'.

Access has six components (or 'objects').

♦   **Tables** - are areas of the database where the data is held

♦   **Queries** - are views of the database and the source of data for a form or report

♦   **Forms** - are input screens, or selective views of the data within the database

♦   **Reports** - are standard format outputs from the database, designed using a report writer and viewed on the screen or printed to hard copy

♦   **Macros** - are like small programs; they automate a series of common tasks

♦   **Modules** - are part of the source code, or programming language, used to create the database and objects.

To exit Microsoft Access - on the **File** menu, click **Exit**. Alternatively, click on the **X** in the top right hand corner of the Window.

3.3   Creating a database

We are going to start from scratch and build a car database. The steps to create this database are specific for Access. Other applications have similar facilities but this text will not be covering them.

Open Microsoft Access and select the blank database and then press OK.

You will now give the database a name - Enter **Cars** in the File name box.

After you have been prompted and given the database a name, click on **Create** and **New**.

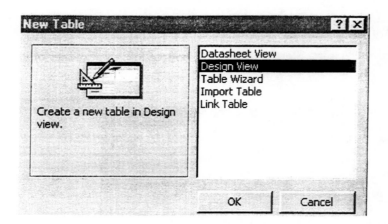

Select **Design View**, click on **OK** and fill in the fields as shown below.

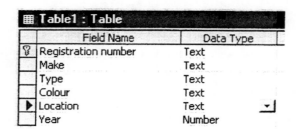
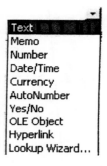

You can choose the Data Type field from a drop down menu or type in the contents.

The first field is the **Key** field that will used to identify each car. This is a unique number for each car. When you enter this field, click on the button in the toolbar that looks like a key, or click on the right hand side of the mouse and select **Primary Key**.

When you have entered all the fields, click on **View** on the menu bar and select Datasheet View.

You will be advised to save the table and give it a name.

For this example, we have called our table **Cars**.

Because this is only an exercise to enable you to process data using a database, we are not going to make it large.

3.4   *Entering and amending data*

After clicking on **View** and selecting **Datasheet View**, you can then fill in the following entries for the fields. The screen should look similar to the one below.

Registration number	Make	Type	Colour	Location	Year
L296NCT	Ford	Saloon	Red	Chester	1994
L299JDN	Honda	Estate	Red	Chester	1994
L392RPC	Ford	Estate	Green	Wallasey	1994
L493ERH	Ford	Saloon	Red	Wallasey	1994
L978PKN	Honda	Saloon	Blue	Manchester	1994
M219ERK	Honda	Hatchback	Green	Wallasey	1995
M297BDJ	Honda	Saloon	Yellow	Wallasey	1995
M297EMH	Ford	Saloon	Yellow	Manchester	1996
M298FQO	Honda	Estate	Blue	Wallasey	1995
M302FNG	Honda	Saloon	Blue	Chester	1995
M392RLX	Ford	Estate	Blue	Wallasey	1995
M491WPN	Ford	Estate	Red	Chester	1995
M492RTH	Ford	Hatchback	Red	Manchester	1995
M962EPK	Ford	Hatchback	Red	Chester	1994
N295GHW	Honda	Saloon	Green	Manchester	1996
N826BUR	Honda	Saloon	Red	Wallasey	1996
					0

(Cars : Table)

You have now set up your database so make sure that you save it.

3.5   *Formatting*

As with most Windows packages, there are many facilities to help you to format your sheet. Click on Format at the top of the screen and experiment. You can change the font, alter the height of rows and width of columns, rename columns and hide columns.

Try out the sort facilities of Access by clicking in different columns on your table and then clicking on the sort ascending button and seeing ⒜↓ what happens. From the point of view of retrieving or amending data at a later stage, it is easier to have one of the fields sorted.

When you are happy with the look of your sheet, press **Save** and then close it, by pressing the X in the top right hand corner of the table. You should now be back to **Cars: Database**, the sheet with the six 'objects'.

3.6   *Adding and amending records*

When the database structure has been established, you can input data and create new files. Most databases must be kept up-to-date and so there will be additions of new records, removal of unwanted records and amendments to existing records.

Activity 3 *(The answer is in the final chapter of this book)*

You are required to add a new car to your database. It is a Ford hatchback, Registration number L386UWN - 1994. It is blue and located in Manchester. You have also noticed that the Honda saloon, registration number L978 PKN is located in Chester - not Manchester as shown.

3.7 Interrogating the database

Data can be retrieved and manipulated in a variety of ways.

♦ You can sort on any specified field, eg sorting cars according to Make.

♦ You can perform calculations such as totals and averages. To find the cars which are older than 1995, you would use >1995 in the criteria range under the Year field. Only 1996 cars should be highlighted.

♦ You can retrieve data by specifying the required parameters, eg Honda cars located in Manchester.

We are going to produce a report to show all the cars located in Manchester. To do this we are going to access the datasheet. On the toolbar menu select Records, Filter, then Advanced Filter/Sort.

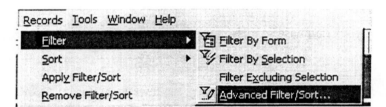

A screen to filter the data is shown. In the first field, double click on Location in the top box and it will be placed in the bottom one. Sort: Ascending will refer to the registration number. Manchester is the criteria to sort by.

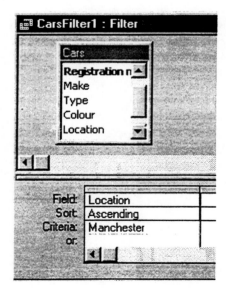

Click on the Filter icon on the tool bar and select **Apply Filter/Sort**

This should produce the following:

Registration number	Make	Type	Colour	Location	Year
L386UWN	Ford	Hatchback	Blue	Manchester	1994
M492RTH	Ford	Hatchback	Red	Manchester	1995
M297EMH	Ford	Saloon	Yellow	Manchester	1996
N295GHW	Honda	Saloon	Green	Manchester	1996

Cars : Table

The main information that is required from this report can be condensed to the following:

Make	Type	Colour	Year
Ford	Hatchback	Blue	1994
Ford	Hatchback	Red	1995
Ford	Saloon	Yellow	1996
Honda	Saloon	Green	1996
			0

Cars : Table

This type of manipulation is done by highlighting the **Registration number** column, clicking on **Format** and then **Hide column**. Similarly do the same for the **Location** column.

To get back to the full database, click on the Return icon on the tool bar again and select **Remove Filter/Sort**. To Unhide, select Format and Unhide columns.

3.8 Creating a query

Creating a query in Access is another way of interrogating the database. To produce our report on the cars available in Manchester, we can choose Query from the Tools menu. Then select New, Design View and OK.

You must then add the Cars database and Close the box. You will then have a series of boxes to fill in as follows:

Field:	Make	Type	Colour	Location	Year	
Table:	Cars	Cars	Cars	Cars	Cars	
Sort:						
Show:	☑	☑	☑	☐	☑	
Criteria:				"Manchester"		
or:						

You do not want to show the location but you need it to determine the criteria for your report, so take the tick from the Show box. Click on the red apostrophe to run the query. When you save it, you must give it a title - Manchester cars.

3.9 *Creating and printing the report*

You can create a report on your own or have Access create one for you using AutoReport or a Report Wizard. When you use Report Wizard it prompts you for information and creates a report based on your answers. Even when you have created many reports, you may want to use Report Wizard to lay out the report and then switch to Design View to customise it.

Creating a report using Report Wizard - to produce the report on cars available in Manchester we are going to access **Reports** on the toolbar.

Select Report Wizard and choose Manchester cars as the query where the object's data comes from, then **OK.**

The Wizard asks a number of questions:

♦ Which fields you want in your report - click on the double arrow pointing right to select all the selected fields. Press **Next.**

♦ Ignore the grouping levels and press **Next.**

♦ Ignore the sort order and press **Next.**

♦ Choose a columnar layout. Press **Next.**

♦ Choose the style you would like and press **Next.**

♦ Give it a title - Manchester cars. Press **Finish.**

You can preview the report before printing by clicking on **Preview.** Then it can be changed in Design View if there are aspects that you are not happy with.

Click on the View button in the top left corner to get a report that looks similar to the following:

Manchester cars

Make	Type	Colour	Year
Honda	Saloon	Green	1996
Ford	Saloon	Yellow	1996
Ford	Hatchback	Red	1995
Ford	Hatchback	Blue	1994

If the report is complete and will not be part of a larger document or need an accompanying letter or memo, you can print it as seen in the preview. Select the report in the Database window, or open the report in Design view, Print Preview, or Layout Preview.

Before you print a report for the first time, you might want to check the margins, page orientation, and other page set up options with a supervisor or someone who has experience. The procedure for printing a report was discussed earlier in this chapter.

Most reports will form part of another document, which may be produced in Word. In this section, we will assume that we have to transfer the report to a Word file.

From the 'objects' screen, click on **Reports** and choose Manchester cars. Click on preview and then click on the Word icon on the toolbar.

A message will appear telling you that the report is outputting to 'Manchester cars.rtf' (rich text file).

When you are completing the rest of the report in Word, you can import this file into your Word document.

4   *Summary*

In this chapter we have used both Excel and Access to demonstrate how to create a database and produce reports from it.

Because it is a 'hands on' learning experience, you should practise using these packages and experimenting with some of the features. The syllabus does not require you to have a thorough knowledge of these packages but you must have an understanding of the ways the data is set up, amended and interrogated in the database.

CHAPTER 16

Using an accounting package

ASSESSMENT FOCUS

This chapter covers the following Knowledge and Understanding and Performance Criteria of the AAT Syllabus.

♦ The purpose and application of accounting packages *(Knowledge and Understanding element 20.1)*

♦ Data is input and stored in the appropriate location *(Performance Criteria element 20.1)*

In order to cover these, the following topics are considered:

♦ Types of data held on a computer system

♦ How to save, transfer and print documents

♦ House style for the presentation of documents

♦ Location of information sources

♦ Examples of accounting software

♦ Show examples of a sales ledger and a purchase/bought ledger

Introduction

The aim of this chapter is to give you an overview of a typical accounting package.

We will be using a package produced by Sage. If you are more familiar with other packages then they can be used. The basic elements of each accounting package and the way that data is output should be the same, only in a different format.

Your main aim must be to achieve competence in the performance criteria by matching your own experiences or performance in simulation to those criteria using whichever software package you consider to be the most appropriate.

You may need to load the software packages if they are not already loaded onto your system. To do this, follow the *manuals* for both your computer system and your chosen software. It is vitally important that you check with your tutor or supervisor that you are allowed to access this software.

1 Components of the accounts package

1.1 The double entry

First let us revise accounting systems. Remember that the double-entry system is contained *only* within the **nominal ledger**.

Each transaction recorded in the **nominal ledger** must be recorded twice. This is the **dual effect**. For every debit there is an equal credit and for every credit a debit.

The nominal ledger contains **ledger accounts** in which the transactions are recorded. This makes it easier to summarise and analyse the transactions at month or year-end.

The **debtors and creditors ledgers** are memorandum accounts. This means that they are not part of the double entry. They contain the same information about debtors and creditors as you find in the nominal ledger, but the information is *analysed* in a different way.

The **books of prime entry** are diaries of the transactions. They are not part of the double-entry system, but they contain information, which is repeated within the nominal ledger.

1.2 The system

Let us next visualise how the program works. Let us think of it in terms of a **manual system**. In a manual system, you would find the following **books of prime entry**:

♦ cash book

♦ petty cash book

♦ sales day book

♦ sales returns day book

♦ purchase day book

♦ purchase returns day book

♦ journal

You would also find the following **ledgers**:

♦ subsidiary debtors ledger

♦ subsidiary creditors ledger

♦ nominal ledger

And you would find the following information:

♦ **standing data** (eg customer names and addresses, nominal ledger codes)

♦ **opening balances** brought forward

♦ transactions in the **current period**

Within a computerised system you will find the same basic components, although they may be slightly different depending upon the program you use. For example some packages do not have a detailed cash book.

1.3   Dealing with credit sales

Let us look first at **credit sales**. Note how the debtors ledger and nominal ledger are updated independently from the same source. This is how your ledger program works in outline. You will input the details of the credit sales (invoices) into the sales input screen and the program will update both ledgers **automatically**.

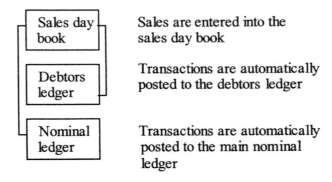

Sales day book	Sales are entered into the sales day book
Debtors ledger	Transactions are automatically posted to the debtors ledger
Nominal ledger	Transactions are automatically posted to the main nominal ledger

Some programs also have the ability to generate the original invoices. We will look at that later.

1.4   Dealing with credit purchases

The system for recording **credit purchases** is identical to the system for recording credit sales.

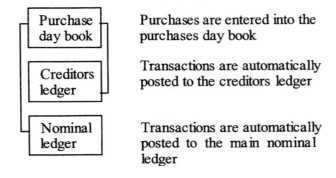

Purchase day book	Purchases are entered into the purchases day book
Creditors ledger	Transactions are automatically posted to the creditors ledger
Nominal ledger	Transactions are automatically posted to the main nominal ledger

1.5   Recording cash receipts

Most packages do not have a separate cash book, instead having a cash account in the nominal ledger. How they work is that receipts from debtors are input through a **cash posting screen** which records the receipts in the debtors ledger and the nominal ledger in much the same way as credit sales.

Other types of receipts (which are not from debtors) must be input directly into the nominal ledger (normally via the **journal** or another **cash posting screen**). This also applies to **petty cash transactions**.

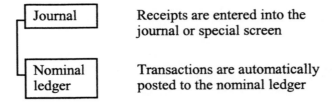

Journal	Receipts are entered into the journal or special screen
Nominal ledger	Transactions are automatically posted to the nominal ledger

1.6 Recording cash payments

Cash payments (whether from a bank account or from petty cash) must be divided into two types: **payments to creditors** and **other payments**.

The two types of payment are then input into two different parts of the program (as above with receipts). Payments to creditors are input through a creditors payment screen in the creditors ledger option. Other payments are input by journal or by a cash payment screen in the nominal ledger option.

Activity 1 *(The answer is in the final chapter of this book)*

Which receipts and payments might a business have other than receipts from debtors and payments to creditors?

---

2 Control features

2.1 Verification

One of the key features of accounting software is that it encourages good control over data, particularly at the input stage, because it has facilities for verification and validation of data.

Verification is the comparison of input data with the source document. Although this might be done by means of the software, requiring double input, it is more likely to be a case of the operator being asked to check and confirm the accuracy of the input data. It is important to recognise that the software is not capable of checking accuracy, as it cannot see the source document. It can only check to see if the input is reasonable, according to pre-defined parameters.

2.2 Validation

Validation is the application of pre-programmed tests and rules by the software, to determine the reasonableness of the data input.

There are a number of different forms of validation control, and each part of the software will use the most appropriate. Some examples are as follows:

♦ **Range checks** - test that the data is within an appropriate range, for example all product prices should be between £10 and £100. This will prevent somebody keying in a price of £22.99 as £2,299 in error. These checks can also be applied to dates.

♦ **Existence checks** - compare the input data with some other piece of data in the system, to see if it is reasonable. For example a customer code might be compared with a list from the customer records file.

♦ **Format checks** - test the data in each input area against rules governing whether it should be numeric, alphabetic or a combination of the two. For example the software might not allow an alphabetic entry in the **Invoice Number** or **Quantity** fields.

♦ **Completeness or sequence checks** - ensure that all data items in a series have been processed. For example confirmation of an invoice number being 3456 may be required if 3454 was the previous invoice raised.

♦ **Check digits** - may be built in to certain data items.

2.3   Codes

To improve the speed and accuracy of the processing, data is normally organised using a system of codes. In most accounting systems all the nominal ledger accounts, suppliers, customers, stock items and documents are referenced using different coding systems. This allows more of the validation checks to be carried out. Coding systems also help to make all the necessary postings from a single data input. Each input field can be set up to perform both sides of the appropriate double entry automatically.

In Sage, all the nominal ledger accounts are given a unique four-digit code. As you will see, all the Working Capital codes begin with 1, the Stock with 10, the Debtors with 11 and so on. This is known as a hierarchical code structure, and makes it easier for the user to find items on a code list, as the related accounts are grouped together.

3   Sage Line 50

3.1   Introduction

A common design thread flows throughout the Sage range of software. The main screen is uncluttered and comprises a toolbar that displays all the accounting features available. Icons depict the various functions in bookkeeping. You will see buttons for customers, suppliers, nominal, bank, etc.

Within the **Sales ledger,** the system maintains detailed customer records. It stores information about what has been sold, at what price and when, when payment is due and the length of time it has been outstanding, as well as credit details and discounts given. You can also obtain a full history of all customer transactions, outstanding balances, invoices and the status of outstanding debts.

The **Purchase ledger** records supplier details. It maintains information about items bought, dates and prices, when payments are due and discount entitlement. A full history of all supplier transactions, outstanding payments and invoices is available.

The **Nominal ledger** collates the entries in other ledgers to produce a balance sheet and profit and loss account. The cashbook is integrated with the nominal ledger and provides for bank and petty cash account payment and receipt postings.

3.2   Accessing Sage Line 50

Make sure that you are authorised to use the software by checking with your supervisor or tutor. Ask whether there are any specific procedures or passwords that you will need to gain access to the package. To start Sage Line 50, open the **Sage** folder on your Windows desktop and then double click **Sage Line 50**.

To close **Sage Line 50** click **Exit** on the **File** menu or click on the **X** in the top right hand corner of the Window.

When you open Sage, the basic Window is displayed. Before you begin working with this software, it is a good idea to familiarise yourself with the interface and the general work procedures common to all parts of the system.

♦ The Green icon in the left hand corner allows you to manipulate the Window, and the title bar at the top of the screen shows the name of the Window.

♦ The menu bar, just below the title bar, displays the menu commands - File, Edit, etc. To select commands on menus, point to the menu you want and click to open it.

♦ The tool bar under the menu bar contains buttons that let you run the main accounting options. When you choose any of these options, a secondary window appears on the desktop. Each of these Windows represents one of the main accounting ledgers. Because there are so many options available on both of the toolbars, there are pointer arrows at the ends of the toolbars to allow you to see options that are difficult to display. If you click on one of them, you can see more options.

3.3 *Setting up a company*

To help you become familiar with an accounting package, you are going to go through the procedure of setting up a small business, Greensleeves Ltd, on the computer. This company sells environmentally friendly adult and children's clothing to small retail outlets.

The company is registered for VAT but has not yet started trading. The business intends to make both cash and credit sales and purchases.

If you are unfamiliar with accounting software on a Windows environment, you may want to open and look at the Demonstration Data. Alternatively, you can begin by setting up the new company, using the Easy Startup Wizard on the File menu.

The **Easy Startup Wizard** guides you through the procedure of entering the default settings you need to start up your company.

To run the **Easy Startup Wizard**, click on the file menu and select **Run Easy Startup Wizard**.

Your progress through the start up procedure is controlled using the Next, Back and Cancel buttons. The fields that you are unsure of can be ignored, eg bank details.

Here are the details of the company, Greensleeves Ltd, which we are going to look at in this first case study. Input these details carefully.

Company name	Greensleeves Ltd
Address	123 Greenwood Road
	Withington
	Manchester
	M20 4TF
Telephone	0161 460 7488
Fax	0161 460 3442
VAT reg. no.	456 3344 12

The business has five prospective customers and five prospective suppliers. The credit limit for each account is £1,000.00 and the VAT code for all of them is GB.

Now that you have created the company, the data you may need to input before you can get started includes:

♦   customer names, addresses and account numbers;

◆ supplier names, addresses and account numbers;

◆ product details; and

◆ nominal ledger codes (only where they do not exist in the default chart).

3.4   Customers

You must set up the names and addresses of the customers you are dealing with. This list can be amended whenever necessary. These are:

00001	Fred Brown Associates 234 Barlow Moor Road West Didsbury Manchester M19 5DG	Telephone: 0161 456 8833 Contact: Fred Brown VAT No: 888 999 0101 22
00002	Everett Enterprises 122 Wilbraham Road Chorlton Manchester M21 9JK	Telephone: 0161 860 3345 Contact: Sid Francis VAT No: 070 545 2233 01
00003	Thornwood Manufacturing Ltd 89 Glendale Street Ancoats Manchester M1 3GH	Telephone: 0161 236 1903 Contact: Sarah Marshall VAT No: 200 200 6666 05
00004	Taylor and Atkins 34 Lightbowne Road Moston Manchester M15 1TF	Telephone: 0161 556 4785 Contact: Steve Hardy VAT No: 123 456 7777 88
00005	White Brothers 239 Darnell Way Oldham OL1 4NM	Telephone: 0161 940 378 Contact: Heather Thomas VAT No: 999 000 1234 55

Using Sage, you can set up the new customers' details with the Wizard or you can access the empty Record to fill in without help. Click on **Customers** then **New** (for the wizard) or **Record** and fill in the details given above. Remember to **Save** after each entry. The Save button is at the bottom of the Record sheet.

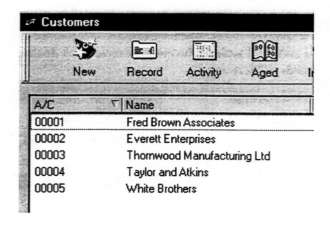

You can produce a report to check that all the customers have been entered onto the system correctly. To do this, click on the Reports icon.

With the customer details in the main Window, highlight each one by clicking on it. When they are all highlighted, click on the Reports icon. This opens the Customer Reports Window. Scroll down until you find **Customer Address List**, and click on it.

At the bottom of this Window, you will see five boxes: New, Edit, Delete, Run and Close. Choose **Run**.

If you click on Preview, the criteria box is displayed and you must select the criteria for the report. There are drop down menu boxes to help you identify the beginning and end of the customer list. The boxes below show the From and To criteria to select. Press OK.

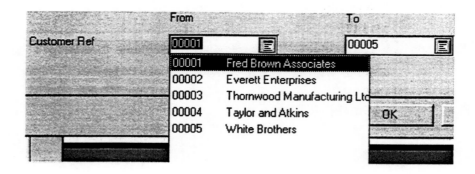

The report will then be produced as a print preview and you can change the format. After viewing it on the screen by scrolling down the page, you can save it to a file or print it.

If you decide to print the report, check that there is paper in the printer and that no one else is using it before clicking on **Print**.

Close the report by clicking on Close at the bottom of the Window. Close the Customer Reports Window by clicking on the X in the right hand corner of the Window (the lowest of the Xs). To return the customers back to a non-highlighted state, press the **Clear** button at the bottom of the screen.

3.5   *Suppliers*

This section contains the names and addresses of the suppliers. For the supplier account number, it is company policy to use the first three letters of the company name followed by a number.

For example when you are entering the details of Dryer Supplies Ltd, the account number will be DRY001. The number part of the code allows for expansion within the range of names beginning with DRY. Subsequent suppliers whose names begin with DRY will be numbered DRY002, DRY003, etc.

The suppliers' details are entered onto the computer by clicking on **Suppliers** then **New** if using the Wizard. Alternatively, you can enter the details directly into the Record - saving after each entry.

The list of suppliers to enter:

Trevor Manufacturing Ltd 345 Taylforth Road Sale Manchester M24 2KN	Telephone: 0161 345 2234 Contact: Harold Goodman VAT No: 33 444 5555 66
Olympic Design Studio 34 Weaver Street Withington Manchester M20 2JL	Telephone: 0161 404 4654 Contact: Betty Davies VAT No: 77 888 9999 01
Joseph Parker & Sons 7 Hillside Drive Chorlton Manchester M21 4DF	Telephone: 0161 403 5712 Contact: Laura Jackson VAT No: 12 333 4545 66
Hill and Saint 566 Burton Road Withington Manchester M20 8JN	Telephone: 0161 723 3887 Contact: Kevin Birch VAT No: 777 888 9090 11
Dryer Supplies Ltd 899 Regency Way Bolton BL1 4RT	Telephone: 01204 5734 Contact: David Warren VAT No: 222 345 6789 22

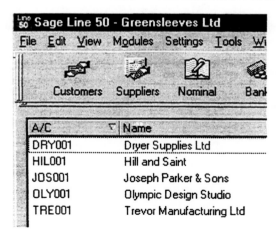

Activity 2 *(Note: There is no printed answer for this activity)*

Identify which part of your program you need to use to input this standing data. Make a note of the procedure followed.

Once you have input all the details, **print out** a list of customers and a list of suppliers.

3.6   Nominal codes

The nominal codes that will be required are as follows:

4000	Sales type A
5009	Discounts taken
5000	Materials purchases
4009	Discounts allowed
6900	Miscellaneous expenses
1100	Debtors control account
2200	Tax control account (VAT)
1200	Bank current account (cash at bank)
1230	Petty cash
2100	Creditors control account
3000	Ordinary shares
1001	Stock

Although there are many default nominal codes, you may need to add a few to cater for your particular type of activities.

To do this, click on Nominal.

Select **Record** and the Nominal Ledger Window appears.

You can then add your Nominal code, eg:

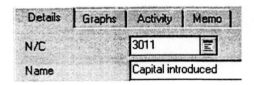

4   Posting transactions

4.1   Introduction

Before you begin posting transactions to a new accounting system, you must transfer the current balances from your existing system to the new one. Outstanding customer and supplier invoices must be entered to reflect what is owed from customers and to suppliers.

Careful consideration should be given to posting opening balances with respect to VAT periods. Some opening balance transactions may belong to VAT periods prior to your first 'live' computerised accounts period and will have been included in a VAT return submitted by other means.

After the ledgers have been set up and opening balances sorted out, then the day to day transactions can be entered into the ledgers.

Most of these transactions are going to be routine, eg purchase and sales on credit and transactions affecting the company's cash. However, transactions other than these routine ones do occur, but they are not so numerous as to warrant special ledgers for each class. This is where the journal is used.

The entries into the journal are different because both aspects of each transaction are recorded. Since the Journal is not reserved for any one kind of transaction, an explanatory note (narration) is made with each entry.

4.2   Journal entries

As Greensleeves Ltd is starting from scratch it has no opening balances to transfer. The first entry you need to post is to record the capital introduced by the owner. He has bought £10,000 of share capital. He has introduced £7,500 in cash and stock of £2,500.

These transactions will be recorded as Journal entries and will be posted to the appropriate accounts in the Nominal Ledger. For every journal transaction, there will be a debit entry in one Nominal Ledger account and a corresponding credit entry in another Nominal Ledger account.

Activity 3 *(The answer is in the final chapter of this book)*

What is the double entry for the above transaction?

Using Sage, as soon as you enter the nominal code and press return, the type of account is entered for you by the software.

If you have postings that need to be made on a regular basis, such as standing orders, direct debits, depreciation postings, etc then most accounting packages will allow you to set up these journals once and then post them automatically.

Recurring journals can be repeated continuously or set for a number of postings, after which they will be cancelled.

4.3 *Posting sales invoices*

To enter the sales invoices into the program you click on **Customers** and then **Invoices**. The mouse is pointing at the customer number and, when you input the unique code number, the Account name and nominal code are filled in from the details on file.

You only need to enter the Net amount because the VAT and Gross are calculated automatically.

Here are the sales invoices for the first month of trading. Do not worry about dates for this exercise. Make sure you complete each field (ie section, box or space) correctly. Check the details carefully before you go on to the next screen.

Customer	Net £	VAT £	Gross £
Everett Enterprises	245.00	42.88	287.88
Taylor and Atkins	45.37	7.94	53.31
Thornwood Manufacturing Ltd	137.99	24.15	162.14
White Brothers	49.26	8.62	57.88
Taylor and Atkins	87.20	15.26	102.46

Remember that although you have only input the sales invoice details into a screen, the program has completed the double entry for you.

The program has also updated the individual accounts in the debtors ledger.

Activity 4 *(The answer is in the final chapter of this book)*

What is the double entry for the total of the above transactions?

4.4 *Posting purchase invoices*

To post the purchase invoices to the accounts, you click on Suppliers then Invoices and enter the details. As with the sales invoices, posting the unique code gives you the supplier's details. The Net figure is all you need to enter - the other boxes are calculated automatically.

Here is the first batch of purchase invoices.

Supplier	Net £	VAT £	Gross £
Hill and Saint	123.76	21.66	145.42
Dryer Supplies Ltd	76.66	13.42	90.08
Joseph Parker & Sons	34.22	5.99	40.21
Hill and Saint	16.78	2.94	19.72
Trevor Manufacturing Ltd	68.34	11.96	80.30

Remember that although you have only input the purchase invoice details into a screen, the program has completed the double entry for you.

The program has also updated the individual accounts in the creditors ledger.

4.5   Draft trial balance

You have now completed posting the first batches of transactions.

To produce a draft trial balance using Sage, click on **Financials** then **Trial.**

You are asked for the criteria, ie the month and the type of output. You can choose to have a preview, to print or to put it in a file. Print the trial balance. It should be the same as the trial balance below.

Greensleeves Ltd Trial balance

N/C	Name	Debit £	Credit £
1001	Stock	2,500.00	
1100	Debtors control account	663.67	
1200	Bank current account	7,500.00	
2100	Creditors control account		375.73
2200	Tax control account (VAT)	55.97	98.85
3000	Ordinary shares		10,000.00
4000	Sales type A		564.82
5000	Materials purchased	319.76	
	Totals	11,039.40	11,039.40

5   *Recording cash transactions*

5.1   *Cash receipts*

Let us move on in time. Let us assume the **customers all pay the full amount**. (Again do not worry about the date for the moment.) The information required to record the receipt includes:

♦   The nominal code for the bank

♦   The customer's account reference number

♦   The amount

♦   The cheque number or reference number

To enter a customer receipt: click on **Bank** and highlight the bank account for receipts. Click on **Customer** button. The Customer Receipt window is displayed.

Enter the account code and all the items that you have invoiced, which are not fully paid, appear automatically on the item table. If you do not know the number you can activate the pull down menu which shows the customers' details and double click on the one you want.

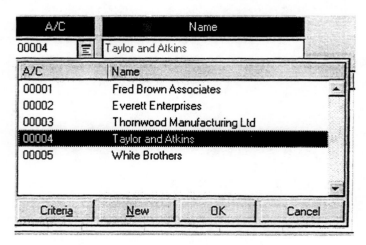

The system date is entered automatically. Enter the amount received. Allocate this same amount against specific invoice items by entering the amount for each of their payment boxes.

Enter the following customers' payments:

00003	Thornwood Manufacturing Ltd	£162.14
00002	Everett Enterprises	£287.88
00005	White Brothers	£57.88
00004	Taylor and Atkins	£155.77

Use your package's allocation facility to pay off each invoice. Note how the receipt from Taylor and Atkins pays off two invoices.

When you have posted the receipts do not forget to print the audit trail. Display the accounts in the debtors' ledger on the screen. Note how they have all been updated automatically.

5.2 *Recording cash payments*

At any time you can check on whether there are any payments due to suppliers. To obtain a report on suppliers' invoices choose the **Report** button from the **Suppliers** Window.

The information required to record a payment includes:

♦ The cheque number or reference number

♦ The net amount owed

♦ The amount of discount (in pounds and pence)

♦ The supplier's account reference number

♦ The nominal code for the bank account

To record a supplier payment: from the toolbar, choose the **Bank** Option.

Bank

The **Bank Accounts** Window is displayed. Select the account that you are using to pay this invoice then select the **Supplier** tool from the toolbar.

Bank Current Account | | | | | | | Date: | 11/09/2000 | |

Payee: DRY001 ☰ Dryer Supplies Ltd

Ninety Pounds and 8p

_____ Greensleeves Ltd

No.	Tp	A/c	Date	Ref	Details	Tc	Amount	d	P
10	PI	DRY001	11/08/2000			n/a	90.08		90

Bank Balance 7928.17 Analysi

The Supplier Payment Window is displayed. The top half of the Supplier Payment Window looks like a cheque. The cheque number is a useful identifier when it comes to reconciling the bank accounts. The date is entered automatically.

Enter the account code of the supplier. There is a drop down menu bar to help. Amounts for all supplies that have been invoiced but not paid for, as well as payments on account and credit notes, appear automatically in the table in the bottom half.

The Payment details and cheque amount should be entered automatically.

The cheque book shows the following payments.

HIL001	Hill and Saint	£145.42
DRY001	Dryer Supplies Ltd	£90.08
JOS001	Joseph Parker & Sons	£40.21
TRE001	Trevor Manufacturing	£80.30

5.3   *Settlement discounts offered to customers*

To improve cash flow let us offer a 2% settlement discount to customers who pay within 7 days.

To set this up on the computer click on Customers, Record then access the customer account and fill in the details in Credit Control.

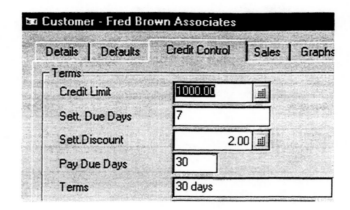

Here is the next batch of sales invoices to input.

Customer	Net £	VAT £	Gross £
Everett Enterprises	236.44	40.54	276.98
Fred Brown Associates	38.56	6.61	45.17
Taylor and Atkins	112.70	19.32	132.02

The VAT charge is based on the lowest amount the customer could pay ie, 98% of the net value. For Everett Enterprises this is £236.44 x 0.98 x 0.175 = £40.54.

Post these transactions using the screen identified earlier.

We later have the following receipts, each customer taking the 2% discount.

Customer	Cash	Discount
Everett Enterprises	£272.26	£4.72
Fred Brown Associates	£44.40	£0.77
Taylor and Atkins	£129.77	£2.25

For Everett Enterprises this is calculated as (£236.44 x 0.98) + £40.54 = £272.26.

Post these transactions using the screen identified earlier.

Activity 5 *(The answer is in the final chapter of this book)*

Note how the cash paid plus the discount clears each invoice in full.

What would happen if the customer paid the full amount and did not take the discount? Would the customer pay the extra VAT?

5.4 Taking advantage of settlement discounts

Let us look at an invoice from a new supplier who is prepared to **give a settlement discount** if Greensleeves settles its account within 10 days. There is a 1.5% settlement discount.

Here is the invoice from the supplier.

Supplier	Net £	VAT £	Gross £
00006 Farmer Manufacturing Ltd 122 High Lane Gorton M8 2DJ Phone: 0161 345 7766 Contact: Wendy Hillby VAT No: 987 654 3210 12	167.88	28.93	196.81

You will have to set up a new supplier account first, before processing this invoice.

Activity 6 *(The answer is in the final chapter of this book)*

How much will the company pay the new supplier, if it takes advantage of the discount?

5.5   *Sending out remittance advices*

Pay off the following invoice then print out the remittance advice.

Hill and Saint   £19.72

To print the remittance advice, from the Sage Line 50 toolbar, choose the Bank option. The Bank Accounts window appears.

From the Bank Accounts list box, select the appropriate bank account and choose the Supplier option from the Bank Accounts toolbar. The Supplier Payment window appears.

Enter the details you require.

If you want to print a remittance advice note to send to your supplier with your payment, then choose the Remittance button at the bottom of the screen now.

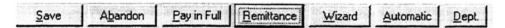

The Remittance Advice Printing window appears.

Select from the Layout list box the remittance layout you require, select the output type you require and choose the Run button. You are returned to the Supplier Payment window.

The remittance advice should look something like the one on the following page.

Greensleeves Ltd
123 Greenwood Road
Withington
Manchester
M20 4TF
Tel: 0161 4607 488

Hill and Saint
566 Burton Road
Withington
Manchester
M20 8JN

REMITTANCE ADVICE

ACC REF	4	DATE	*	TRANS REF		PAGE	1

DATE		REF		OUTSTANDING	PAID THIS MONTH	REMAINING	THIS PAYMENT
*	Inv	4		19.72	19.72		19.72

	TOTAL DUE		
19.72	19.72		19.72

Total paid	
	19.72
Less discount	
Cheque enclosed	19.72

5.6   *Cash sales and purchases*

There may be occasions where customers pay immediately for their goods or services. You do not have to produce an invoice and the transaction does not need entering in the Customers Ledger.

The transaction is recorded as a sale and a bank receipt. To do this type of recording:

Select the **Bank** button on the toolbar and the bank account for recording the payment.

Select **Receipt** and enter the details. The nominal code for Sales is 4000.

Post the following cash sales that Greensleeves made:

Narrative	Net £	VAT £	Gross £
Cash sales	354.25	61.99	416.24

The principle is the same for payments through the bank, which are made to non-credit suppliers.

Select the **Bank** button on the toolbar and the bank account for recording the payment.

Select **Payment** and enter the details.

Here are some payments for you to post.

Narrative	Net £	VAT £	Gross £
Materials purchases	98.56	17.25	115.81
Miscellaneous expenses	34.44	nil	34.44

The nominal codes for Materials purchases is 5000 and for Miscellaneous expenses it is 6900. The 'expenses' payment is VAT exempt. Use T9 as the VAT code.

Activity 7 *(The answer is in the final chapter of this book)*

What is the double entry to record the above payments?

5.7   *Petty cash payments*

Petty cash comes initially from the main bank account. It has been estimated that the business needs £150 a month petty cash to cover minor cash expenses.

The business maintains a manual **petty cash book** in which payments are recorded (including the analysis of VAT where applicable).

Transfer the money to petty cash and post these petty cash payments. The payments are summarised as follows (note some of the expenses are zero rated for VAT).

Narrative	Net £	VAT £	Gross £
Purchases	22.34	3.91	26.25
Expenses	11.38	0.31	11.69

To transfer from the current bank account to petty cash, you need to click on the Nominal then Journals. The entries are shown below:

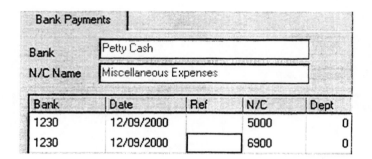

N/C	Name	Dept	Details	Tc	Debit	Credit
1230	Petty Cash	0	Transfer from bank account	T9	150.00	0.00
1200	Bank Current Account	0	Transfer to petty cash	T9	0.00	150.00

To make payments out of petty cash select the **Bank** button on the toolbar and the bank account for recording the payment.

Select **Payment** and enter the details. See below for the codes to use:

Bank Payments

Bank	Petty Cash
N/C Name	Miscellaneous Expenses

Bank	Date	Ref	N/C	Dept
1230	12/09/2000		5000	0
1230	12/09/2000		6900	0

Activity 8 *(The answer is in the final chapter of this book)*

What is the double entry to post the above payments?

5.8 At month-end

Let us assume that all of these transactions have taken place in the first month of trading. The final trial balance should look like the one below (print yours out and compare). To produce the trial balance you click on Financials and then Trial.

Financials

Greensleeves Ltd Trial balance

Code	Code	Debit £	Credit £
1001	Stock	2,500.00	
1200	Bank current account	8,156.06	
1230	Petty cash	112.06	
2100	Creditors control account		
2200	Tax control account		120.94
3000	Ordinary shares		10,000.00
4000	Sales type A		1,306.77
4009	Discounts allowed	5.23	
5000	Material purchases	608.54	
6900	Miscellaneous expenses	45.82	
1100	Debtors control		
	Total	**11,427.71**	**11,427.71**

Save your work and back up your disk if you wish to rework this case study.

6 Accounting for sales and debtors

6.1 Producing sales invoices

We are now going to look at the **debtors ledger** in more detail, in particular **producing sales invoices**.

We will also look in more detail at **how sales are analysed**.

For this section, you will also need the following nominal ledger accounts.

4000	Sales A - men's
4001	Sales B - women's
4002	Sales C - children's
8100	Bad debt write-off
1100	Debtors control
2200	Tax control account (VAT)
9998	Suspense account

Note how the business has three different types of sales. These sales are different types of supply for VAT purposes.

Category	Goods supplied	VAT rate
1	Men's T-shirts	Standard
2	Women's T-shirts	Standard
3	Children's T-shirts	Zero

Standard rate is currently 17.5% and **zero rate** is 0%. (Do not confuse this with items which are exempt or outside of the scope of VAT.)

6.2 VAT rates for sales

You will probably have to set up the **rates of VAT,** which are currently charged in the debtors ledger. This will probably include codes for **exempt** and **outside of scope.**

Sage Line 50 sets the code T1 - standard rate (currently at 17.5%) as the default tax code. If you need to add or change VAT Codes, use the Tax Code Setup dialogue box.

Tax codes are used to identify the rate of VAT to be applied to a given transaction. You can specify up to 100 VAT rates, each one identified by a code from T0 to T99. You can then select which rates are to be included in the VAT Return calculations and which relate to EC transactions.

On installation, Sage Line 50 automatically sets up the following VAT Rates for you:

T0   zero rated transactions

T1   standard rate

T2   exempt transactions

T4   sales to customers in EC

T7   zero rated purchases from suppliers in EC

T8   standard rated purchases from suppliers in EC

T9   transactions not involving VAT

Sage Line 50 has already set these rates up for this purpose, but you can change these and all other VAT codes if you wish. You can set up your VAT codes to be automatically included in your VAT Return. To change or add VAT codes click on Settings in the tool bar and then Tax Codes. You will be given the opportunity to amend the details.

6.3 Setting up product categories

To save typing out the items sold on each individual invoice you can set up a product file. Here are the products for you to input. **These prices exclude VAT.**

Check in your manual that product prices should be stated exclusive of VAT.

Stock code	Description	Unit of sale	Unit Price £	VAT rate
001	Green (men's)	Each	7.50	Standard
002	Blue (men's)	Each	7.50	Standard
003	Red (men's)	Each	7.50	Standard
004	Yellow (men's)	Each	7.50	Standard
005	Green (women's)	Each	6.50	Standard
006	Blue (women's)	Each	6.50	Standard
007	Red (women's)	Each	6.50	Standard
008	Yellow (women's)	Each	6.50	Standard
009	Green (children's)	Each	4.00	Zero
010	Blue (children's)	Each	4.00	Zero
011	Red (children's)	Each	4.00	Zero
012	Yellow (children's)	Each	4.00	Zero

You need to enter the details onto the system. On the toolbar, click on the Products Icon: this should change the toolbar to the Products Toolbar:

Products

| New | Record | Activity | In | Out | Transfer | Reports |

Click on **New** and the Wizard allows you to enter the details of the products. You progress through the procedures by using the tab to move about the separate screens and, on completion of the screen, pressing **Next** to continue. Ignore the entries where you have no information to enter.

Alternatively, select **Products** and then **Records** and enter the details.

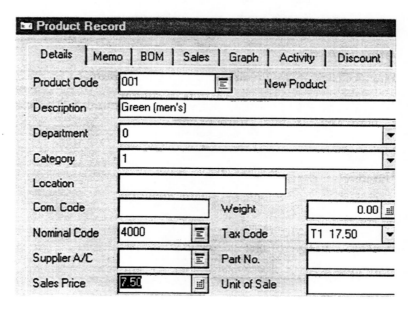

Before we can invoice customers you will have to put some goods into stock.

Stock code	Description	Quantity	Cost £
002	Blue	5	6.00
004	Yellow	10	5.00
008	Yellow	5	3.50
009	Green	5	3.50
010	Blue	8	3.50
007	Red	10	5.00

We need to update **opening stock**. To do this click on Product then Record and find the stock code. In the right hand corner of this screen there is a blank box with O/B, labelled **In Stock**.

Enter the details as shown below:

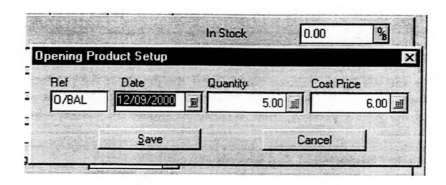

6.4   *Generating an invoice*

To generate an invoice click on the **Invoicing** icon and then Product.

You are required to invoice **Fred Brown Associates** (account number 1) as follows.

Date	As per system
Invoice number	1
Order number	23
Discount rate	0% or ignore

Product no.	002	008	009
Quantity	3	4	5

You will need to amend the customer record because he is currently receiving a 2% settlement discount.

Make sure you allocate each sale to the correct nominal code (shown below).

A/C Name	Fred Brown Associates						Tax Rate			17.50
N/C Name	Sales Type C						Batch Total			80.49

A/C	Date	Ref	Ex.Ref	N/C	Dept	Details	Net	T/C	VAT
00001	12/09/2000			4000	0		22.50	T1	3.94
00001	12/09/2000			4001	0		26.00	T1	4.55
00001	12/09/2000			4002	0		20.00	T1	0.00

Now generate and print out the invoice (it should look something like the one on the next page).

Greensleeves Ltd
123 Greenwood Road
Withington
Manchester
M20 4TF
Tel: 0161 460 7488
VAT No: 456 3344 12

Fred Brown Associates
234 Barlow Moor Rd
West Didsbury
Manchester
M19 5DG

INVOICE

INVOICE	1
DATE/TAX POINT	*
ORDER	23
ACCOUNT NO.	000001

QUANTITY	DETAILS	DISC	NET PRICE	VAT
3.00	Blue (men's)	0.00	22.50	3.94
4.00	Yellow (women's)	0.00	26.00	4.55
5.00	Green (children's)	0.00	20.00	0.00

... AS INVOICED ...

NET	68.50
VAT	8.49
CARRIAGE	0.00
TOTAL	76.99

View Fred Brown Associates' **transaction history** on screen. It should look like this. The unpaid items are marked with a star.

				Transaction History			
A/C Ref.		000001			Balance:		76.99
A/C Name:		FRED BROWN ASSOCIATES			Amount paid:		44.40
Credit limit:		1000.00			Turnover:		121.39
No.	*Tp*	*Date*	*Ref*	*Details*	*Value*	*Debit*	*Credit*
23	SI	040698	7		45.17	45.17	
27	SD	040698		Discount	0.77		0.77
28	SR	040698		Sales receipt	44.40		44.40
48	SI	070698	1	Blue (men's)	26.44*		
49	SI	070698	1	Yellow (women's)	30.55*		
50	SI	070698	1	Green (children's)	20.00*	76.99	

	Future	Current	30 Days	60 Days	90 Days	Older
Aged:	0.00	76.99	0.00	0.00	0.00	

6.5 Offering settlement discounts

Fred Brown has just been complaining to customer services that he did not get the 2% discount he expected on his last invoice.

Let us now offer Fred Brown Associates a 2% discount if he settles his invoices within 10 days.

You must amend his customer record again so that he gets his discount.

Now generate the following invoice.

Date	As per system
Invoice no.	2
Order no.	24
Discount rate	2% 10 days
Product no.	002 008
Quantity	1 1

Before printing out the invoice, calculate the amount of VAT which will be charged at each rate. We also need to post this invoice to the ledger.

Activity 9 *(The answer is in the final chapter of this book)*

What is the double entry to record the above sale?

Print the invoice (as before). It should look something like the one on the next page. Note that the "discount" box on the invoice refers to quantity discounts and not settlement discounts.

Greensleeves Ltd
123 Greenwood Road
Withington
Manchester
M20 4TF
Tel: 0161 460 7488
VAT No: 456 3344 12

Fred Brown Associates
234 Barlow Moor Rd
West Didsbury
Manchester
M19 5DG

INVOICE

INVOICE	2
DATE/TAX POINT	*
ORDER	24
ACCOUNT NO.	000001

QUANTITY	DETAILS	DISC	NET PRICE	VAT
1.00	Blue (men's)	0.00	7.50	1.29
1.00	Yellow (women's)	0.00	6.50	1.11

... AS INVOICED ...	NET	14.00
	VAT	2.40
Discount of £0.28 may be deducted for payment in 10 days	CARRIAGE	0.00
	TOTAL	16.40

6.6 *Printing the aged debtors' report*

Next we want to run the month-end procedure. We will assume that we are now moving into the next month. You may have to exit the program and change the run date (or actual date) to one month later than the actual date.

Generate the following invoice to Fred Brown Associates at that later date.

Date	As per system
Invoice no.	3
Order no.	25
Discount rate	2% 10 days

Product no.	004	007	010
Quantity	10	3	2

Print it out - it should look like the one on the next page.

There are two ways that you can produce an aged debtors' report. The first way is to click on Customers, then Aged. Highlight the account that you are interested in and specify the dates that you are interested in:

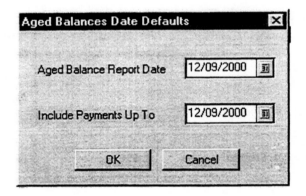

The second way is to click on Reports, then Customer and then the CSTAGED.SRT to produce a more professional looking report.

Try both ways and print out the **aged debtors' report (or listing)** - see below

Sales Ledger - Account Balances (Aged)								
A/C	Account name	Credit limit	Balance	Current	30 days	60 days	90 days	Older
00001	Fred Brown Associates	1000.00	212.09	118.70	93.39	0.00	0.00	0.00

Greensleeves Ltd
123 Greenwood Road
Withington
Manchester
M20 4TF
Tel: 0161 460 7488
VAT No: 456 3344 12

Fred Brown Associates
234 Barlow Moor Rd
West Didsbury
Manchester
M19 5DG

INVOICE

INVOICE	3
DATE/TAX POINT	*
ORDER	25
ACCOUNT NO.	000001

QUANTITY	DETAILS	DISC	NET PRICE	VAT
10.00	Yellow (men's)	0.00	75.00	12.86
3.00	Red (women's)	0.00	19.50	3.34
2.00	Blue (children's)	0.00	8.00	0.00

... AS INVOICED ...	*NET*	102.50
Discount of £2.05 may be deducted for payment within 10 days	*VAT*	16.20
	CARRIAGE	0.00
	TOTAL	118.70

6.7 Printing out statements of account

Once you are satisfied that the ageing is correct, you can then print out the **statement of account** to send to the customer. The statement is essentially the same as the ledger accounts, but you would print them on special stationery to make them look more professional.

Sending your customers statements on a regular basis is a good way of keeping them informed and it can also gently remind them of payments that are now overdue.

An example is shown on the next page.

From the **Customers** window select the customers required and choose the **Statement** button. The Customer Statements window appears.

Statement

From the Layout list box, select the statement layout with the combination of options you require.

The statement options available are:

♦ 11"or A4;

♦ 2 Part or Tear Off;

♦ Individual or Grouped;

♦ O/S Only or All.

By default, the software remembers which layout you used the last time you printed your customer statements, and automatically selects this layout for you.

Select the type of output you require from the option buttons provided. Choose the Run button to continue with the Statement printing. The Criteria dialogue box appears for you to enter your date range. All aged balance transactions are aged to the End Date.

In the From and To boxes, enter the date range required. All customer transactions falling on or within these dates are included in the Statements.

Select the Exclude Later Payments check box if you want to exclude any future sales receipts and sales payments on account from your statement. This gives you the flexibility to run retrospective statements, ie to include or exclude invoices depending on the payment date.

Choose the OK button to continue.

STATEMENT

Fred Brown Associates
234 Barlow Moor Road
West Didsbury
Manchester
M19 5DG

	A/C Ref	000001
	Date	*
	Page	1

Date	Ref	Details	Debit	Credit
*	1	Blue (men's)		
*	1	Yellow (women's)		
*	1	Green (children's)	76.99	
*	2	Blue (men's)		
*	2	Yellow (women's)	16.40	
*	3	Yellow (men's)		
*	3	Red (women's)		
*	3	Blue (children's)	118.70	

Current	30 Day	60 Day	90 Day	120+ Day
118.70	93.39	0.00	0.00	0.00

Amount due	212.09

REMITTANCE ADVICE

Fred Brown Associates
234 Barlow Moor Road
West Didsbury
Manchester
M19 5DG

	A/C Ref	000001
	Date	*
	Page	1

Date	Ref	Details	Debit	Credit
*	1	Blue		
*	1	Yellow		
*	1	Green	76.99	
*	2	Blue		
*	2	Yellow	16.40	
*	3	Yellow		
*	3	Red		
*	3	Blue	118.70	

Amount due	212.09

6.8 Posting credit notes

As with invoices, there are usually two methods of posting credit notes. These are:

♦ generating the credit notes by using the option within the program; or

♦ inputting manual (ie generated by some other means) credit notes.

To produce a credit note click on **Invoicing** and then **Credit**.

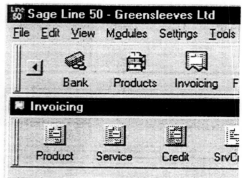

You can raise and print out a credit note for the products you have invoiced a customer, in exactly the same way that you would raise a product invoice. The only difference is that you can't record any Payment Received details, as this is not applicable to credit notes.

When you update your ledgers with the credit note, your customer's account will show the value of the credit on account, which you can then allocate to the relevant outstanding invoice items using the Bank, Customer Receipt option.

All postings to the Nominal Accounts are the opposite of those made when an invoice is raised.

From your program, generate the following credit note for Fred Brown Associates to refund the customer for an item on invoice no. 1, which was faulty.

Date   As per system

Credit note no. 4

Product no.   008

Quantity   4

The VAT is calculated on the discounted amount, as charged on the original invoice (£26 × 98%) × 17 ½% = £4.46. Your credit note should look like the one below:

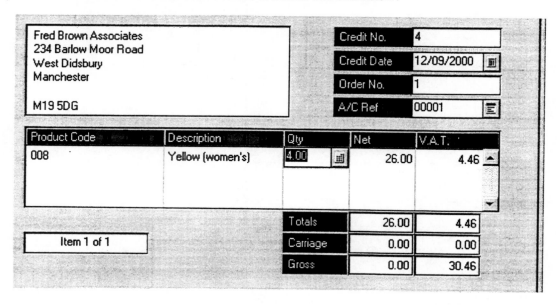

Make sure you remembered to discount the VAT because the **original invoice offered a settlement discount**.

If you display the individual ledger account the credit note will appear as a **negative entry**.

Obviously this credit note relates to one particular invoice and you will want to **allocate it against that invoice**. The method of allocating will depend upon the package you are using. See the manual for the exact procedure.

Activity 10 *(The answer is in the final chapter of this book)*

What is the double entry to record the above detailed credit note?

6.9   Bad debts

Bad debts must be written off within the **debtors ledger** if the debt clearly cannot be recovered.

Four types of bad debts can be written off - accounts; transactions; transactions below a specified value; and overpayments. All the appropriate adjustments to the nominal ledger are generated automatically, and customer and supplier account transactions are added accordingly.

Note that the VAT and sales accounts in the nominal ledger are unaffected by the write-off. The VAT account is unaffected because the company *cannot* reclaim the VAT unless the customer has gone into liquidation. If this is so then the company must fill out certain forms and receive permission from HM Customs & Excise.

If you are using a credit note to write off bad debts, it must be allocated against the bad debt nominal ledger account code, not sales.

If you are using an automatic bad debt routine, the system will post the entries to the correct accounts for you. The double entry involves debiting the Bad debt write off and crediting the Debtors control account.

Let us say we want to write off invoice 3, which we now have to admit will not be paid. The original invoice totalled £118.70, including VAT of £16.20.

To do this in Sage: click on **Tools** then **Write Off, Refund, Return**.

The result is a Wizard that goes through the steps to produce the write off.

7   Summary

You have completed the first months trading for a small company. In that time, you have created the company, set up the standing data, entered transactions and produced reports.

You should now be in a position where you could demonstrate your competence in many of the performance criteria required for this AAT Unit.

CHAPTER 17

Payroll

ASSESSMENT FOCUS

This chapter covers the following Knowledge and Understanding and Performance Criteria of the AAT Syllabus.

- The purpose and application of accountancy packages *(Knowledge and Understanding element 20.1)*

- Data to be input into the computer system is clarified with the appropriate person *(Performance Criteria element 20.1)*

- Confidentiality of data is maintained at all times *(Performance Criteria element 20.1)*

- Data is stored in the appropriate location *(Performance Criteria element 20.1)*

In order to cover these, the following topics are considered:

- Types of inputting: addition of new information, some of which requires the generation of unique reference codes, modification of existing information, deletion/cancelling of existing information

Introduction

This chapter must assume that you are either reasonably familiar with payroll processing, but need some guidelines as to the facilities offered by a payroll software package or you are a complete beginner and need an overview of what is available. Either way, there is not much that can be taught by reading and you really need to sit in front of a computer with a software package and try out the exercises.

We will be using Metro Payroll, which is an example of an icon-led easy-to-use package with a friendly user interface. Whatever software you are using, check with your tutor or supervisor that you are authorised to access it. If passwords are needed, make sure you keep yours safe.

1 Payroll packages

1.1 Introduction

Every pay day, a wages clerk will calculate how much money each employee has earned and will arrange for their payment.

Out of this payment there will usually be two deductions, Income Tax and National Insurance. These are deducted on behalf of the Government to ensure that monies are available for public services, social security and other benefits. In the United Kingdom, the Government operates a system known as Pay As You Earn (PAYE), whereby these deductions are automatically taken out of your gross pay, ie your wages before deductions, by your employer.

Computerising the payroll has several advantages for a business.

♦ It is more accurate than using the tables, and thus prevents the possibility of over or underpayment of deductions.

♦ It is far faster than using the tables, which saves an account clerk's time and money over the traditional method.

♦ Due to its ease of use, the payroll may not have to be contracted out to a third party - it can all be done in house at a fraction of the cost.

♦ The program also keeps track of payments to employees, helping with filling in the payments to the Inland Revenue.

1.2 Features

All the payroll packages on the market will have similar facilities. They should all:

♦ process weekly, fortnightly, four-weekly and monthly payrolls;

♦ provide for all tax codes, standard (contracted in) and contracted out National Insurance contributions;

♦ produce payment details that can be printed on pre-printed payslips and forms;

♦ calculate Statutory Sick Pay and Maternity Pay entitlements;

♦ record and report absence periods; and

♦ process holiday pay and pension schemes payments.

Using a package means that you are able to create detailed employee records, which are easy to access. All packages allow you to update the data quickly.

The main activities associated with payroll processing fall into four main categories:

♦ Adding, removing and amending employee details

♦ Entering payments and processing the payments

♦ Updating the payroll records and paying the Inland Revenue

♦ Producing reports and payslips

1.3 Opening and closing the Payroll package

If you are using Sage Payroll or Pegasus Payroll, the procedure for opening the software will be the same as we have already covered, but you will be looking for the relevant Payroll package.

If it is a different package, eg Metro, click on the Start button in the bottom left hand corner of your desktop then click on Programs. Select the relevant folder and then the right file.

Because the payroll database contains sensitive information, there should be some security procedures associated with the package. At the very least a password will be required.

The system defaults to the current date, but you can change it if necessary and there will be a reminder of the **Last Updated** date displayed with most packages. This is because you must confirm the processing date and this must be a date **after** the last date the payroll was updated.

All of the modern integrated packages, designed for a Windows environment, will have a friendly user interface. The icons should be self-explanatory. Sage Payroll has a different layout to the screen from Line 50 because it incorporates a stacked toolbar on the left of the Window. The menu items at the top of the Window are similar to those encountered in the Accounting software.

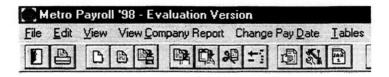

On the menu bar, the facilities that you should be familiar with are:

♦   The **File** menu - you can Back up and Restore data and process Year end data.

♦   The **Employee** menu - gives access to Employee Details and Defaults and lets you print Employee Records, Lists and Labels.

♦   The **Pay** menu - has all the facilities for processing the payroll and producing reports. You can enter pay variations, eg pay codes, and produce essential reports, eg payslips, company totals and payroll summaries. The optional reports list includes NI Summary, Pay elements analysis, P45 certificates, Cheques, Bank Giros, etc.

1.4   *Government legislation*

All packages will have a file where the latest government rates for income tax, NI contributions, SSP and SMP are stored. The system uses the information to apply the right rates from the correct table in the relevant file when processing the payroll. However, most users pay for and rely on the originating company to send out support software at the beginning of each tax year.

The tables that we will be using as examples in this chapter are out of date. This is not important because the package that you are or will be using should have the latest tables. You must make allowances for any variation in results, when practising some of the procedures.

2   *Inputting data*

2.1   *Company details and information*

We are going to continue using the same company as in the last chapter. Here are the payroll details for Greensleeves Ltd. Input the data for the company into the Payroll package you are using to set up the basic company information.

Company name	Greensleeves Ltd
Address	123 Greenwood Road, Withington, Manchester, M20 4TF
Tax office reference	345/6789
Rounding indicator	0.00
Bank name	Southern Bank plc
Branch	10 High Street, Withington, Manchester M20 6NM
Sort code	22–11–58
Account name	Payroll account
Account number	90239151

Now we will input the different ways of paying the Greensleeves employees. Employees are paid on a **monthly** or **hourly** basis. **Overtime** is also paid and **bonuses** are given to some employees, so we will need to input three pay elements:

♦ Monthly basic

♦ Hourly basic

♦ O/time - hours

(Leave all the columns at their default settings if appropriate).

2.2 Basic employee records

Now that we have set up the basic company details we can set up the records of some of Greensleeves' employees.

We will look at two employees, one of whom is paid monthly, the other weekly. To input the data you go through the menu and select 'Employee Record' or similar option to select or create a new employee. Your programme may have an **Employee Wizard** on the screen, which will guide you through the input.

Select **New employee details**. Now key in the following details for two employees (using the tab button to move from entry to entry, or use your mouse, as directed in your program manual).

Employee no.	1	2
Title	Mrs	Mr
First name	Jane	Kevin
Surname	Howard	Baker
Address	567 Whitchurch Rd	28 Bard Road
	Withington	Withington
	Manchester	Manchester
	M20 1XX	M20 3YY
Works number	1	1
Payment type	QM (cheque monthly)	CW (cash weekly)
Holiday scheme	0	0
Pension scheme	0	0
Auto SSP/SMP	Y	Y
Birth date	05/04/67	20/09/71
Join date	12/12/94	19/05/92
Tax code	300L	419L
Tax basis	Normal cumulative	Normal cumulative
Effective from	06/04/98	06/04/98
NI number	NA 68 35 03 B	HR 23 18 15 A
NI category	A	A
Marital status	M	S
Director	No	No

As Jane is paid by cheque you do not want to enter banking information. Jane is normally paid £1,000 per month - enter this onto her record.

Kevin is paid in cash weekly, based on a standard week of 40 hours at an hourly rate of £5.048, with double time (£10.096) for overtime; enter this information.

The following illustration shows the type of screen, with pull down menus and easy boxes to fill in that is most common.

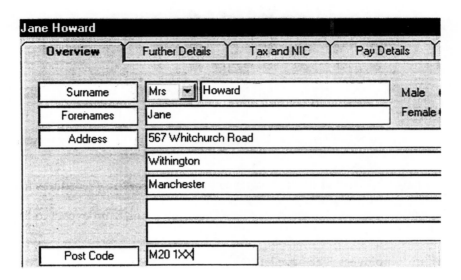

Assuming it is week 4 in the **income tax calendar**, this means that Kevin has already been paid three times this tax year (£605.76), for the first 3 weeks. The payments for these 3 weeks need to be entered on his record - using the **Year to Date input options**:

You will have to input the following **brought forward figures**, that is the cumulative figures so far this tax year. (Remember this is all for *this* employment.)

Total gross pay	£605.76
Gross pay for NIC	£605.76
Taxable gross pay	£605.76
Tax paid	£76.04
Standard NI earnings	£603
NI Total contribution	£87.39
NI contributions to date	Employee - £45.09 (Employer - £42.30)

Save this information.

Let us assume that in the fourth week/first month these employees are going to be paid their **basic rate only**; that is, no overtime or other variations.

2.3   Calculating the pay

Most Payroll systems have **pre-set 52 tax weeks** and 12 tax months based on the year 6 April to 5 April. As a result, to process week 1 you must enter a run day between **6 April** and **12 April**. To process the payroll for month 1 you must enter a date between **6 April** and **5 May**.

To process week 4 and month 1, the payroll run date should be set as **28 April**, with each run advancing one week or month as appropriate.

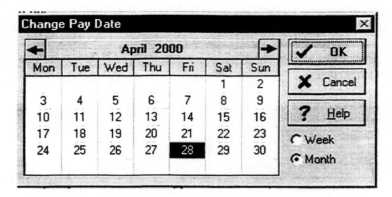

Only the weekly payroll should be processed each week, whilst the monthly payroll should be processed every 4 or 5 weeks.

Before entering payments and updating the payroll, there are certain procedures to adopt.

♦   Check for employees who have joined in the last period and who expect to be paid in the current payroll run.

♦   Check for any employees who have left or are leaving since the previous payroll run.

♦   Note the return of any employees from sick leave, holiday or maternity leave.

♦   Ensure that the correct Government parameters are being used and that any changes in legislation that have come into effect since the last payroll run are entered correctly.

♦   Make sure that you have the information you need to complete the payroll run quickly. During a payroll run, no employee details can be changed between printing the reports and updating the records.

You are now ready to start entering the payments (where necessary).

For Sage users: click on the Enter Payments icon on the stacked toolbar. The Process Window lets you enter the payment details for every employee receiving pay in this payroll run.

The Window lists all the pay items that the employee might receive. The cursor is in the Hours box. For Kevin Baker, we need to enter the hours that he has worked. Once these are entered his weekly pay can be calculated. Using Metro the button to press is Calculate. The employee's gross salary will appear automatically in the box to the right of the screen. This will interact with employee details to calculate gross pay, tax and NICs. The computer will automatically calculate PAYE, NIC and net pay. Move onto the next employee.

When you have completed one entry, click on the Next button at the top of the screen.

Continue in this way until all the weekly paid employees have had payments entered or accepted, then you can Close and return to the main Window.

We will now run the payroll for Greensleeves for week 4, month 1 and produce a payslip for both employees.

Follow the instructions on screen, and in the manual.

(You may be able to check figures prior to printing the reports.)

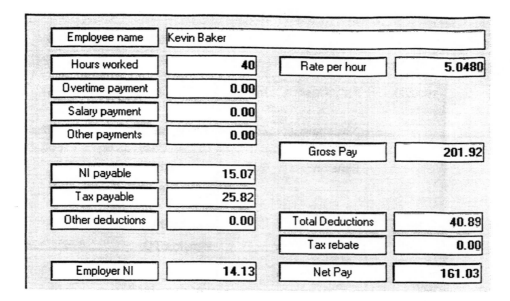

Employee name	Kevin Baker		
Hours worked	40	Rate per hour	5.0480
Overtime payment	0.00		
Salary payment	0.00		
Other payments	0.00		
		Gross Pay	201.92
NI payable	15.07		
Tax payable	25.82		
Other deductions	0.00	Total Deductions	40.89
		Tax rebate	0.00
Employer NI	14.13	Net Pay	161.03

2.4   Printing out payslips

This is a good time to print out payment analyses to check the accuracy of the inputting and compare the figures with our manual payroll figures.

If there are any mistakes, you can return to the Enter Payments/Pay Variations to correct any errors that are detected.

For **Sage** users: - Click on the **Pre-update Reports** icon in the Payroll Stacked toolbar. Choose a report to check and compare with our manual figures, eg a Payment Summary or sample payslips.

When you are satisfied that the payroll run is correct, **Print** the payslips - firstly for Kevin, then repeat with the processing selected for the monthly employees to run the program for Jane Howard.

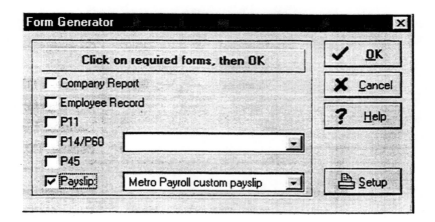

Select a payslip that conforms to your printer and click on OK.

Greensleeves Ltd

Dept - No Dept   Payment Method - Cheque   Payment Period - Monthly

Monthly basic 1000.00	1000.00	PAYE Tax	161.51	Total Gross Pay TD	1000.00
		National Insurance	77.76	Gross for Tax TD	1000.00
		Pension	0.00	Tax paid TD	161.51
				Earnings for NI TD	998.00
				National Ins TD	77.76
				Pension TD	0.00
Sick Pay	0.00			Earnings for NI	998.00
Maternity Pay	0.00	Rounding c/f	0.00	Gross for Tax	1000.00
Holiday Pay	0.00	Rounding b/f	0.00	Total Gross Pay	1000.00
				National Ins No	NA683503B

1   01/05/2000   0   300L   1   Mrs J Howard   £760.73

Greensleeves Ltd

Dept - No Dept   Payment Method – Cash   Payment Period - Weekly

Hourly basic 40.00	5.048	201.92	PAYE Tax	25.82	Total Gross Pay TD	807.68
			National Insurance	15.07	Gross for Tax TD	807.68
			Pension	0.00	Tax paid TD	101.86
					Earnings for NI TD	804.00
					National Ins TD	60.16
					Pension TD	0.00
Sick Pay		0.00			Earnings for NI	201.00
Maternity Pay		0.00	Rounding c/f	0.00	Gross for Tax	201.92
Holiday Pay		0.00	Rounding b/f	0.00	Total Gross Pay	201.92
					National Ins No	HR23181 A

4   01/05/2000   0   419L   2   Mr K Baker   £161.03

(Remember the above figures have been calculated using old tables and differences will no doubt occur between these figures and your computer payroll package solution.)

With special stationery you can print out **cheques** incorporating logos and designs.

2.5   *Printing the payroll summary*

Print out the **payroll summaries (weekly and monthly)**. You may be able to do this by department as well as for the company as a whole.

You will need to study the manual carefully to find out which reports are available and which you *must* print out. For instance, you must have a report which **summarises payroll totals**. You need this to prepare the **journal entry** to record the payroll charge in the nominal ledger.

You must also have a report which summarises the **amount owed to the Collector of Taxes** under the PAYE system.

3   *Updating and finalising*

3.1   *Closing off the payroll period*

Once you are certain that the payroll has been completed correctly and you have printed out all the reports you need, then make a back-up of your payroll data files, using the automatic back-up routines. If you back-up to disk, label it clearly as Pre-update back-up.

When the back-up routine is complete, you must close off the payroll period by updating the employee records. This is a vital process; if you fail to update the records, the cumulative totals are incorrectly stated in subsequent periods and so tax and National Insurance Contributions will be incorrectly calculated.

Select the commands to do this. The computer will often inform you as to **how many employees** in which payment category have been updated.

Then you can proceed in the knowledge that this month's/week's processing is saved. Remember to update both monthly and weekly employees - this may have to be done separately, so follow the instructions.

3.2   *P32 Payment Record*

Within 14 days of the end of the tax month employers must pay the PAYE and National Insurance contributions they have deducted from their employees to the Collector of Taxes. The payment must be accompanied by the PAYE Remittance Report.

Because you can amend the records at any time until the Update routine has been run, there is a danger of changes to stored values. That is why the PAYE Remittance Report can only be printed and the report totals cleared after the Update process.

Now move into the Company Reports and select Form P32 - **Employer's Payment Record.** The Criteria box needs to have **1** typed in both the **From** and **To** boxes to specify the month range for the report. Print the PAYE remittance report, P32. This can be sent to the Inland Revenue with the month's payment of NI and PAYE, assuming Greensleeves has to account monthly to the IR.

When this procedure is completed, close the form, the Window and the system.

4   *Summary*

In this chapter we have had a brief look at the four main features of a payroll package. We have added and amended employee details, entered payments and processed them, updated the payroll records and produced payslips and reports for paying the Inland Revenue.

CHAPTER 18

Solutions to chapter activities

Chapter 8

ANSWER 1

This type of input device is often a badge reader or a swipe card.

ANSWER 2

An example would be PC with scanner and printer.

PC is a Pentium P2/400 with 128 Mb RAM; 13 Gb hard disk; 3.5 inch floppy drive; 19 inch super VGA colour monitor; mouse; 102 key keyboard. Scanner is a Black Widow. The printer is a Hewlett Packard laser jet printer.

ANSWER 3

Print.

ANSWER 4

The subsidiary sales ledger, bought ledger, main (nominal) ledger and payroll are generally linked to form an integrated accounting system.

ANSWER 5

Examples of spreadsheet packages include Microsoft Excel and Lotus 1-2-3.

ANSWER 6

Examples include: Windows 98, Office 2000 incorporating Word, Excel, Access and Powerpoint, Pegasus Gold, Internet Explorer 5.

ANSWER 7

♦ the line minimises the window, reducing it to an icon on the task bar;

♦ the two squares overlapping makes the window smaller so that you can see other windows on the screen. When the window is reduced, clicking the single square makes it bigger;

♦ the X closes the window.

ANSWER 8

The answer is (b).

ANSWER 9

(1) **Word-processing** involves the generation, manipulation, modification, storage and communication of data in the form of text. The main packages on the market have the following features:

    (i) Text can be entered, edited, stored and printed in large volumes very easily.

    (ii) Documents and data can be validated for accuracy using spell-checkers.

    (iii) Text can be combined from many sources to form a new document.

    (iv) Special layouts can be generated to improve the appearance of text and give a 'corporate image'.

    (v) Diagrams, graphs and other graphic features can be incorporated into documents.

    (vi) A mail-merge feature allows personalised letters to be sent to individuals.

(2) **Spreadsheets** are analytical tools facilitating the construction and analysis of numerically expressed models. The main features of spreadsheet packages include:

    (i) Data is entered in a matrix form using columns (labelled A, B, C, etc) and rows (labelled 1, 2, 3, etc).

    (ii) At the intersection of these rows and columns are 'cells' and data can be entered into these cells.

    (iii) Any numerical data entered into cells can be manipulated and arithmetic operations can be carried out on it as well as more complex operations.

    (iv) The cells can be referenced in the spreadsheet and linked together in performing the necessary operations required by the model. These operations can be done very quickly.

    (v) Graphs can be drawn and plotted from data within the spreadsheet model.

(3) **Database** packages allow the storage of data which may be accessed in some systematic way to retrieve the data for further processing at a later date.

The main features of database packages include:

    (i) The ability to store numeric or textual data for subsequent use.

    (ii) Updating or expanding the data relating to a particular record or entry in the database.

    (iii) Retrieving data previously stored and transferring it to another system for further processing.

    (iv) Retrieving the total group of data stored in some specified sequence or retrieving individual records or elements in a random or ad hoc manner.

    (v) Printing out user-defined reports.

Chapter 9

ANSWER 1

They are used to input to a stock control and purchase ledger system.

ANSWER 2

Excel is a type of spreadsheet.

ANSWER 3

It takes you to the start of a document of written text.

ANSWER 4

The processing may include a selection from the following:

♦   Recording;

♦   Conversion into other units or media;

♦   Classification;

♦   Sorting;

♦   Storage;

♦   Calculation;

♦   Interpretation;

♦   Summarisation;

♦   Retrieval;

♦   Destruction;

♦   Communication.

Chapter 10

ANSWER 1

Examples include ISBN numbers on books, catalogue numbers for goods and aeroplane flight numbers.

ANSWER 2

The sequence of weights for a six-digit number are 6, 5, 4, 3, 2, 1. The check sum can be calculated using the following formula.

4	1	6	7	9	2
6	5	4	3	2	1
24	5	24	21	18	2

Check sum = 24 + 5 + 24 + 21 + 18 + 2

= 94

This check sum is not exactly divisible by 11 and therefore the number is invalid.

ANSWER 3

Shown below is the check digit calculation, by the formula known as Modulus 11, of the food processor coded 412 -125:

4	1	2	1	2	5	
7	6	5	4	3	2	
28	6	10	4	6	10	Total = 64

The sum of products is now divided by the Modulus = 64/11

= 5 REM 9

The check digit is the Modulus - the remainder = 11 - 9

= 2

The full product code with check digit is thus 412 - 125 - 2.

Chapter 11

ANSWER 1

Most floppy disks hold 1.44 MB.

ANSWER 2

Disks are divided into folders and the folders contain a collection of files.

ANSWER 3

> J Brown
>
> M Brown
>
> Mary Brown
>
> C Browne

ANSWER 4

The five-figure number is similar to the number used for purchase invoices and may lead to confusion.

Similar lines of stock are not linked in any way.

A better system would be to give stock items a number based on their type. For example: 01 02 1123 where

> 01   Clothes
>
> 02   Men
>
> 1123 Unique reference for this stock line

ANSWER 5

The operation of this method is shown in the following diagram:

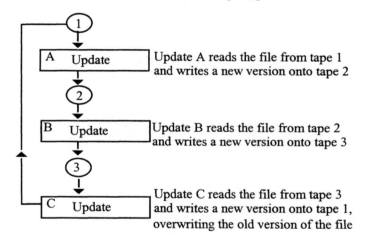

The three versions of the file are known as grandfather, father and son. The principle of the system is that only two generations are on the computer at the same time, so that even if both are spoiled the file can be reconstructed from the third.

Chapter 12

ANSWER 1

A user may easily forget that when the machine is switched off at the end of the day, it will not be able to receive fax messages. Stand alone fax machines tend to be left on-line all the time.

Chapter 13

ANSWER 1

There are several ways of minimising the risk:

♦   Burglar alarms can be fitted.

♦   Access to the building can be controlled.

♦   Smaller items can be locked away securely. Larger pieces of equipment can be bolted to the surface.

♦   The organisation can maintain a log of all equipment so that its movement can be monitored.

♦   Disks containing valuable data should not be left lying around.

ANSWER 2

Examples include:

♦   Theft of assets, eg computers, stock or software

♦   Theft of incoming cheques

♦   Invented personnel on the payroll

♦   Unauthorised discounts given to customers

♦   False supplier accounts

♦   Corruption and bribery, eg when selecting suppliers

♦   Abuse of organisation's credit card facilities, eg company car fuel allowance used privately

Chapter 14

ANSWER 1

In the Excel worksheet that is used in this chapter it is IV65536.

ANSWER 2

To do this you should make a copy of your spreadsheet so that you can experiment with it without losing the original information. Highlight the worksheet and go to the Edit menu and select **Copy**. Click on another area of the spreadsheet and press the return key or go to the Edit menu and choose **Paste**.

In the copy version, remove all entries for AB Plastics Ltd and raise the price from 20 pence to 22 pence. The total would now be £1,595.72, which would be more than previously and therefore would be beneficial to the organisation.

ANSWER 3

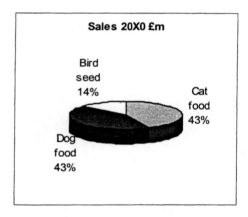
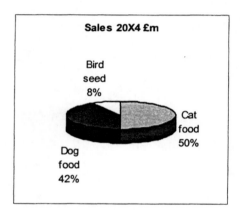

Chapter 15

ANSWER 1

To do this, highlight all the entries in the database except the titles. From the Data menu select Sort. Choose the column containing the firm (probably B) and choose Ascending to sort the firms in alphabetical order. You can then sort the Gross invoice value by selecting row G under Data Sort and Sort Descending.

ANSWER 2

Your results should look as follows:

Part (i)

Invoice	Firm	Items	Price	Net	VAT	Gross
	J Hoggs Ltd					
Invoice	Firm	Items	Price	Net	VAT	Gross
1007	J Hoggs Ltd	300	£0.20	£60.00	£10.50	£70.50
1012	J Hoggs Ltd	350	£0.20	£70.00	£12.25	£82.25
1014	J Hoggs Ltd	400	£0.20	£80.00	£14.00	£94.00

Part (ii)

I	J	K	L	M	N	O
Invoice	Firm	Items	Price	Net	VAT	Gross
				>£25.00		
Invoice	Firm	Items	Price	Net	VAT	Gross
1005	J Cables Ltd	500	£0.20	£100.00	£17.50	£117.50
1007	J Hoggs Ltd	300	£0.20	£60.00	£10.50	£70.50
1008	L Quick Ltd	1000	£0.20	£200.00	£35.00	£235.00
1012	J Hoggs Ltd	350	£0.20	£70.00	£12.25	£82.25
1013	L Quick Ltd	1500	£0.20	£300.00	£52.50	£352.50
1014	J Hoggs Ltd	400	£0.20	£80.00	£14.00	£94.00
1015	L Quick Ltd	1250	£0.20	£250.00	£43.75	£293.75
1018	L Quick Ltd	500	£0.20	£100.00	£17.50	£117.50

ANSWER 3

From the Cars: Database screen select **Open.**

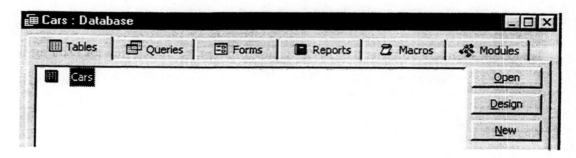

To add a car to the database, position the mouse in the next free cell in the Registration number. Enter the details (the same format as the rest). Then complete the other fields. Change the location of the Honda saloon to Chester. Save the data sheet and close it.

Chapter 16

ANSWER 1

Receipts

◆ Proceeds from sale of fixed assets

◆ VAT refunds

◆ Capital received from owners of the business

◆ Long-term loans received

Payments

◆ Wages and salaries

◆ VAT payments

◆ PAYE payments

◆ Purchases of fixed assets

◆ Capital repaid

◆ Long-term loans repaid

ANSWER 3

For the initial entry, the nominal codes for the Stock account and the Bank account will be debited by the amounts shown and the nominal code for Capital Introduced will be credited with £10,000.

Nominal account	Debit	Credit
1001 Opening stock account	£2,500	
1200 Bank current account	£7,500	
3000 Share capital introduced		£10,000

ANSWER 4

		Code	£
Dr	Debtors Control Account	1100	663.67
Cr	Sales type A	4000	564.82
	Tax control	2200	98.85

ANSWER 5

The customer would pay the total as invoiced. The customer would not be expected to pay the extra VAT. This practice has been agreed by HM Customs and Excise as a practical solution to an otherwise difficult problem.

ANSWER 6

	Cash	Discount
Farmer Manufacturing Ltd	£194.30	£2.51

ANSWER 7

Narrative	Code	Debit £	Credit £
Materials purchases	5000	98.56	
Miscellaneous expenses	6900	34.44	
Tax control	2200	17.25	
Bank current account	1200		150.25

ANSWER 8

Narrative	Code	Debit £	Credit £
Materials purchases	5000	22.34	
Miscellaneous expenses	6900	11.38	
VAT	2200	4.22	
Petty cash	1230		37.94

ANSWER 9

	Code	Debit £	Credit £
Debtors	1100	16.40	
Sales A - men's	4000		7.50
Sales B - women's	4001		6.50
Tax control	2200		2.40

ANSWER 10

	Code	Debit £	Credit £
Sales B- women's	4001	26.00	
Tax control	2200	4.46	
Debtors control account			30.46

UNIT 20

DEVOLVED ASSESSMENT

QUESTIONS

Practice Devolved Assessment 1: George Jones, Scrapmerchants

FACTFILE

Business name	George Jones Scrapmerchants
Address	134 High Street Lees Oldham OL4 6ER
Telephone	0161 626 7788
Fax	0161 626 4922
VAT Reg. No.	411 2344 98
Personnel	George Jones – the boss Betty Foster – does all the paperwork
Business	Buying and selling all types of scrap metal
Type of business entity	Sole trader
Number of accounts	20 each for customers and suppliers

Business profile

Business has always been good.

George has dealt with most of the customers for years. They either collect the scrap from the yard or George delivers it in the business's van.

He does not expect immediate payment from his long standing customers, so they send cheques or postal orders by post.

Occasionally casual customers turn up at the yard to buy odd bits of scrap. They must pay cash.

The ledgers have recently been transferred to a computerised system.

Terms of trade

The business has recently registered for VAT. All customers have a credit limit of £500.

A 2% discount is offered on all invoices which are paid within 30 days of the invoice date.

None of the business's suppliers offers settlement discounts.

Tasks

Today is 30 April 20X1.

You are required to set up the standing data within the computerised ledger system.

You are then required to enter the transactions for April from the cash book into the computerised ledger system.

Print out the **nominal ledger listing** (trial balance) (individual accounts are not required).

Print out individual **ledger accounts** in the debtors' and creditors' ledgers.

File any **audit trails** at the back of your work.

STANDING DATA

Customers

Code	Name	Address	Contact	VAT No.
1	J F Lawrence	22 Dougal Street Chadderton Oldham OL9 9TH Tel: 0161 626 5536	John Lawrence	111 2222 33
2	Acme Scrap	Horseshoe Lane Overton Preston PR5 3RF Tel: 0161 335 7686	Sid Fredericks	222 3333 44
3	Alfred Stocker	Sam Road Diggle Oldham OL15 4PL Tel: 0161 667 2349	Alfred Stocker	333 4444 55
4	Foster Brothers	409 Edgeware Street Newton Heath Manchester M3 4ED Tel: 0161 236 7766	Edward Foster	444 5555 66
5	Palatine Supplies	404 Palatine Road Withington Manchester M20 Tel: 0161 338 8769	George Fox	555 1666 77

6	Sid Pearl	Scrapmerchants 48 Canal Walk Newton Heath Manchester M3 7BJ Tel: 0161 366 9880	Sid Pearl	666 7777 88
7	Terrence James & Co Ltd	35 Fleet Road Beswick Manchester M28 6EW Tel: 0161 334 4566	Terrence James	777 8888 99
8	Proctor & Proctor	366 New Earth Street Leeds Oldham OL4 8BE Tel: 0161 366 8678	Fred Proctor	888 9999 00

Suppliers

Code	Name	Address	Contact	VAT No.
1	Graham Metals	167 Fortune Street Clayton Manchester M16 4MC Tel: 0161 488 7677	John Graham	121 3333 99
2	C R Carson	219 Merry Street Chadderton Oldham OL9 5WF Tel: 0161 776 4533	Charlie Carson	232 4444 99
3	Derek Taylor & Co	359 Diggle Road	Derek Taylor Uppermill Oldham OL14 5GJ Tel: 0161 244 5787	343 5555 99
4	S R Grant	Old Works	Steve Grant Priest Lane Middleton M36 9US Tel: 0161 377 4566	454 6666 99

5	Davies and Hughes	Allen Street	Terry Davies St Marys Oldham OL1 4EL	565 7777 99
			Tel: 0161 337 8799	
6	Yates' Yard	Whitely Lane	Ted Boulton Prestwich Manchester M14 4MF	676 8888 99
			Tel: 0161 377 6733	

Opening balances

Code	Account	Invoice	Net £	VAT £	Gross £
1	JF Lawrence	1032	34.68	5.94	40.62
2	Acme Scrap	1027	27.44	4.70	32.14
3	Alfred Stocker	1040	36.48	6.25	42.73
4	Foster Brothers	1023	18.90	3.24	22.14
5	Palatine Supplies	1038	267.90	45.94	313.84
6	Sid Pearl Scrapmerchants	1025	344.98	59.16	404.14
		1039	27.99	4.80	32.79
7	Terrence James & Co Ltd	1024	189.30	32.46	221.76
		1041	45.77	7.84	53.61
8	Proctor & Proctor	1026	18.90	3.24	22.14
		1028	122.48	21.00	143.48
	Total				1,329.39

1	Graham Metals	2399	112.45	19.67	132.12
2	C R Carson	2396	54.39	9.51	63.90
		2400	130.89	22.90	153.79
3	Derek Taylor & Co	2397	99.09	17.34	116.43
4	S R Grant	2401	178.67	31.26	209.93
5	Davies and Hughes	2403	23.46	4.10	27.56
6	Yates' Yard	2398	28.90	5.05	33.95
		2402	174.98	30.62	205.60
	Totals				943.28

Nominal codes and opening balances

		Dr £	Cr £
4000	Sales		14,689.34
5000	Purchases	8,813.40	
4009	Discounts allowed	212.60	
7003	Staff salaries	2,435.78	
7200	Electricity	443.66	
7502	Telephone	245.89	
7504	Office stationery	123.90	
6900	Miscellaneous expenses	87.40	
7900	Bank interest	122.45	
0020	Plant and machinery	5,219.95	
1100	Debtors	1,329.39	
2200	Tax control		514.15
1200	Current account		2,344.68
1230	Petty cash	70.00	
2100	Creditors		943.28
3000	Ordinary shares		2,000.00
3200	Profit & loss account		1,068.64
1001	Stock	2,455.67	
		21,560.09	21,560.09

CASH BOOK RECEIPTS

Date	Narrative	Invoices paid	Folio	Account code	Bank £	VAT £	Discount £
3/4	Foster Brothers	1023	DL	4	22.14		
7/4	Cash sale		NL	1	73.48	10.94	
10/4	Paletine Supplies	1038	DL		308.48		5.36
14/4	JF Lawrence	1032	DL	1	39.93		0.69
17/4	Terrence James & Co	1024	DL	7	221.76		
21/4	Cash sale		NL	1	44.66	6.65	
23/4	Sid Pearl	1025, 1039	DL	6	436.38		0.55
24/4	Acme Scrap	1027	DL	2	32.14		
28/4	Cash sale		NL	1	89.33	13.30	
29/4	Capital: New shares issued		NL		5,000.00		
	Totals				6,268.30	30.89	6.60

CASH BOOK PAYMENTS

Date	Narrative	Cheque no.	Invoices paid	Folio	Account code	Cash £	Bank £	VAT £	Disc. £	Station-ery £
12/4	Stationery	233		NL						50.00
15/4	Graham Metals	234	2399	CL	1		132.12			
15/4	CR Carson	235	2396	CL	2		63.90			
15/4	Derek Taylor	236	2397	CL	3		116.43			
15/4	Yates' Yard	237	2398	CL	6		33.95			
29/4	Wages – Betty	238		NL	54		395.44			
29/4	Fixed assets	239		NL	134		1,566.34	233.28		
29/4	English Telecomm	SO		NL	62		137.66	20.50		
29/4	Petty cash	–		NL	166	38.75				
30/4	Bank interest/charges	–		NL	115		23.45			
	Totals					38.75	2,469.29	253.78		50.00

PETTY CASH BOOK

Receipts	Date	Details	Voucher	Total payment	Analysis					
£				£	VAT	Stationery	Postage	Travel	Sundries	Oth
70.00	1/4	b/f								
	3/4	Stamps	67	6.55			6.55			
	14/4	Taxi	68	2.50				2.50		
	16/4	Rail fare	69	11.45				11.45		
	20/4	Stamps	70	3.45			3.45			
	22/4	Coffee etc.	71	8.09	1.20				6.89	
	24/4	Stationery	72	4.04	0.60	3.44				
	28/4	Cleaning goods	73	2.67					2.67	
38.75	29/4									
				38.75	1.80	3.44	10.00	13.95	9.56	
	30/4	c/f		70.00						
108.75		Totals		108.75						

Practice Devolved Assessment 2: Paperbox Express Ltd

FACTFILE

Business name	Paperbox Express Ltd
Address	Braebank Mill Inverkip Road Greenock PA16 8FT
Telephone	01475 33446
Fax	01475 36778
VAT Reg. No.	220 5564 12
Number of accounts required	20 each (debtors, creditors and products)

Personnel		
	Managing director	Lothar Meyer
	Sales director	Tony Bernadotti
	Financial director	Adrian Eastwood
	Financial controller	Angela Rumbold
	Ledger assistant	You
Business	Wholesale of computer stationery supplies	

Business profile

Paperbox Ltd was started in 1975 by Lothar Meyer and Tony Bernadotti. Originally the business was a partnership, but in 1985 the partners formed a limited company.

That company now sells a wide variety of stationery products by mail order and to stationery retailers. A sales team covers the whole country, visiting retailers. The company produces a catalogue twice a year.

Following the success of Paperbox Ltd the directors set up Paperbox Express Ltd. This company offers rapid despatch on a small range of computer accessories.

The company has been financed mostly by a loan from the parent company. It has no fixed assets.

Terms of trade

Sales to retailers are on credit terms. Normal terms are a 2% discount for invoices paid within 14 days of the invoice date. All invoices are payable within 30 days. All customers have a credit limit of £1,000.–

The company is registered for VAT. VAT is charged on all supplies made by the company at standard rate.

The company buys goods from a limited number of suppliers.

Sales and despatch procedures

Sales orders are taken by the telesales team. A record of all sales orders is kept centrally. Goods are then despatched from one of four sites around the country.

Goods despatched are accompanied by a despatch note. Sales invoices are prepared from a listing of despatch notes. All sales invoices are issued and recorded centrally.

Purchasing procedures

Invoices are approved, coded and batched prior to input. The source document for inputting is the *batch summary*.

Tasks

The company has only been trading for two days.

1   You have just received the first details of despatches from around the country. You are required to generate a **sales invoice** for each despatch. Print out **audit trails** for filing.

   Two copies of each invoice should be produced. (You may use multi-copy stationery if supplies are available.)

2   You have also received a purchase invoice **batch summary**. You are required to input the details shown on the summary. Print out **audit trails** for filing.

3   Print out the **trial balance** at the end of processing. Individual ledger accounts (debtors', creditors' and nominal) are **not** required.

4   Print out an **aged debtors' listing** and a **creditors' listing**.

5   Prepare **statements of account** to send to customers.

Paperbox Express Ltd
Product Listing

Code	Product	Size/colour	Price (excl. VAT) £
1	Datasaver envelope	330 × 254mm	104.02
2	(100)	406 × 304mm	137.64
3	Diskbox	CD	12.95
4		3¹/₂"	9.95
5	Expanding diskbox	3¹/₂"	10.95
6	Multibox	CD	21.95
7		3¹/₂"	18.95
8	Microfiche ring binder	325 × 272mm	14.60
9	Labels (10,000 box)	89 × 37mm	48.50
10		102 × 37mm	51.00
11		89 × 49mm	71.20
12		102 × 49mm	71.20
13		127 × 49mm	83.70
14	Printout paper (2,000)	279 × 370mm	31.57
15	Multicopy 2-part (1,000)	295 × 235mm	54.22
16	Multicopy 3-part (700)	295 × 235mm	56.86
17	Re-cyclone (1,000)	279 × 370mm	25.98
18	Printout binder	Black	52.60
19	(universal) (10)	Blue	52.60
20		Red	52.60

Paperbox Express Ltd
Nominal code listing (extract)

4000	Sales A (Computer supplies)
5000	Purchases (Computer supplies)
4009	Discounts allowed
1100	Debtors
2200	Tax control account
2100	Creditors control
3000	Share capital
2300	Loan creditors (Inter-company)
1001	Stock

Before recording the first trading transactions the company has share capital of £2.00, stock of £4,765.96, VAT recoverable of £834.04 and an inter-company loan of £5,598.00.

DESPATCH RECORD

No.	Customer	VAT Reg.	Product No.	Quantity
1	Abraham and Matthews Ltd 152 High Street Romford Essex RM1 1JU	111 2222 33 GB	5 6 12	24 10 3
2	Qwerty Office Supplies 192 High Street Barnet Herts EN6 4ES	444 5555 66 GB	14 15 18	1 1 1
3	Ronald Earl Group Limited 245 Holliday Street Birmingham B1 5VT	777 8888 99 GB	1 4	2 3
4	Giftbox Ltd 76 Queensway Redhill Surrey RH1 3WE	010 1212 33 GB	13 18	2 2
5	Denton Stationery Suppliers 87 Crown Street Guide Bridge Manchester M23 4EF	222 3333 44 GB	11 13 18 19	1 3 3 1

PURCHASE INVOICE BATCH SUMMARY

Inv. No.	Supplier	Supplier ref.	NL code	Net £	VAT £	Gross £
1	First Class Supplies	1	5000	344.78	60.34	405.12
2	Computerise Ltd	3	5000	123.89	21.68	145.57
3	Plastics Unlimited	5	5000	445.66	77.99	523.65
4	Davidson Stationers Ltd	2	5000	234.55	41.05	275.60
5	Paper Products Ltd	4	5000	2,988.89	523.06	3,511.95
				4,137.77	724.12	4,861.89

SUPPLIER DETAILS

		VAT No.	Credit limit
1	First Class Supplies 56 The Cross Worcester WR1 2PQ	333 4545 66 GB	3,000
2	Davidson Stationers Ltd 23 St Andrews Street Cambridge CB2 3AH	555 6767 88 GB	3,000
3	Computerise Ltd 288 West Regent Street Coventry CV1 5DF	666 7878 99 GB	3,000
4	Paper Products Ltd 199 Spon Street Glasgow G2 2RQ	888 9090 11 GB	3,000
5	Plastics Unlimited 18 Belvoir Way Colchester CO1 2FG	999 0101 22 GB	3,000

Mock Devolved Assessment: Natural Products Ltd

FACTFILE

Business name	Natural Products Ltd	
Location	Taunton, Somerset	
Personnel	Managing director	Cindy Taylor
	Sales director	Jason Taylor
	Production director	Tracy Yard
	Financial director	Steve Roberts
Address	151 Green Lane	
	Taunton	
	TA20 6GH	
Telephone	01823 452211	
Fax 01823 348899		
VAT Reg. No.	322 5833 23	
Number of accounts	20 of each	
Last invoice no.	5445	
Business	Manufacture, wholesale and mail order sale of toiletries and cosmetics	

Business profile

The business was started in 1978 by Cindy Taylor. Early success in supplying natural products to a famous retail chain led to Cindy's husband, Jason, and brother-in-law, Steve, joining the company.

The company originally based its business on products marketed under the customer's own label. Major customers continue to be supermarket and drugstore chains.

Sales increased steadily throughout the 1980s. In 1989, encouraged by her own staff, Cindy launched a new range of products marketed under the company's own name. These products are only available by mail order. A catalogue is produced annually.

The company hopes to be floated on the stock market soon, although the directors appreciate certain improvements will be required first in the accounting systems.

The company specialises in products which use as many natural ingredients as possible. The directors are leading campaigners against animal testing.

Accounts department

Accounts supervisor	Caroline Everley
Ledger clerk	You

Administration and payroll   Robert Foster
Cashier and petty cashier   Trudi Roberts

Terms of trade

The company is registered for VAT. All sales are standard-rated.

All wholesale customers are allowed settlement discounts of 2% if invoices are paid within 14 days of the date of the invoice and all customers have a credit limit of £3,500.

Certain suppliers offer settlement discounts.

System changeover

The company has decided to change over to a new computerised system. As part of this changeover it has decided to analyse sales in a more complex way.

Sales procedures

All sales are despatched from the main warehouse. Sales invoices are raised from *despatch listings*. The company has an integrated debtors' ledger and nominal ledger system.

Credit notes are raised from *returns listings*.

Mail order receipts and sales in the staff shop are input through a sales invoice.

Purchasing procedures

All purchases are made by two purchasers who work within the production department. The purchasers maintain *masterfiles* of supplier details and pricelists.

Letters of enquiry are sent to various suppliers requesting *quotations* for the supply of specific goods. The quotations are then compared and an official *purchase order* is sent. (The production director approves all purchase orders.)

The administration assistant checks and processes all *purchase invoices*. The ledger clerk makes the postings to the creditors' and nominal ledgers (from batch headers) and deals with all queries.

Credit notes are included on purchase order batch headers as *negative amounts*.

YOUR ASSIGNMENT

Setting up files

1   This is the first day of the new accounting year and the first day of the changeover.

     Record all the opening balances using the current run date. Perform the month-end procedures to re-set the ageing, etc.

     Set up stock categories and product codes, and enter opening quantities.

2   Leave the system then re-enter. Set the run-date to one month later. (This makes the assumption that the opening balances in the debtors' and creditors' ledgers are unpaid amounts from the previous month only.)

If your package does not allow this function, use the current run date, but the ageing on your reports will be different from the solution. NP Ltd does not wish to produce stock value reports so you do not need to input unit costs into the stock system.

Processing transactions

1   Raise sales invoices for the latest batch of despatches. The next invoice number is 5446.

2   Raise sales credit notes for the latest batch of returns.

3   Post purchase invoices and credit notes received from the batch header.

4   Record cash receipts and payments from the cash book.

5   Write off sales invoice no. 5330 as a bad debt.

Printing out reports

1   Print out statements of account to send to customers.

2   Print out the aged purchase ledger listing and the aged sales ledger listing.

3   Print out the trial balance (nominal ledger listing) and the VAT return analysis.

Customers

Code		Invoice No.	Net £	VAT £	Gross £
1	Dehlavi Kosmetayos	5330	345.67	59.28	404.95
	388 Commercial Road	5439	234.45	40.21	274.66
	Bristol				
	BS1 3UH				
	Richard Allen				
2	Cosmetic Co Ltd	5331	123.45	21.17	144.62
	234 Grange Road	5334	23.44	4.02	27.46
	Twickenham	5345	1,564.66	268.34	1,833.00
	TW23 5TR				
	Lawrence Deardon				
3	Mexican Products Ltd	5333	455.67	78.15	533.82
	356 Union Street	5340	177.88	30.51	208.39
	London				
	N14 5TH				
4	Green & Green Ltd	5339	567.45	97.32	664.77
	356 Royal Way	5443	23.56	4.04	27.60
	Chelmsford				
	Essex				
	CM2 6FG				
	Chris Bailey				
5	Health Promotions Ltd	5335	876.56	150.33	1,026.89
	289 Park Road North				
	Newcastle				
	NE13 5RD				
	Bob Rimmer				
6	Mail order and staff sales				

Suppliers

Code		Invoice No.	Net £	VAT £	Gross £
1	Adler Electrical Supplies	23445	677.45	118.55	796.00
	223 Blackwood Road	23447	134.66	23.57	158.23
	St Albans				
	AL1 1SA				
	Fred Smith				
2	Blackwood Foodstuffs & Additives Ltd	23449	187.56	32.49	220.05
	244 Parker Street	23488	344.70	59.72	404.42
	Leatherhead				
	KT22 8AG				
	Peter Forrest				
3	Arthur Chong Ltd	23455	366.46	64.13	430.59
	233 Leigh Street	23481	845.66	147.99	993.65
	Leeds				
	LS21 4YH				
	Lee Chong				
4	English Gas plc	23457	768.45		768.45
	South West House				
	12 Bennetts Court				
	Bristol				
	BS12 3WE				
	Business users dept				
5	Green Chemical Co Ltd	23466	270.05	46.31	316.36
	Imperial Avenue	23480	47.44	8.14	55.58
	Nottingham				
	NG24 4RE				
	Stuart Frost				

Nominal codes and opening trial balance income

Income

4000	Sales: Type A, B, C and D – Shampoo and conditioner
4001	Sales: Type A, B, C and D – Bath products
4002	Sales: Type A, B, C and D – Soap
4100	Sales: Type A, B, C and D – Baby products
4101	Sales: Type A, B, C and D – Cosmetics
4904	Rent income
5009	Discounts taken

Purchases

5000	Materials purchases	

Expenditure

4009	Discounts allowed
7003	Staff salaries
7100	Rent
7201	Gas
7502	Telephone
7501	Postage and carriage
7504	Stationery
7400	Travel and subsistence
8204	General insurance
7800	Repairs and renewals
7803	Building expenses (misc.)
7304	Miscellaneous motor expenses
6900	Miscellaneous expenses
8205	Refreshments
7801	Cleaning
8100	Bad debts write-off
7900	Bank interest paid
7903	Loan interest paid

Assets

		£
0010	Fixed assets – Freehold property	150,779.50
0020	Fixed assets – Plant and machinery	167,345.67
0040	Fixed assets – Fixtures and fittings	45,234.67
1001	Stock	25,789.45
1100	Debtors control account	5,146.16
1200	Bank (current account)	12,345.45
1210	Cash at bank (deposit account)	250,000.00
1230	Petty cash	200.00

Liabilities

2100	Creditors control account	4,143.33
2310	Hire purchase	10,786.45
2200	Control account (current VAT)	Nil
2201	Tax VAT balance b/f	25,564.33

Capital and reserves

3000	Ordinary shares	50,000.00
3100	Reserves	15,875.00
3200	Profit and loss account	550,471.90

Product listing
Wholesale price list and units in stock

		£ *(excl. VAT)* *each*	*Quantity*
Shampoo and conditioner			
1	Lavender shampoo	2.49	0
2	Travel wash	1.49	0
3	Coconut grove	2.49	40
4	Untangled	1.49	40
5	Egg whip	1.49	20
Bath products			
6	Raspberry treat	1.49	0
7	Lemon treat	1.49	20
8	Pretty bubbles	1.99	40
9	Passionfruit	2.49	40
Soap			
10	Soapy Molloy	0.99	20
11	Sand rub	1.99	25
12	Fruit fool	1.49	6
Baby products			
13	Baby bubbles	1.49	0
14	Baby soap	0.99	15
15	Baby shampoo	1.49	6
Cosmetics			
16	Day	9.49	30
17	Evening	9.49	30
18	Summer	5.49	0
19	Spring	5.49	20
20	Autumn	5.49	0

DESPATCH LISTING

Batch No.   345
Date   *

Customer	Account	Product No.	Quantity
Cosmetic Company Ltd	2	5	10
		10	20
Health Promotions Ltd	5	4	30
		7	10
		9	40
Dehlavi Kosmetayos	1	11	15
		14	10
		19	10
Mexican Products Ltd	3	8	20
		17	20
Cosmetic Company Ltd	2	3	30
		16	20

RETURNS LISTING

Batch No.   346
Date   *

RN No.	Customer	Account No.	Product	Quantity	Reason for credit
122	Green & Green Ltd	4	5	5	Damaged
123	Health Promotions Ltd	5	6	10	Overdelivery

BATCH HEADER

Invoice No.	Supplier	Nominal code	Net	VAT £	Total £
23490	Adler Electrical Supplies	7800	23.56	4.12	27.68
23491	Blackwood Foodstuffs	5000	422.10	73.13	495.23
23492	Green Chemical Co.	5000	556.45	95.43	651.88
23493	Arthur Chong Ltd	5000	755.02	132.13	887.15
23494	Green Chemical Co.	5000	344.23	59.04	403.27

STAFF & MAIL ORDER SALES SUMMARY

Return No. 1
Date *

Category of sale	Nominal code	Net	VAT £	Total £
Shampoo and conditioner	4000	223.56		
Bath products	4001	156.77		
Soap	4002	133.44		
Baby products	4100	244.03		
Cosmetics	4101	87.56		
Totals		845.36	147.93	993.29

CASH BOOK RECEIPTS

Date	Narrative	Invoices paid	Total £	Debtors £	Rent £	Other £	VAT £	Discount £
*	Mexican Products Ltd	5333	524.71	524.71				9.11
*	Green & Green Ltd	5339	644.84	644.84				11.20
*	Cosmetic Company	Unknown	1,026.89	1,026.89				
*	Transfer (deposit account)		10,000.00			10,000.00		
*	Mail order and staff sales		993.29	993.29				
*	Freeman & Jenkins		600.00		600.00			
	Totals		13,789.73	3,189.73	600.00	10,000.00		20.31

CASH BOOK PAYMENTS

Date	Narrative	Cheque no.	Invoices paid	Total £	Debtors £	Rent £	Other £	VAT £	Disc £
*	Alder Electrical Supplies	655	23445 23447	954.23	954.23				
*	Arthur Chong Ltd	656	23455	310.88	310.88				
*	Green Chemical Co.	657	23466	310.96	310.96				5.40
*	Kingsbury Insurance	DD		123.66			123.66		
*	Monthly salaries	CT		16,345.39			16,345.66		
	Totals			18,045.39	1,576.07		16,469.32		5.40

UNIT 20

DEVOLVED ASSESSMENT

ANSWERS

Practice Devolved Assessment 1: George Jones, Scrapmerchants

Note: When inputting the opening debtors' and creditors' balances, the full value of invoices must be allocated to the nominal code for suspense, not sales, as these invoices have already been accounted for in an earlier period.

Double-entry

(This is shown for the sake of completeness. Remember that receipts from creditors/debtors are posted through the purchase/sales ledgers and other items are posted through the nominal ledger.)

		Code	£	£
Dr	Bank current account	1200	6,268.30	
	Discounts allowed	4009	6.60	
Cr	Debtors (1,060.83 + 6.60)	1100		1,067.43
	Sales	4000		176.58
	Tax control	2200		30.89
	Ordinary shares	3000		5,000.00

To record cash receipts

		Code	£	£
Dr	Office stationery	7504	50.00	
	Creditors	2100	346.40	
	Wages	7003	395.44	
	Telephone	7502	117.16	
	Fixed assets	0020	1,333.06	
	Petty cash	1230	38.75	
	Bank interest/charges	7900	23.45	
	Tax control	2200	253.78	
Cr	Bank current account	1200		2,558.04

To record cash payments

		Code	£	£
Dr	Tax control	2200	1.80	
	Stationery	7504	3.44	
	Postage (sundry)	6900	10.00	
	Travel (sundry)	6900	13.95	
	Miscellaneous	6900	9.56	
Cr	Petty cash	1230		38.75

To record petty cash payments

George Jones Scrapmerchants Ltd
Trial Balance

		£	£
0020	Plant and machinery	6,553.01	
1001	Stock	2,455.67	
1100	Debtors control	261.96	
1200	Bank current account	1,365.58	
1230	Petty cash	70.00	
2100	Creditors		596.88
2200	Tax control		289.46
3000	Ordinary shares		7,000.00
3200	P&L account		1,068.64
4000	Sales		14,865.92
4009	Discounts allowed	219.20	
5000	Purchases	8,813.40	
6900	Miscellaneous expenses	120.91	
7003	Staff salaries	2,831.22	
7200	Electricity	443.66	
7502	Telephone	363.05	
7504	Office stationery	177.34	
7900	Bank interest	145.90	
		23,820.90	23,820.90

George Jones Scrapmerchants Ltd

Sales Ledger Reports – Transaction History

Date: *

Page: *

Account 1: JF Lawrence

No	Tp	Date	Ref	N/C	Details	Value	Debit	Credit	V	B
*	SI	*	1032	9998	Opening balance	40.62	40.62			
*	SR	*	–	1200	Sales receipt	40.62		40.62		B

Amount outstanding	0
Amount paid this period	40.62
Credit limit	500.00
Turnover year to date	40.62

Account 2: ACME Scrap

No	Tp	Date	Ref	N/C	Details	Value	Debit	Credit	V	B
*	SI	*	1027	9998	Opening balance	32.14	32.14			
*	SR	*	–	1200	Sales receipt	32.14		32.14		B

Amount outstanding	0
Amount paid this period	32.14
Credit limit	500.00
Turnover year to date	32.14

Account 3: Alfred Stocker

No	Tp	Date	Ref	N/C	Details	Value	Debit	Credit	V	B
*	SI	*	1040	9998	Opening balance	42.73*	42.73			

Amount outstanding	42.73
Amount paid this period	0
Credit limit	500.00
Turnover year to date	42.73

Account 4: Foster Brothers

No	Tp	Date	Ref	N/C	Details	Value	Debit	Credit	V	B
*	SI	*	1023	9998	Opening balance	22.14	22.14			
*	SR	*	–	1200	Sales receipt	22.14		22.14	V	

Amount outstanding	0
Amount paid this period	22.14
Credit limit	500.00
Turnover year to date	22.14

Account 5: Palatine Supplies

No	Tp	Date	Ref	N/C	Details	Value	Debit	Credit	V	B
*	SI	*	1038	9998	Opening balance	313.84	313.84			
*	SR	*	–	1200	Sales receipt	313.84		313.84		B

Amount outstanding   0
Amount paid this period   313.84
Credit limit   500.00
Turnover year to date   313.84

Account 6: Sid Pearl Scrapmerchants

No	Tp	Date	Ref	N/C	Details	Value	Debit	Credit	V	B
*	SI	*	1025	9998	Opening balance	404.14*	404.14			
*	SI	*	1039	9998	Opening balance	32.79	32.79			
*	SR	*		1200	Sales receipt	436.93		436.93		

Amount outstanding   0
Amount paid this period   436.93
Credit limit   500.00
Turnover year to date   436.93

Account 7: Terrence James & Co Ltd

No	Tp	Date	Ref	N/C	Details	Value	Debit	Credit	V	B
*	SI	*	1024	9998	Opening balance	221.76	221.76			
*	SI	*	1041	9998	Opening balance	53.61*	53.61			
*	SR	*		1200	Sales receipts	221.76		221.76		B

Amount outstanding   53.61
Amount paid this period   221.76
Credit limit   500.00
Turnover year to date   275.37

Account 8: Proctor & Proctor

No	Tp	Date	Ref	N/C	Details	Value	Debit	Credit	V	B
*	SI	*	1026	9998	Opening balance	22.14*				
*	SI	*	1028	9998	Opening balance	143.48*				

Amount outstanding   165.62
Amount paid this period   0
Credit limit   500.00
Turnover year to date   165.62

Creditors Ledger – George Jones Scrapmerchants Ltd

Purchase Ledger Reports – Transaction History

Account 1: Graham Metals

No	Tp	Date	Ref	N/C	Details	Value	Debit	Credit	V	B
*	PI	*	2399	9998	Opening balance	132.12		132.12	V	
*	PP	*	234	1200	Purchase payment	132.12	132.12			B

Amount outstanding	0
Amount paid this period	132.12
Credit limit	0.00
Turnover year to date	132.12

Account 2: CR Carson

No	Tp	Date	Ref	N/C	Details	Value	Debit	Credit	V	B
*	PI	*	2396	9998	Opening balance	63.90		63.90	V	
*	PP	*	2400	9998	Opening balance	153.79*		153.79		
*	PP	*	235	1200	Purchase payment	63.90	63.90			B

Amount outstanding	153.79
Amount paid this period	63.90
Credit limit	0.00
Turnover year to date	217.69

Account 3: Dereck Taylor & Co

No	Tp	Date	Ref	N/C	Details	Value	Debit	Credit	V	B
*	PI	*	2397	9998	Opening balance	116.43		116.43	V	
*	PP	*	236	1200	Purchase payment	116.43	116.43			B

Amount outstanding	0
Amount paid this period	116.43
Credit limit	0.00
Turnover year to date	116.43

Account 4: SR Grant

No	Tp	Date	Ref	N/C	Details	Value	Debit	Credit	V	B
*	PI	*	2401	9998	Opening balance	209.93*		209.93*	V	

Amount outstanding	209.93
Amount paid this period	0.00
Credit limit	0.00
Turnover year to date	209.93

Account 5: Davies and Hughes

No	Tp	Date	Ref	N/C	Details	Value	Debit	Credit	V	B
*	PI	*	2403	9998	Opening balance	27.56*		27.56*	V	

Amount outstanding	27.56
Amount paid this period	0.00
Credit limit	0.00
Turnover year to date	27.56

Account 6: Yates Yard

No	Tp	Date	Ref	N/C	Details	Value	Debit	Credit	V	B
*	PI	*	2398	9998	Opening balance	33.95		33.95		
	PI	*	2402	9998	Opening balance	205.60*		205.60*		
*	PP	*	234	1200	Purchase payment	33.95	33.95			B

Amount outstanding	205.60
Amount paid this period	33.95
Credit limit	0.00
Turnover year to date	239.55

Practice Devolved Assessment 2: Paperbox Express Ltd

Trial balance

		£	£
4000	Sales 1 – Computer supplies		1,877.48
5000	Purchases 1 – Computer supplies	4,137.77	
4009	Discounts given		
1100	Debtors	2,199.47	
2200	Tax control	1,236.17	
2100	Creditors		4,861.89
3000	Share capital		2.00
2300	Loan creditors		5,598.00
1001	Stock	4,765.96	
		12,339.37	12,339.37

Note that discounts given are not accounted for until the cash is received from the customer.

Paperbox Express Ltd
Braebank Mill
Inverkip Road
Greenock
PA16 8FT
Tel: 01475 33446
Fax: 01475 36778
VAT No: 220 5564 12

Abraham and Matthews Ltd
152 High Street
Romford
Essex
RM1 1JU

INVOICE

INVOICE NO.	1
DATE/TAX POINT	*
ACCOUNT REF.	001

QUANTITY	DETAILS	DISC	NET PRICE	VAT
24	Expanding diskbox	0.00	262.80	45.07
10	Multibox 5¹/4	0.00	219.50	37.65
3	Labels 102 × 49	0.00	213.60	36.63
... AS INVOICED ...			*NET*	695.90
			VAT	119.35
			TOTAL	815.25

Paperbox Express Ltd
Braebank Mill
Inverkip Road
Greenock
PA16 8FT
Tel: 01475 33446
Fax: 01475 36778
VAT No: 220 5564 12

Qwerty Office Supplies
192 High Street
Barnet
Herts
EN6 4ES

INVOICE

INVOICE NO.	2
DATE/TAX POINT	*
ACCOUNT REF.	002

QUANTITY	DETAILS	DISC	NET PRICE	VAT
1	Printout 2000	0.00	31.57	5.41
1	Multicopy 2-part	0.00	54.22	9.30
1	Printer binder	0.00	52.60	9.02

... AS INVOICED ...		*NET*	138.39
		VAT	23.73
		TOTAL	162.12

Paperbox Express Ltd
Braebank Mill
Inverkip Road
Greenock
PA16 8FT
Tel: 01475 33446
Fax: 01475 36778
VAT No: 220 5564 12

Ronald Earl Group Ltd
245 Holliday Street
Birmingham
B1 5VT

INVOICE

INVOICE NO.	3
DATE/TAX POINT	*
ACCOUNT REF.	003

QUANTITY	DETAILS	DISC	NET PRICE	VAT
2	Datasaver env.	0.00	208.04	35.68
3	Diskbox 3^1/2	0.00	29.85	5.12

... AS INVOICED ...		
NET	237.89
VAT	40.80
TOTAL	278.69

Paperbox Express Ltd
Braebank Mill
Inverkip Road
Greenock
PA16 8FT
Tel: 01475 33446
Fax: 01475 36778
VAT No: 220 5564 12

Giftbox Ltd
76 Queensway
Redhill
Surrey
RH1 3WE

INVOICE

INVOICE NO.	4
DATE/TAX POINT	*
ACCOUNT REF.	004

QUANTITY	DETAILS	DISCOUNT	NET PRICE	VAT
2	Labels 127 × 49	0.00	167.40	28.71
2	Printout binder	0.00	105.20	18.04
... AS INVOICED ...			*NET*	272.60
			VAT	46.75
			TOTAL	319.35

Paperbox Express Ltd
Braebank Mill
Inverkip Road
Greenock
PA16 8FT
Tel: 01475 33446
Fax: 01475 36778
VAT No: 220 5564 12

Denton Stationery Suppliers
87 Crown Street
Guide Bridge
Manchester
M23 4EF

INVOICE

INVOICE NO.	5
DATE/TAX POINT	*
ACCOUNT REF.	005

QUANTITY	DETAILS	DISC	NET PRICE	VAT
1	Labels 89 × 49	0.00	71.20	12.21
3	Labels 127 × 49	0.00	251.10	43.06
3	Printout binder	0.00	157.80	27.06
1	Printout binder	0.00	52.60	9.03
... AS INVOICED ...			*NET*	532.70
			VAT	91.36
			TOTAL	624.06

STATEMENT					REMITTANCE ADVICE				

Paper Box Express Ltd
Braebank Mill
Invertrip Road
Greenock

A/C ref	000001
Date	*
Page	1

Abraham & Matthews Ltd
152 High Street
Romford
Essex
RM1 1JU

Paper Box Express Ltd
Braebank Mill
Invertrip Road
Greenock

A/C ref	000001
Date	*
Page	1

Abraham & Matthews Ltd
152 High Street
Romford
Essex
RM1 1JU

Date	Ref	Details	Debit	Credit	Date	Ref	Details	Debit	Credit
* .	1	Expanding diskbox			*	1	Expanding diskbox		
*	1	Multibox $5^1/4$			*	1	Multibox $5^1/4$		
*	1	Labels 102×49	815.25		*	1	Labels 102×49		815.25

Current	30 Day	60 Day	90 Day	120+ Day
815.25				

Amount due	815.25

Amount due	815.25

Sales ledger account balances (aged)

A/C	Account name	Turnover	Credit limit	Balance	Current	30 days	60 days	90 days	Other
1	Abraham & Matthews	815.25	1,000	815.25	815.25				
2	Qwerty Office Supplies	162.12	1,000	162.12	162.12				
3	Ronald Earl Group	278.69	1,000	278.69	278.69				
4	Giftbox Ltd	319.35	1,000	319.35	319.35				
5	Denton Stationery	624.06	1,000	624.06	624.06				
	Totals	2,199.47	5,000	2,199.47	2,199.47				

Purchase ledger account balances (aged)

A/C	Account name	Turnover	Credit limit	Balance	Current	30 days	60 days	90 days	Other
1	First Class Suppliers	405.12	3,000	405.12	405.12				
2	Davidson Stationers Ltd	275.60	3,000	275.60	275.60				
3	Computerise Ltd	145.57	3,000	145.57	145.57				
4	Paper Products Ltd	3,511.95	3,000	3,511.95	3,511.95				
5	Plastics Unlimited	523.65	3,000	523.65	523.65				
	Totals	4,861.89	15,000	4,861.89	4,861.89				

Note: not all programs produce an aged creditors report.

Mock Devolved Assessment

Opening balances

When inputting opening balances for debtors and creditors via the debtors' and creditors' ledger routines, the full value of each invoice must be allocated to the nominal ledger code for contras/suspense. The VAT account is unaffected.

When inputting the opening trial balance the balances on the debtors' and creditors' accounts must be allocated to contras/suspense as the individual balances have already been input through the debtors' and creditors' ledgers.

Staff sales

These have been input by creating an invoice within the debtors' ledger and then allocating the cash received against it. The value on this account within the debtors' ledger should always be nil once processing has been completed.

Other receipts and payments

If these are to appear correctly on VAT reports, invoices must be posted in the debtors' and creditors' ledger against which the receipts and payments are then allocated.

The alternative approach is to post these as journal entries. Although this is adequate for this exercise, it would not be acceptable outside this course.

Bad debts

When writing off a bad debt, the full value of the invoice must be posted to the nominal ledger code for bad debts. The VAT account is unaffected.

Allocation of cash

The cash received from the Cosmetic Company has been allocated against the oldest invoices first.

Sales invoices

Note that some software will not allow you to input Natural Products Ltd as a company heading and that the sales invoices will not display the discount deduction available for prompt settlements.

NATURAL PRODUCTS LTD

151 Green Lane, Taunton TA20 6GH

Tel: 01823 452211
Fax: 01823 348899
VAT no: 322 5833 23

Cosmetic Company Ltd 234 Grange Road Twickenham TW23 5TR	Invoice no: Date: Order A/c ref:	5446 * 0 2	

Quantity	Details	Discount	Net price	VAT
10.00	EGG WHIP	0.00	14.90	2.56
20.00	SOAPY MOLLOY	0.00	19.80	3.40

AS INVOICED

Settlement discount

£0.69 may be deducted if payment is made strictly within 14 days.

Net	34.70
VAT	5.96
Carriage	0.00
	40.66

NATURAL PRODUCTS LTD

151 Green Lane, Taunton TA20 6GH

Tel: 01823 452211
Fax: 01823 348899
VAT no: 322 5833 23

| Health Promotions Ltd
289 Park Road North
Newcastle
NE13 5RD | | Invoice no:
Date:
Order
A/c ref: | 5447
*
0
5 |

Quantity	Details	Discount	Net price	VAT
30.00	UNTANGLED	0.00	44.70	7.67
10.00	LEMON TREAT	0.00	14.90	2.56
40.00	PASSIONFRUIT	0.00	99.60	17.08

AS INVOICED

Net	159.20
VAT	27.31
Carriage	0.00
	186.51

Settlement discount

£3.18 may be deducted if payment is made strictly within 14 days.

NATURAL PRODUCTS LTD

151 Green Lane, Taunton TA20 6GH

Tel: 01823 452211
Fax: 01823 348899
VAT no: 322 5833 23

Dehlavi Kosmetayos
388 Commercial Road
Bristol
BS1 3UH

Invoice no:	5448
Date:	*
Order	0
A/c ref:	1

Quantity	Details	Discount	Net price	VAT
15.00	SAND RUB	0.00	29.85	5.12
10.00	BABY SOAP	0.00	9.90	1.70
10.00	SPRING	0.00	54.90	9.42

AS INVOICED

Net	94.65
VAT	16.24
Carriage	0.00
	110.89

Settlement discount

£1.89 may be deducted if payment is made strictly within 14 days.

NATURAL PRODUCTS LTD

151 Green Lane, Taunton TA20 6GH

Tel: 01823 452211
Fax: 01823 348899
VAT no: 322 5833 23

Mexican Products Ltd
356 Union Street
London
N14 5TH

Invoice no:	5449
Date:	*
Order	0
A/c ref:	3

Quantity	Details	Discount	Net price	VAT
20.00	PRETTY BUBBLES	0.00	39.80	6.83
20.00	EVENING	0.00	189.80	32.55

AS INVOICED

Net	229.60
VAT	39.38
Carriage	0.00
	268.98

Settlement discount

£4.59 may be deducted if payment is made strictly within 14 days.

NATURAL PRODUCTS LTD

151 Green Lane, Taunton TA20 6GH

Tel: 01823 452211
Fax: 01823 348899
VAT no: 322 5833 23

| Cosmetic Company Ltd
234 Grange Road
Twickenham
TW23 5TR | | **Invoice no:**
Date:
Order
A/c ref: | 5450
*
0
2 |

Quantity	Details	Discount	Net price	VAT
30.00	COCONUT GROVE	0.00	74.70	12.81
20.00	DAY	0.00	189.80	32.55

AS INVOICED

Settlement discount

£5.29 may be deducted if payment is made strictly within 14 days.

Net	264.50
VAT	45.36
Carriage	0.00
	309.86

NATURAL PRODUCTS LTD

151 Green Lane, Taunton TA20 6GH

Tel: 01823 452211
Fax: 01823 348899
VAT no: 322 5833 23

Green & Green Ltd
356 Royal Way
Chelmsford
Essex
CM2 6FG

Credit no: 122
Date: *
Order 0
A/c ref: 4

Quantity	Details	Discount	Net price	VAT
. 5.00	EGG WHIP	0.00	7.45	1.28

AS INVOICED

Net	7.45
VAT	1.28
Carriage	0.00
	8.73

NATURAL PRODUCTS LTD

151 Green Lane, Taunton TA20 6GH

Tel: 01823 452211
Fax: 01823 348899
VAT no: 322 5833 23

Health Promotions Ltd
289 Park Road North
Newcastle
NE13 5RD

Credit no:	123
Date:	*
Order	0
A/c ref:	5

Quantity	Details	Discount	Net price	VAT
10.00	RASPBERRY TREAT	0.00	14.90	2.46

AS INVOICED

Net	14.90
VAT	2.56
Carriage	0.00
	17.46

SAMPLE CUSTOMER STATEMENTS

(You must print all five statements)

STATEMENT

DEHLAVI KOSMETAYOS   **A/C REF:**   1
388 COMMERCIAL RD   **DATE:**   *
BRISTOL   **PAGE:**   1
BS1 3UH

DATE	REF	DETAILS	DEBIT	CREDIT
*	5439	OPENING BALANCE	274.66	
*	5448	SAND RUB		
*	5448	BABY SOAP	110.89	
*	5448	SPRING		

Current	30 day	60 day	90 day	Older
110.89	274.66	0.00	0.00	0.00

Amount due   385.55

REMITTANCE ADVICE

DEHLAVI KOSMETAYOS   **A/C REF:**   1
388 COMMERCIAL RD   **DATE:**   *
BRISTOL   **PAGE:**   1
BS1 3UH

DATE	DETAILS	DEBIT	CREDIT
*	OPENING BALANCE	274.66	
*	SAND RUB		
*	BABY SOAP	110.89	
*	SPRING		

Amount due   385.55

SALES LEDGER – ACCOUNT BALANCES (AGED)

A/c	Account name	Turnover	Credit limit	Balance	Current	30 days	60 days	90 days	Older
1	Dehlavi Kosmetayos Richard Allen	774.26	3,500.00	385.55	110.89	274.66	0.00	0.00	0.00
2	Cosmetic Company Ltd Lawrence Deardon	2,304.28	3,500.00	1,328.71	350.52	978.19	0.00	0.00	0.00
3	Mexican Products Ltd	971.81	3,500.00	477.37	268.98	208.39	0.00	0.00	0.00
4	Green & Green Ltd Chris Bailey	684.92	3,500.00	27.60	– 8.73	36.33	0.00	0.00	0.00
5	Health Promotions Ltd Bob Rimmer	1,171.19	3,500.00	1,195.94	169.05	1,026.89	0.00	0.00	0.00
	Totals	5,906.46	17,500.00	3,415.17	890.71	2,524.46	0.00	0.00	0.00

PURCHASE LEDGER – ACCOUNT BALANCES (AGED)

A/c	Account name	Turnover	Credit limit	Balance	Current	30 days	60 days	90 days	Older
1	Adler Electrical Supplies Fred Smith	977.79	0.00	27.68	27.68	0.00	0.00	0.00	0.00
2	Blackwood Foodstuffs Peter Forrest	1,046.57	0.00	1,119.70	495.23	624.47	0.00	0.00	0.00
3	Arthur Chong Ltd Lee Chong	2,179.26	0.00	2,000.51	887.15	1,113.36	0.00	0.00	0.00
4	English Gas plc Business Users Dept	768.45	0.00	768.45	0.00	768.45	0.00	0.00	0.00
5	Green Chemical Co Stuart Frost	1,272.62	0.00	1,110.73	1,055.15	55.58	0.00	0.00	0.00
	Totals	6,244.69	0.00	5,027.07	2,465.21	2,561.86	0.00	0.00	0.00

NOMINAL LEDGER REPORTS - TRIAL BALANCE

Ref	Accounts name	Debit	Credit
0010	Freehold property	150,779.50	
0020	Plant and machinery	167,345.67	
0040	Furniture and fixtures	45,234.67	
1001	Stock	25,789.56	
1100	Debtors control account	3,415.17	
1200	Bank current account	8,089.79	
1210	Bank deposit account	240,000.00	
1230	Petty cash	200.00	
2100	Creditors control account		5,027.07
2200	Tax control account	85.51	
2201	VAT liability		25,564.33
2310	Hire purchase		10,786.45
3000	Ordinary shares		50,000.00
3100	Reserves		15,875.00
3200	Profit and loss account		550,471.90
4000	Sales type A		350.41
4001	Sales type B		296.17
4002	Sales type C		183.09
4009	Discounts allowed	14.91	
4100	Sales type D		253.93
4101	Sales type E		522.06
4904	Rent income		600.00
5000	Materials purchases	2,077.80	
7003	Staff salaries	16,345.66	
7800	Repairs and renewals	23.56	
8100	Bad debt write-off	404.95	
8204	Insurance	123.66	
		659,930.41	659,930.41

MANAGEMENT REPORTS - VAT RETURN ANALYSIS

Note: Please check all figures thoroughly before transferring them to your VAT return form.

		£
VAT due in this period on sales	1	278.34
VAT due in this period on EC acquisitions	2	0.00
Total VAT due	3	278.34
VAT reclaimed in this period on purchases	4	363.85
Net VAT to be paid or reclaimed by you	5	– 85.51
Total value of sales, excluding VAT	6	2,206.00
Total value of purchases, excluding VAT	7	2,102.00
Total value of all supplies to EC member states	8	0.00
Total value of acquisitions from EC member states	9	0.00

VAT DUE IN THIS PERIOD ON SALES

Code: Rate:	T0 0.00	T1 17.50	T2 0.00	T3 0.00	T4 0.00	T5 0.00	T6 0.00	T7 0.00	T8 17.50	T9 0.00
Sales invoices	0.00	282.18	0.00	0.00	0.00	0.00	0.00	0.00	0.00	0.00
Sales credits	0.00	3.84	0.00	0.00	0.00	0.00	0.00	0.00	0.00	0.00
Bank receipts	0.00	0.00	0.00	0.00	0.00	0.00	0.00	0.00	0.00	0.00
Cash receipts	0.00	0.00	0.00	0.00	0.00	0.00	0.00	0.00	0.00	25,564.30
Journal credits	0.00	0.00	0.00	0.00	0.00	0.00	0.00	0.00	0.00	0.00
Totals	0.00	278.34	0.00	0.00	0.00	00.00	0.00	0.00	0.00	25,564.30

Total for return (Box 1)   278.34 (Excluding T9 transactions)

VAT DUE IN THIS PERIOD ON EC ACQUISITIONS

Code: Rate:	T7 0.00	T8 17.50
Purchase invoices	0.00	0.00
Purchase credits	0.00	0.00
Bank payments	0.00	0.00
Cash payments	0.00	0.00
Journal debits	0.00	0.00
Totals	0.00	0.00

Total for return (Box 2)   0.00 (Excluding T9 transactions)

VAT RECLAIMED IN THIS PERIOD ON PURCHASES

Code:	T0	T1	T2	T3	T4	T5	T6	T7	T8	T9
Rate:	0.00	17.50	0.00	0.00	0.00	0.00	0.00	0.00	17.50	0.00
Purchase invoices	0.00	363.85	0.00	0.00	0.00	0.00	0.00	0.00	0.00	0.00
Purchase credits	0.00	0.00	0.00	0.00	0.00	0.00	0.00	0.00	0.00	0.00
Bank payments	0.00	0.00	0.00	0.00	0.00	0.00	0.00	0.00	0.00	0.00
Cash payments	0.00	0.00	0.00	0.00	0.00	0.00	0.00	0.00	0.00	0.00
Journal debits	0.00	0.00	0.00	0.00	0.00	0.00	0.00	0.00	0.00	0.00
Totals	0.00	363.85	0.00	0.00	0.00	0.00	0.00	0.00	0.00	0.00

Total for return (Box 4)   363.85 (Excluding T9 transaction)

TOTAL VALUE OF SALES, EXCLUDING VAT

Code:	T0	T1	T2	T3	T4	T5	T6	T7	T8	T9
Rate:	0.00	17.50	0.00	0.00	0.00	0.00	0.00	0.00	17.50	0.00
Sales invoices	0.00	1,628.01	0.00	0.00	0.00	0.00	0.00	0.00	0.00	5,146.10
Sales credits	0.00	22.35	0.00	0.00	0.00	0.00	0.00	0.00	0.00	425.20
Bank receipts	0.00	0.00	600.00	0.00	0.00	0.00	0.00	0.00	0.00	10,000.00
Cash receipts	0.00	0.00	0.00	0.00	0.00	0.00	0.00	0.00	0.00	0.00
Journal credits	0.00	0.00	0.00	0.00	0.00	0.00	0.00	0.00	0.00	631,276.60
Totals	0.00	1,605.66	600.00	0.00	0.00	0.00	0.00	0.00	0.00	645,997.50

Total for return (Box 6)   2,205.66 (Excluding T9 transaction)

TOTAL VALUE OF PURCHASES, EXCLUDING VAT

Code: Rate:	T0 0.00	T1 17.50	T2 0.00	T3 0.00	T4 0.00	T5 0.00	T6 0.00	T7 0.00	T8 17.50	T9 0.00
Purchase invoices	0.00	2,101.36	0.00	0.00	0.00	0.00	0.00	0.00	0.00	4,143.30
Purchase credits	0.00	0.00	0.00	0.00	0.00	0.00	0.00	0.00	0.00	5.40
Bank payments	0.00	0.00	0.00	0.00	0.00	0.00	0.00	0.00	0.00	16,469.30
Cash payments	0.00	0.00	0.00	0.00	0.00	0.00	0.00	0.00	0.00	0.00
Journal debits	0.00	0.00	0.00	0.00	0.00	0.00	0.00	0.00	0.00	656,841.00
Totals	0.00	2,101.36	0.00	0.00	0.00	0.00	0.00	0.00	0.00	677,448.20

Total for return (Box 7)   2,101.36 (Excluding T9 transaction)

TOTAL VALUE OF ALL SUPPLIES TO EC MEMBER STATES

Code.	*T4*	
Rate:	*0.00*	
Sales invoices	0.00	
Sales credits	0.00	
Bank receipts	0.00	
Cash receipts	0.00	
Journal credits	0.00	
	————	
Totals	0.00	
	————	

Total for return (Box 8) 0.00

TOTAL VALUE OF ACQUISITIONS FROM EC MEMBER STATES

Code:	*T7*	*T8*
Rate:	*0.00*	*17.50*
Purchase invoices	0.00	0.00
Purchase credits	0.00	0.00
Bank payments	0.00	0.00
Cash payments	0.00	0.00
Journal debits	0.00	0.00
	————	————
Totals	0.00	0.00
	————	————

Total for return (Box 9) 0.00

MARKING GUIDE

As there are no workings as such for this simulation, the student can only be given credit for the final output. The following mark allocation attempts to approximately reflect the relative amount of work (input, etc.) necessary to produce the particular document or report. It should be used as a guide only – the markers will need to use their discretion as to the percentage of maximum marks to award to each part of the student's answer.

Sales invoices/credit notes

		Marks
Invoices	3	15
Credit notes	2	4

Note that the company name and discount information may not appear. This should not be penalised. Check invoice numbers, a/c ref, quantities, correct product name and price.

Customer statements

The information and data on these will reflect the accuracy of input of opening balances, cash postings and bad debt adjustments as well as the invoices and credit notes. The marks allocated to each statement take these into account.

Customer a/c ref	1		5
	2		5
	3		4
	4		4
	5		3
			——
			21

Note that the ageing may be different from the answer.

Ledger listings

Sales	5	
Purchases	20	
	——	
		25

The marks for the purchase ledger listing reflects the work involved in the input of opening balances, purchase invoices and credit notes, and cash postings. These have already been taken into account above for sales.

Nominal ledger listing

1 mark per correct balance	27	
Account references and names	3	
	——	
		30
VAT return analysis		5
		——
		100
		——

COMMENTARY

This simulation concentrates on the setting up of accounts and their updating through the input of everyday credit and cash transactions. Some routine reports are also required.

If your figures differ from those in the answer, read through the important points to note, which may help you to discover why.

As there are no workings as such to show as part of your answer, credit can only be awarded on the basis of correct final output. It is therefore very important that you take care to be totally accurate when inputting your data so that you do not start to lose marks simply for being careless.

INDEX